The Development of Child Protection Law and Policy

This book examines how child protection law has been shaped by the transition to late modernity and how it copes with the ever-changing concept of risk.

The book traces the evolution of the contemporary child protection system through historical changes, assessing the factors that have influenced the development of legal responses to abuse over a 130-year period. It does so by focusing on the Republic of Ireland where child protection has become emblematic of wider social change. The work draws on a wide range of primary and secondary sources including legislation, case law and official and media reports of child protection inquiries. It also utilises insights developed through an extensive examination of parliamentary debates on child protection matters. These materials are assessed through the lens of critical discourse analysis to explore the relationship between law, social policy and social theory as they affect child protection. While the book utilises primarily Irish sources, this multi-disciplinary approach ensures the argument has international applicability.

The book will be a valuable resource for all those with an interest in the development of child protection law.

Kieran Walsh is a Senior Lecturer in Family and Child Law at the University of Portsmouth, UK.

Studies in Citizenship, Human Rights and the Law

Series Editor:

Leïla Choukroune *is Professor of International Law and Director of the University of Portsmouth Research and Innovation Theme in Democratic Citizenship. Her research focuses on the interactions between international trade and investment law, human rights, development studies, jurisprudence and social theory. It is also applied to emerging countries, India, China and East Africa in particular.*

The series *Studies in Citizenship, Human Rights and Law* encourages a pluralistic vision of citizenship. The aim is to promote inclusiveness and rights at the local and global levels while approaching citizenship from a socio-legal perspective. The series may include comparative approaches along with books that focus on single jurisdictions, and brings together research monographs and edited collections which allow the expression of different schools of thought. Grounded in law and legal theory, where relevant, the series also welcomes contributions that take an interdisciplinary approach to rights and citizenship.

Titles in this series:

The Development of Child Protection Law and Policy
Children, Risk and Modernities
Kieran Walsh

For more information about this series, please visit: https://www.routledge.com/Studies-in-Citizenship-Human-Rights-and-the-Law/book-series/StudiesCHRL

The Development of Child Protection Law and Policy

Children, Risk and Modernities

Kieran Walsh

Routledge
Taylor & Francis Group
LONDON AND NEW YORK

First published 2020
by Routledge
2 Park Square, Milton Park, Abingdon, Oxon OX14 4RN

and by Routledge
52 Vanderbilt Avenue, New York, NY 10017

Routledge is an imprint of the Taylor & Francis Group, an informa business

British Library Cataloguing-in-Publication Data
A catalogue record for this book is available from the British Library

Library of Congress Cataloging-in-Publication Data
A catalog record has been requested for this book

ISBN: 978-0-367-27631-7 (hbk)
ISBN: 978-0-429-29698-7 (ebk)

Typeset in Galliard
by Deanta Global Publishing Services, Chennai, India

For Sarah and Benjamin

Contents

Cases

Ireland

United Kingdom

United States of America

Legislation and other legal instruments

Ireland

Constitutional documents

Legislation

United Kingdom

International legal materials

Acknowledgements

This book has had a long gestation. Over the years, I have accumulated a great many debts, only some of which I can mention here. First and foremost, I would like to acknowledge the contributions of Professor Harry Ferguson and Professor Aoife Nolan. Over the years they have been a wonderful source of advice, encouragement and support. Their intellectual rigour and good humour as well as the crucial support they gave me when writing had to give way to other parts of my life are deeply appreciated.

A great many friends and colleagues I have met over the years were helpful in sharing ideas, differing points of view and the benefit of their own experiences. I would like to particularly thank Dr Geoffrey Shannon; both his work and his encouragement have been invaluable. Professor Leila Choukroune also provided significant encouragement and support all through the process. Several people have provided help by reading various sections and drafts of this work, and providing helpful comments, including Professor Caroline McGregor, Professor Ralph Sandland and Éilis Philips. I would also like to thank the staff at Routledge for their assistance all through this process. I am also indebted to the library staff and archivists at several institutions whose assistance greatly assisted the sourcing of materials. In this respect, I am especially grateful to both Robert O'Brien and Sinéad O'Callaghan who not only helped with chasing unusual sources but provided diverting conversations about the finer points of citation styles, cataloguing and tea-making. No library has yet replicated that alchemy.

My greatest debts are owed to Sarah, and to Benjamin. For the entirety of Benjamin's life, I have been working on this book. I can only hope that I have returned the warmth and affection that he has shown to me, and that I have been a positive example to him. Sarah's love has been a constant throughout this project. It showed itself in the practical support that she gave me, and in the intellectual challenges she presented me with, especially when acting as a sounding board for nascent ideas. Most importantly, she showed me that another life was possible. Without her, this work would not have been possible.

Introduction

The construction of children and the risks they face have been radically transformed over the last 130 years. This book charts that transformation in the context of child protection law and policy. In particular, I argue that these changes are due in large part to a radical reorientation in the constitution of modern society, characterised by detraditionalization, individualization, and new ways of thinking about risk. Taken together, these social forces indicate that a new form of modernity, reflexive modernity, has begun to take root. This process is bringing about a radical change in social structures, lessening the importance of tradition as a means of determining how people act and how they view the world around them. As a result of this, children themselves have been reconceptualised in law and social policy, and indeed culturally. Our understanding of childhood, which was once based entirely on the ideas of children as incapable, immature, innocent or even intimidating is being replaced by one more informed by the recognition of children's differing capabilities, their rights, their needs; in short, their humanity.

This historical perspective on childhood is important, as I will argue that to fully understand contemporary law and policy it is necessary to trace trends in child protection law back to their roots in the late nineteenth century. In that time, the role of the individual, the family, the state, tradition, regulation and rights have all changed immensely. The argument will, therefore, be framed in terms of the transition from "simple modernity" to "reflexive modernity". It will not merely focus on the content of a series of laws, but also on why those laws developed the way they did, and the ways in which those laws represented and reconstructed children and the risks they face. In doing so, it aims to tell a dynamic history of child protection and the concept of risk.

Key concepts

Telling the story of childhood and risk necessitates engaging with several traditionally independent disciplines. I have chosen to focus on law, sociology and history, as this book essentially presents a sociologically informed view of the historical development of our present laws and policies affecting child protection. From a sociological perspective, the argument draws heavily on the two related, but slightly differing, accounts of reflexive modernity offered by Ulrich

Beck and Anthony Giddens. In summary, this approach to modern life and society posits that there has been a decline in respect for "traditional, given, or taken-for-granted models for identity",[1] leading to a disentanglement from traditional social institutions.[2] In early or simple modernity, identity was "comparatively stable ... whatever you were was not your own choice".[3] This freedom from social roles determined by tradition opened up space for agency and the need to be reflexive, to take control over one's own identity and biography, as the possibilities were now virtually limitless.[4] In order to be considered properly reflexive, individuals require something more than the capacity to merely reflect; reflexivity requires action in order to adapt to new circumstances.

This also leads to a change in how societies deal with the risks associated with everyday life. Societies which could be considered modern only in a "first" or "simple" sense attempted to tame or eliminate risks, or in some cases reward those who took economic risks. Yet the recognition of an ever-expanding range of risks, some of which were the unintended consequences of earlier steps on the road to the development of a complex society, led to the development of what has been termed a risk society, where the public contemplates risk to a much greater degree than ever before. According to Giddens, "to recognise the existence of a risk or set of risks is to accept not just the possibility that things might go wrong, but that this possibility cannot be eliminated."[5] Not only do we think about risks, but we also attempt to reflexively act on them, accounting for them in our daily lives.

This book focuses primarily on the Irish law and policy framework. While this may seem a narrow jurisdictional focus for examining the impact of wide-reaching sociological forces, it in fact provides an exemplary case study in both the process of passing from one form of modernity to another and the ways in which this passage can impact on a particular area of social policy. Many of the features of the Irish system or the events which shaped that system will have their parallels in other countries. However, the process of social change was both so radical and truncated in Ireland that it acts as an ideal setting in which to observe the interaction between sociological forces and legal and policy decisions.

One of the central claims which I aim to substantiate in later chapters is that, in the late twentieth century, Irish society underwent a major period of modernization, thereby entering what is commonly referred to as late modernity. This "second modernity" was much more reflexive than the first, in that individualization loosened people from traditional social structures, meaning that individuals

1 David Farrugia, 'Addressing the Problem of Reflexivity in Theories of Reflexive Modernisation: Subjectivity and Structural Contradiction' (2015) 51(4) *Journal of Sociology* 872, 874.

2 Ulrich Beck, *World Risk Society* (Wiley Blackwell 1999).

3 Peter Wagner, *A Sociology of Modernity: Liberty and Discipline* (Routledge 1994).

4 See generally, Anthony Giddens, *The Consequences of Modernity* (Polity Press 1990), Anthony Giddens, *Modernity and Self-Identity: Self and Society in the Late Modern Age* (Polity Press 1991) and Anthony Giddens, *The Transformation of Intimacy: Love, Sexuality and Eroticism in Modern Societies* (Polity Press 1993).

5 Giddens, *Consequences* (n 3) 111.

came to have a greater amount of agency than before. Law and regulation took on an expanded role, and social institutions came to reflect the concerns of a risk society.[6] Child protection work, the institutions built to carry out that work, the children it sought to protect and the kinds of activity it targeted were particularly affected by this transition between modernities.

The first period of modernization in Ireland occurred, as in many other west European states, in the period between the mid-nineteenth century and the early twentieth century. This "first modernity", or "simple modernity", has several indicators, among them an association with the nation-state; second, a limited form of individualization whereby individuals were "theoretically free and equal and their associations are voluntary. But their freedom and equality are moulded by social institutions" in ways which often mirrored coercion.[7] Simple modernity ordered individual life around gainful employment, in that "[s]tatus, consumption and social security all flow from participation in the economy."[8] Other indicators include the exploitation of nature, an emphasis on rationalization and instrumental control and the use of functional differentiation, which permitted the division of society into various subgroups which made social structures more complex than they had previously been. The development of social structures such as the nation-state, a sexually divided labour market, the nuclear family, a reconfigured class system and a new hierarchical distinction between experts and laypeople based on the instrumental control of knowledge has been claimed as characteristic of a society in the midst of first modernity.

This was the modernity in which the Irish child protection system initially developed. From the late nineteenth century onwards, Ireland did undergo the kind of institutional and governmental development commonly associated with simple modernity. For instance, from the 1860s onwards, new state agencies were established, creating a new bureaucratic infrastructure governing everything from the management of public records,[9] to the construction and management of railways,[10] to the establishment and management of the census.[11] Social life was also organised along the fault lines commonly associated with simple modernity – society and the labour market were divided along class and gender lines, while the welfare state provided meagre assistance when compared with gainful employment.[12] As Lee argues of this time period, "the proliferation of government boards, the diffusion of popular literature, the growth of mass consumption

6 See generally, Ulrich Beck, *Risk Society: Towards A New Modernity* (Sage 1992).

7 Ulrich Beck, Wolfgang Bonss and Christoph Lau, 'The Theory of Reflexive Modernization: Problematic, Hypotheses and Research Programme' (2003) 20(2) *Theory, Culture & Society* 1, 4.

8 Ibid.

9 Public Records (Ireland) Act 1867.

10 Railways (Ireland) Act 1860.

11 Census (Ireland) Act 1890.

12 On this, see Anthony McCashin, *Social Security in Ireland* (Gill and Macmillan 2004) chapter 1.

simply reflected the administrative and cultural requirements of mass society, developments occurring more or less simultaneously in all European countries".[13]

Since the 1990s, however, Ireland has changed radically. Economic modernization has been accompanied by the increasing scope for individuals to exercise agency, and thereby control over their own lives. These changes can be seen in newfound social freedoms – most conspicuously seen in the 22-year gap between the decriminalization of homosexuality and the legalization of same-sex marriage, as well as the ability to divorce and greater reproductive autonomy to women. These are classic indicators of detraditionalization as well as indicating a higher level of agency for Irish people. This heightened possibility for agency has simultaneously led to the decline of traditional sources of power and authority – concepts like religion, family and geography now determine people's lives less than they used to. Power structures like the traditional patriarchal, marital family and the Roman Catholic Church also exercise less influence than they used to. The Church now plays a much smaller role in legal discourse than before.

Children's lives have also been the subject of legal regulation since before Irish independence, and children continued to be part of legal discourse in the decades following the establishment of an independent Irish state through occasional reform. Since the early 1990s, however, the legal and social landscape affecting children has become unrecognisable. As such, the development of child protection law and policy mirrors the shift from simple to reflexive modernity itself, being almost contemporaneous with that shift. As such, Ireland is a useful focal point for inquiry into the extent to which the development of a second modernity preoccupied with risk influences legal and policy change in child protection.

Child protection in Ireland has been convulsed by a series of crises and scandals since the publication of the Report of the Kilkenny Incest Inquiry in 1993.[14] Since then, there have been a series of reports into abuse within families,[15] examinations of failures by the state to adequately implement or follow best practice,[16] and reports into historic systematic maltreatment of children by individuals in religious organizations.[17] Following two major Supreme Court decisions in 2006 relating to the age of consent, criminal liability and constitutional law,[18]

13 Joseph Lee, *The Modernisation of Irish Society* (2nd edn, Gill and Macmillan 1989) 140.

14 Catherine McGuinness, *The Kilkenny Incest Investigation: Report Presented to Mr Brendan Howlin TD, Minister for Health by South Eastern Health Board* (Stationery Office 1993).

15 North Western Health Board, *West of Ireland Farmer Case: Report of Review Group, presented to North Western Health Board, July 1998* (North Western Health Board 1998), Roscommon Child Care Inquiry, *Roscommon Child Care Case Report of the Inquiry Team to the Health Service Executive* (Stationery Office 2010).

16 Kate Brosnan, *Monageer Inquiry: A Report Presented to Ms Mary Harney TD, Minister for Health and Mr Dermot Ahern TD, Minister for Justice, Equality and Law Reform* (Stationery Office 2007, Shannon and Gibbons, 2012 (n 1)).

17 Commission to Inquire into Child Abuse (CICA), *Report of the Commission to Inquire into Child Abuse* (Stationery Office 2009), Yvonne Murphy, *Report of the Commission of Investigation into the Catholic Archdiocese of Dublin* (Stationery Office 2009).

18 *CC v Ireland* [2006] 4 IR 1 (SC) and *A v Governor of Arbour Hill Prison* [2006] 4 IR 88 (SC).

there appeared to be a heightened political interest in child protection matters when compared to earlier periods in Irish history. It was as if the ground had shifted – the question was no longer whether stronger protections ought to be afforded to children, but what those protections would be. The idea that the Constitution could be amended to provide for new rights for children was more extensively discussed, and the subject of examination by several Oireachtas committees.[19] Previously trusted organizations – such as the religious orders – were now being identified as the sources of threats to children as the image of the "paedophile priest" became a powerful social symbol.[20] As a result of all of these changes, major legal reforms were undertaken including new civil child protection legislation, criminal law safeguards for children, a constitutional amendment designed to strengthen children's position in the constitutional order, and greater levels of participation of children in legal and policy spheres. Many of these changes have been seen in other jurisdictions. While it is outside the scope of the present work to examine whether reflexive modernity may lie behind those changes also, it is unlikely to have affected Ireland alone.

Approach and structure

The law on child protection presents a particularly useful test for the claims of modernity theorists. The hypothesis that the transition from simple modernity to late, reflexive modernity could be witnessed by the presence of heightened agency, risk and the decline of tradition can now be empirically evaluated, given the extensive legal reform of this area since the early 1990s. Doctrinal legal analysis alone would be inadequate to substantiate such an argument. This traditional legal approach will be used in order to explain the nature and limitations of the various rights and the duties imposed by the legal system, and in doing so will rely on constitutional texts, statutes and case law emanating from the courts. But in order to tell an original historical story, where the full range of child protection statutes has been chronologically analysed from a perspective rooted in theoretical sociology, it became necessary to foreground sources which are often marginal in legal scholarship. Particular emphasis has been placed on the parliamentary debates leading to the development of various child protection initiatives.

These debates were supplemented by archival material, official inquiries into child protection scandals and by media commentary and reporting, in particular from *The Irish Times*, commonly thought of as Ireland's newspaper of record.[21] Each of these will play a different role throughout the book, largely influenced by the time period under examination. Archival material including the evidence

19 See Chapter 6 for an outline of the approaches of the Joint Oireachtas Committee on Child Protection, The All-Party Oireachtas Committee on the Constitution and the Joint Oireachtas Committee on the Constitutional Amendment on Children.

20 On this phenomenon, see Harry Ferguson, 'The Paedophile Priest: A Deconstruction' (1995) 84 *Studies: An Irish Quarterly Review* 247.

21 See generally, Mark O'Brien, *The Irish Times: A History* (Four Courts Press 2008).

presented to, and reports of, committees of inquiry and the governmental responses to these inquiries contained in cabinet papers play a much larger role in Chapters 4 and 5. This is due largely to the availability of such sources. The provisions of the National Archives Act 1986 mean that many governmental papers from the 1990s are not yet available. Consequently, the decision was made to use media reporting of child abuse scandals to compensate for the incompleteness of the official historical record throughout Chapters 6, 7 and 8. The use of media reporting of these scandals, which was uncommon before the early 1990s, enabled a different perspective on child abuse and child protection to come to the fore, a perspective framed by victims, and by members of the public now grappling for the first time with a more comprehensive understanding of child abuse. I have chosen 2017 as a cut-off point for my analysis because this was the last major legislative reform impacting on the work – the enactment of legislation to give effect to young people's views on age of consent matters. While other reforms have taken place, such as changes to sentencing in incest cases, these do not add significantly to the understanding of the shift to a reflexive, risk-orientated system. The only exception to the 2017 end date is in respect of Chapter 6, where certain cases relating to the understanding of the new constitutional provisions relating to children are briefly analysed.

Chapter 1 will outline the theoretical framework of the book in greater depth. The ideas of reflexivity and risk will be explored in detail, while also examining the relationship between agency, childhood and law. In Chapter 2, I move to begin my examination of how the child protection system developed. I begin by looking at the positioning of children in the legal reforms undertaken in the late nineteenth and early twentieth centuries, prior to Irish independence. These Victorian and Edwardian reforms are commonly thought of as taking place during a period of significant concern for childhood, although one that placed significant emphasis on children's vulnerabilities, and their potential to be regarded as threatening delinquents. It also represented an approach to reform which was representative of the concerns of traditional modernity, and it was this system which Ireland inherited on independence.

Ireland gained independence in 1921, and so the end of British governance provides an appropriate point at which to examine the position of children in Ireland's constitutional order. This is undertaken in Chapter 3, which covers the period from the early constitutional documents to the early 1990s. This material is treated separately from other types of legal reform, given the supremacy of constitutional law over legislation in the Irish legal system. Thus, it provides background material against which more detailed reform can be discussed, which also demonstrates the limitations imposed on potential legal change. The chapter examines alternative potential drafts of early constitutional texts, the gradual development of children's constitutional rights from the early case law on this from the 1980s and the limitations imposed by the significance accorded to the marital family.

The detail of the child protection system of the first five decades of the Irish state – from its inception to the end of the 1960s – is examined in Chapter 4.

I begin by detailing the reform of the criminal law aspects of child protection, principally the age of consent. This was the subject of a committee known as the Carrigan Committee, a sustained examination of which provides a comprehensive and nuanced view of how children and the risks they faced were thought of. The legislation underpinning the care system, then comprised of industrial and reformatory schools, is also examined, with particular emphasis placed on the construction of children in both official reports into the operation of the system and in parliamentary debates on the legislative reforms undertaken between 1922 and 1970. Towards the end of the chapter, a marked change of approach can be seen in how children were thought about; they began to be regarded as having interests, and in some cases, rights.

This process of the recognition of children as having certain entitlements gathered pace in the period between 1970 and 1993, examined in Chapter 5. During these years, industrial and reformatory schools were closed, constitutional amendments to promote children's rights were first discussed and social work began to develop its own professional ideology. The legal reforms undertaken in this period culminated in the passing of the Child Care Act 1991, which is examined in detail. As will become clear, the structures of simple modernity were dominant in the period until the 1970s, but as the chapter progresses, the first stirrings of reflexivity can be found. This can be seen not only in changing attitudes to children but also to changing attitudes to risk – new guidelines for the assessment and management of information about risk were developed, morality took a less prominent role in the discourse, and so traditional attitudes were becoming less common.

Chapters 6, 7 and 8 analyse the transition to, and entrenchment of, reflexive modernity in Irish child protection. Chapter 6 deals with the constitutional position of children from the early 1990s to 2017. It opens with an account of the criticism of the constitutional relationship between children and family from the Kilkenny Report and then proceeds to outline how the courts dealt with children's issues over the following decade. In doing so it highlights the possibilities within the constitutional text for establishing new rights for children, but also finds significant judicial reluctance to do so, especially when faced with a potential clash with other constitutional principles. Following controversy over the age of consent, the question of constitutional reform entered the political arena; the chapter examines the process leading to eventual constitutional reform via a referendum in 2012 and concludes with a brief overview of constitutional case law on children since then.

Chapter 7 opens with an overview of the child protection scandals uncovered between 1993 and 2006. The Kilkenny Incest Inquiry of 1993 was the first of these to reach a wide audience, and the findings of its report were to have a lasting effect not only on child protection social work but on the construction of children and family life in Ireland. I will argue that this report contributed to the opening of the door to the forces of late modernity. A new awareness of risk was prominent among these forces, especially as it related to previously trusted institutions and persons in positions of authority. Legislation developed in this period, covering both civil and criminal law aspects of child protection, was pre-occupied with these concepts, as demonstrated by how lawmakers reacted to the revelations of abuse. This process developed even further, as outlined in the final chapter, Chapter 8. This begins with the controversies over the age of consent in 2006 and ends with the impact of young people's own views on the reform of these laws, which were implemented in 2017. This chapter again devotes significant coverage to the changed discursive construction of the child among the Irish public, largely driven by abuse scandals. Legislation in the 11 years covered here again shows an approach to childhood and risk that is highly characteristic of late modernity in that it attempts to manage risks, recognises children's agency and shows a radical distrust of traditionally powerful institutions.

References

Beck U, *Risk Society: Towards A New Modernity* (Sage 1992).

Beck U, *World Risk Society* (Wiley Blackwell 1999).

Beck U, Bonss W and Lau C, 'The Theory of Reflexive Modernization: Problematic, Hypotheses and Research Programme' (2003) 20(2) *Theory, Culture & Society* 1.

Brosnan K, *Monageer Inquiry: A Report Presented to Ms Mary Harney TD, Minister for Health and Mr Dermot Ahern TD, Minister for Justice, Equality and Law Reform* (Stationery Office 2007).

Farrugia D, 'Addressing the Problem of Reflexivity in Theories of Reflexive Modernisation: Subjectivity and Structural Contradiction' (2015) 51(4) *Journal of Sociology* 872.

Ferguson H, 'The Paedophile Priest: A Deconstruction' (1995) 84 *Studies: An Irish Quarterly Review* 247.

Giddens A, *The Consequences of Modernity* (Polity Press 1990).

Giddens A, *Modernity and Self-Identity: Self and Society in the Late Modern Age* (Polity Press 1991).

Giddens A, *The Transformation of Intimacy: Love, Sexuality and Eroticism in Modern Societies* (Polity Press 1993).

Joseph Lee J, *The Modernisation of Irish Society* (2nd edn, Gill and Macmillan 1989).

McCashin A, *Social Security in Ireland* (Gill and Macmillan 2004).

O'Brien M, *The Irish Times: A History* (Four Courts Press 2008).Shannon G and Gibbons N, *Report of the Independent Child Death Review Group* (Department of Children and Youth Affairs 2012).

Wagner P, *A Sociology of Modernity: Liberty and Discipline* (Routledge 1994).

1 Modernity, reflexivity, risk and the law

Introduction

The interaction between ideas of modernity, risk and law is complex, but an understanding of it is vital in order to appreciate the development of the child protection system. Concepts such as detraditionalization and juridification provide some of the intellectual scaffolding for the development of the contemporary legal and policy framework surrounding this system while ideas such as agency and constructivist approaches to risk appear to be woven into its very fabric. This was, however, not always the case. Historically, a more traditional approach rooted in the views that risk could be eliminated and that agency ought not to play a significant role appeared to dominate.

This chapter's primary aim is to establish the theoretical framework I will adopt throughout this book. It begins by describing how modernity has been conceptualised in the work of Giddens and Beck. Their understanding of reflexive modernity will help to shape the argument I make throughout this book that Irish child protection legislation and policy has been reformed in a way that bears the hallmarks of a reflexively modern society. The hallmarks of this later form of modernity include detraditionalization of social relationships, the rise of agency and the development of 'subpolitical' actors who help to drive social change, ideas which are outlined below. This understanding of late modernity leads to a consideration of the ways in which risk has been conceptualised, with particular emphasis being placed on Beck's idea of late modern society as a 'risk society'. Central to this is the idea of risk as a construct, a value-laden concept where its meaning is, at least in part, socially determined.

I then consider the relationship between agency and childhood, especially in the context of the construction of childhood by the rest of society and the extent to which children can meaningfully be considered agents. In the course of this examination, I will introduce David Oswell's relational and collective approach to agency as a way of understanding how we can account for the differences in children's capacities and level of involvement in decision-making without having to have recourse to an older, more binary concept of agency which relies on an all or nothing approach. This, in turn, informs the final issue I examine, the role of law and legal regulation. I will examine how law expresses certain sentiments about social actors or situations and how, as the reach of the law extended, it regulated previously unregulated aspects of social life. By marking out conduct or ideas as being worthy of protection or criticism, law plays a standard-setting role within which risks can be governed or conceptualised. This, in turn, leads to an exploration of the ways in which law and risk interact in the context of a risk society.

From simple to reflexive modernity

Since the 1980s, the question of the nature of modernity has occupied a significant role within sociological theory.[1] Prompted by reasonably clear evidence that ways of living and being are, for many people, recognisably different from the patterns that were experienced in earlier decades, social theorists have proposed a variety of narratives to explain and contextualise these changes, ranging from changes within modes of production[2] to explanations more rooted in cultural identity.[3] The role of the individual in modern society has often been at the centre of these inquiries, with questions of the nature and extent of individual freedom, the interactions between citizen and state, and the individual's sense of security all explored across academic disciplines. Social theory has also attempted to explain changes in social systems and institutions, as well as the ways in which thinking about concepts have changed.[4]

This book focuses on the causes and impact of change on both institutions and individuals. The changes under examination occurred within a particular setting – changes in child protection laws – but in exploring these, it is necessary to consider changes in wider society, including changes in how children, child abuse and risks have been conceptualised. This necessitates an understanding of the modernization process in order to develop an argument that places children and child protection in a meaningful socio-historical context.

Despite simple modernity's prizing of certainty, in the face of uncertainty, or risk, in Ulrich Beck's terms, a further phase of modernization is opened "[j]ust as modernisation dissolved the structure of feudal society in the nineteenth century and produced the industrial society, modernisation today is dissolving industrial society and another modernity is coming into being."[5] This has been termed as second modernity, or as late modernity, and has been characterised as "*the*

1 See, for example, works such as Jean-François Lyotard, *The Postmodern Condition: A Report on Knowledge* (Manchester University Press 1984), Jürgen Habermas, *The Philosophical Discourse of Modernity* (MIT Press 1987), David Harvey, *The Condition of Postmodernity: An Enquiry into the Origins of Cultural Change* (Wiley-Blackwell 1989), Fredric Jameson, *Postmodernism: Or, The Cultural Logic of Late Capitalism* (Verso 1992).

2 See Harvey, ibid 141–197, for an argument that a new way of understanding the capitalist process known as flexible accumulation has occurred.

3 One of the best-known examples is Jameson (n 1).

4 See generally, Anthony Giddens, *New Rules of Sociological Method* (Hutchinson 1976) and Anthony Giddens, *The Constitution of Society: Outline of the Theory of Structuration* (Polity Press 1984).

5 Ulrich Beck, *Risk Society: Towards A New Modernity* (Sage 1992) 10.

modernization of modern society."[6] Another characterization has termed it reflexive modernization, "a heightened modernization of society-changing scope".[7] Beck posits that, in this latter stage of modernity, the institutions making up the nation-state – traditional political parties, the nuclear family and the gendered labour market – are thrown into a state of flux. This brings about not only a reconsideration of those institutions but what has been described as a "meta-change" where the ways of understanding these institutions have been called into question due to the unintended consequences of how the first modernity unfolded.[8]

Ulrich Beck and Anthony Giddens present two related but different accounts of reflexive modernity. Both argue that individuals place less emphasis on "traditional, given, or taken-for-granted models for identity",[9] leading to a process of detraditionalization. This leads the conduct of social life to be called into question, resulting in "reflexive subjectivities, or sets of socially constructed identities which work on themselves in order to change themselves."[10] It has been argued that "reflexivity is an expression of the process that happens when we (individuals and institutions) reflect critically on the development we, ourselves, have been a part of creating."[11] According to Beck, this critical reflection leads to "individualization", which means the disentanglement from traditional social institutions.[12]

In early or simple modernity, identity was "comparatively stable ... whatever you were was not your own choice".[13] Late modernity, however, institutionalises a different way of living and being in the world. For Giddens, modern social life requires that social practices are constantly examined and reformed in the light of new information about those practices, meaning that the nature of that character is constantly altered.[14] He placed significant emphasis on the role of the subject, or knowledgeable human agent, in late modernity. He argues that the process of disembedding people from traditional social identities is largely driven by abstract systems or systems of technical expertise, such as social sciences. These abstract forces, along with the processes of cultural and economic globalization, disembed identities from contexts such as locality and break down the cultural basis for traditional identities. This disembeddedness brings about the need to be reflexive, to take control over one's own identity and biography, as the possibilities seem

6 Ulrich Beck, Wolfgang Bonss and Christoph Lau, 'The Theory of Reflexive Modernization: Problematic, Hypotheses and Research Programme' (2003) 20(2) *Theory, Culture & Society* 1, 1, emphasis in original.

7 Ulrich Beck, *The Reinvention of Politics: Rethinking Modernity in the Global Social Order* (Wiley 1997) 17.

8 Beck, Bonss and Lau (n 6) 2.

9 David Farrugia, 'Addressing the Problem of Reflexivity in Theories of Reflexive Modernisation: Subjectivity and Structural Contradiction' (2015) 51(4) *Journal of Sociology* 872, 874.

10 Ibid.

11 Malene Freudendal-Pedersen, *Mobility in Daily Life: Between Freedom and Unfreedom* (Routledge 2009) 29.

12 Ulrich Beck, *World Risk Society* (Wiley Blackwell 1999).

13 Peter Wagner, *A Sociology of Modernity: Liberty and Discipline* (Routledge 1994).

14 Anthony Giddens, *The Consequences of Modernity* (Polity Press 1990) 38.

to be now virtually limitless.[15] This new form of modernity generally relies on individuals possessing high levels of agency. In order to be considered properly reflexive, individuals require something more than the capacity to merely reflect; reflexivity requires action in order to adapt to new circumstances. A consequence of this is the decline in trust and deference towards traditional authorities and institutions, with the notion of expertise itself gradually losing its power when experts are seen to fail, creating even greater space for individuals to control their own biographies. In essence, reflexivity is about responding to the side-effects and dangers produced by modernity itself.[16]

Beck similarly argues for the reflexivity of identity, due to a compulsion for the "construction, self-design and self-staging of one's own biography".[17] These changes in identity had to be managed in a world with a different conception of, and approach to, risk. For Beck, risk has become such a central part of late modern life that the contemporary world can be characterised as a risk society. While it has been argued that individuals are not nearly so free to self-identify and control their own biographies as advocates of reflexivity appear to argue,[18] this misses one fundamental aspect of reflexive modernity. Despite having a greater amount of agency than before due to the decline of traditional social structures, these structures are not "replaced by a void",[19] but by a new way of conducting life based on an idea of the welfare state which has a different attitude towards individuals. Having been disembedded from traditional social roles, new kinds of constraints act to re-embed individuals in this new social structure. Reflexive modernity, therefore, has a "double face",[20] whereby social structures presume high levels of individual agency, where an individual is "*actor*, *designer*, *juggler* and *stage director* of his own biography, identity, social networks, commitments and convictions."[21]

Similarly, Giddens argues that reflexivity is not only a matter for individuals – institutions are also affected by the decline of tradition, by radical doubt over knowledge and by the need to adapt to multiple potential futures, all of which are inherently uncertain. For Giddens, institutional reflexivity means that an increasing number of aspects of social life and relations are amenable to continuous

15 See generally, Giddens ibid, Anthony Giddens, *Modernity and Self-Identity: Self and Society in the Late Modern Age* (Polity Press 1991) and Anthony Giddens, *The Transformation of Intimacy: Love, Sexuality and Eroticism in Modern Societies* (Polity Press 1993).

16 Harry Ferguson, *Protecting Children In Time: Child Abuse, Child Protection and the Consequences of Modernity* (Palgrave Macmillan 2004) 119.

17 Beck (n 7) 96.

18 See Will Atkinson, *Class, Individualization and Late Modernity: In Search of the Reflexive Worker* (Palgrave Macmillan 2010), Carl May and Andrew Cooper, 'Personal Identity and Social Change: Some Theoretical Considerations' (1995) 38(1) *Acta Sociologica* 75, Matthew Adams, 'The Reflexive Self and Culture: A Critique' (2003) 54(2) *British Journal of Sociology* and Margaret Archer, *The Reflexive Imperative in Late Modernity* (Cambridge University Press 2012).

19 Beck (n 7) 95.

20 Beck (n 5) 30.

21 Beck (n 7) 95. Emphasis in original.

revision in light of newly emergent information and knowledge: "the regularized use of knowledge about social life is a constitutive element in its organization and transformation."[22] This, in turn, produces new possibilities for individuals operating within those institutional structures, new possibilities for availing of increased agency. Therefore, the concept of reflexivity can be seen as a "characteristic of macro-level structural, cultural and institutional processes, as well as subjectivities and biographies" which captures "something historically significant about the relationship between subjectivity and the rest of the social world."[23] This more subtle view of the modernization process means that reflexivity cannot be seen solely as the rise of unfettered agency, or as the rise of a fetishised individualism, but more as the complex interplay of individuals trying to find their way in a world rendered increasingly unfamiliar by change.

One important way in which institutions can be influenced by individuals with increased scope for agency is through the political process. The knowledge produced in late modernity leads to increasing scepticism over the ability of traditional institutions to cope with the challenges people face.[24] This can lead to two distinct responses – counter-modernization, which seeks a return to more traditional ways of thinking and being so as to promote a sense of security, and a more radical subpolitics.[25] This latter response signifies a politics that takes place "outside and beyond the representative institutions of the political system of nation-states".[26] This politicises social actors and areas of social life which were previously unpolitical,[27] thereby opening up new areas for political engagement and debate. For Beck, individuals and groups who were previously marginalised and excluded from the political arena take centre-stage, leading to "the contestation of taken-for-granted assumptions of modernity by actors outside the system of formal politics, predominantly social movement."[28] This engagement is ad hoc and direct in nature, allowing the "shaping [of] society from below" by previously marginalised groups or individuals.[29]

A number of test criteria have been proposed to determine whether a second, reflexive stage of modernity has developed. These include attempts to redraw boundaries between social groups or new ways of conducting social life. The demise of traditional, hierarchical notions of expertise, the increased importance of risk and uncertainty, and the rise of the individual subject are also important

22 Giddens 1991 (n 15) 21.

23 Farrugia (n 9) 881. In this way, reflexivity comes quite close to Foucault's concept of responsibilisation, whereby responsibility for avoiding risks is placed on individuals – see Thomas Lemke, 'The Birth of Bio-Politics: Michel Foucault's Lectures at the Collège de France on Neo-Liberal Governmentality' (2001) 30(2) *Economy and Society* 190.

24 Giddens (n 15) chapter 3.

25 Beck (n 7) 18.

26 Ibid.

27 Ibid 93.

28 Boris Holzer and Mads P Sorensen, 'Rethinking Subpolitics: Beyond the Iron Cage of Modern Politics' (2003) 20(2) *Theory, Culture and Society* 79, 82.

29 Ulrich Beck, *World Risk Society* (Wiley Blackwell 1999) 39–40.

indicators of late modernity.[30] Importantly, it must be remembered that these indicators do not crystallise quickly or at the same time; rather, a gradual transition occurs which allows for the ex post facto application of second or reflexive modernity as a methodology as well as a theoretical descriptor.[31]

These indicators of change in the context of child protection will be explored later in this book, and especially in Chapters 6, 7 and 8. In the earlier chapters of the book, a child protection system which was wedded to tradition, morality, and risk elimination will be described. This stands in clear contrast to the later chapters where it will become clear that concepts such as the demise of tradition, the importance of subpolitics and an overriding concern with risk management are among the factors that have shaped the development of the contemporary protection system. During these chapters, the significant legal changes that have taken place since the 1990s will be overlaid with an outline of these social forces. In essence, I argue that the present system is capable, from our present vantage point, of being described as a child protection system of late, reflexive modernity.

The risk society and approaches to risk in social theory

The nature of risk itself differs according to whether the society in which it operates can be characterised as one of simple or late modernity. In order to understand the ways in which risks to children, outlined later in the book, were identified, experienced and managed, it is necessary to outline the social understanding of risk in each of these contexts. As indicated above, risk has taken an increased role in reflexive modernity. Risk, however, cannot simply be thought of as exposure to hazard or misfortune, but as a highly complex, politicised and value-laden concept.[32] It is also a concept which has a significant impact on law and, therefore, on legal responses to social problems.

Risk has always been present in nature. In the pre-modern era, societies tended to conflate risks and fate.[33] As more modern societies developed, a more complicated way of theorising risk developed, with Lupton pointing to three distinct ways of thinking about risk – realism, weak social constructivism and strong social constructivism.[34] Realism can be associated with the view of risk held in simple modernity. This view holds that risks are real and calculable and that a proper scientific investigation will be able to uncover them. Risk was, therefore, conceptualised as an artefact.[35] As societies became increasingly subject to industrialization, risk came to be both tamed and rewarded – risk-taking was central to the development of first mercantile and then capitalist economies. The belief that risk

30 Beck, Bonss and Lau (n 6) 19–26.
31 Ibid 26.
32 Mary Douglas, *Risk and Blame* (Routledge 1992).
33 Judith Green, *Risk and Misfortune: The Social Construction of Accidents* (Routledge 1997).
34 Deborah Lupton, *Risk* (Routledge 1999) 35.
35 Tom Horlick-Jones, 'Meaning and Contextualisation in Risk Assessment' (1998) 59(1) *Reliability Engineering and System Safety* 79.

can be measured and assessed led to the development of risk assessment strategies that have attempted to highlight certain risk factors amenable to control and management.[36] Risk was seen as arising from very specific situations, which could be highly regulated, and the risk potentially eliminated completely. Eventually, natural risks were increasingly brought to heel by technology.[37] However, each step in the process of modernization brought with it the possibility of unintended consequences and unforeseen risks, consequences which would lead to a decision about how it ought to be managed; such decisions would lead to further unintended consequences. The scale of these risks multiplied as society developed, as did social and cultural awareness of them.

Later approaches to risk, especially in the era of the risk society of late modernity, tended towards a more constructivist approach. Weak and strong social constructivism can be differentiated by understanding the difference between the level of "reality" accorded to the risk in question, and to the degree to which social and cultural contingencies are seen to influence the ways risks are perceived. Weak constructivism holds that risks are real, but are partly constructed by social processes.[38] Strong constructivism, on the other hand, places near-total emphasis on the social construction process.[39] Risk may consequently be seen as a product of the "social dynamics of particular relationships or situations",[40] rather than possessing an underlying ontological reality.

Weak constructivist perspectives on risk seem more suitable for understanding the nature of risk in reflexive modernity. While social processes do mediate how risks are perceived and may distort or amplify certain aspects of risks, it would seem unsupportable to deny the reality of certain risks, especially those explored in this book such as the risk of child abuse either within the home or by a person in a position of trust. Another way of approaching this problem is to recognise that while certain risks have commonly been present throughout history, the priority they are accorded shifts with prevailing attitudes. As Beck argued, risks

> can thus be changed, magnified, dramatized or minimized within knowledge, and to that extent they are particularly open to social definition and

36 Hazel Kemshall, *Understanding Risk in Criminal Justice* (Open University Press 2003).

37 Mary Douglas, *Risk Acceptability According to the Social Sciences* (Routledge 1986) 53–65.

38 Kemshall cites the public response to information campaigns relating to safer sex and drink-driving as examples of a constructivist approach to risk – the risk is real, yet expert advice is mediated by social factors – ibid 54.

39 Steve Rayner, 'Cultural Theory and Risk Analysis' in Sheldon Krimsky and Dominic Golding (eds), *Social Theories of Risk* (Praeger 1992). An example of this approach would be the public reaction to the Windscale nuclear inquiry – see Brian Wynne, *Rationality and Ritual: Participation and Exclusion in Nuclear Decision-making* (Routledge 1982).

40 Tim Rhodes, 'Risk Theory in Epidemic Times: Sex, Drugs and the Social Organisation of "Risk Behaviour"' (1997) 19(2) *Sociology of Health and Illness* 208, 216. Michael Thompson and Aaron Wildavsky, 'A Proposal to Create a Cultural Theory of Risk' in Howard Kunreuther and Eryl V Ley (eds), *The Risk Analysis Controversy: An Institutional Perspective* (Springer-Verlag 1982).

> construction. Hence the mass media and the scientific and legal professions in charge of defining risks become key social and political positions.[41]

Kemshall highlights how risk is thus understood as pervasive, leading to a sense of anxiety, while some risks are regarded as more legitimate and the symbolic meaning of selected risks amplified.[42] The risks in question, be they the risk of environmental hazard highlighted by Beck, the risk of crime as conceptualised by Kemshall, or the risk of childhood abuse which will be central to this book, are real phenomena given new meaning in a late modern, reflexive, risk society due to broader sociological factors.

The characterization of contemporary societies as risk societies is central to understanding many of the legal and policy responses which underpin modern child protection systems. Because modern society can be seen as "a society increasingly preoccupied with the future (and also with safety), which generates the notion of risk",[43] it also follows that there is something distinct about the way in which we attempt to deal with risk. While societies operating under conditions of simple modernity attempted to eliminate risk, late modern societies instead recognise that risk must instead be lived with, as the underlying anxiety compels us to design new structures for the management, rather than the eradication, of risk, which in turn creates problems for our relationship with public institutions.[44] This preoccupation with something that cannot be done away with, despite its potentially troubling consequences, brings about a feeling of lack of control. Beck recognised this when he highlighted how the "risks created by the momentum of innovation increasingly elude the control and protective institutions of industrial society."[45] In a risk society, risks are no longer limited in time or space, and so cannot be insured against, and it is more difficult to hold political institutions accountable for them should they come to pass. Also, because risks have become pervasive, the public contemplates risks to a much greater degree, not only with the result that they are subject to much higher degrees of anxiety but the dynamic between public or lay knowledge and expert knowledge is radicalised. This stands in stark contrast to the more optimistic elements of late modernity outlined above, such as increasing agency. This agency is now exercised under conditions of strain, with attempts to build systems that reflect our newfound concerns. In late modernity, individuals and

41 Beck (n 5) 22–23.

42 Kemshall draws on Lupton (n 34), Richard Sparks, 'Risk and Blame in Criminal Justice Controversies: British Press Coverage and Official Discourse on Prison Security' in Mark Brown and John Pratt (eds) *Dangerous Offenders: Punishment and the Social Order* (Routledge 2000) and Richard Sparks, 'Degrees of Estrangement: The Cultural Theory of Risk and Comparative Penology' (2001) 5(2) *Theoretical Criminology* 159.

43 Anthony Giddens and Christopher Pierson, *Conversations with Anthony Giddens: Making Sense of Modernity* (Stanford University Press 1998) 209.

44 Giddens (n 14) 111.

45 Ulrich Beck, 'Risk Society and the Provident State' in Scott Lash, Bronislaw Szerszynski and Brian Wynne, *Risk, Environment and Modernity: Towards a New Ecology* (Sage 1996) 27.

institutions are expected to be accountable,[46] and new systems constructed to manage risks effectively. Our optimism about our ability to build foolproof systems clashes with our anxiety over risk, leading to one of the paradoxes of a risk society – despite increased expectations that our new systems will not fail, the risk that they will fail cannot be eliminated, leading to more attempts to design failure-proof systems that incorporate elements of risk within them, regardless of whether a failure has occurred or not.[47]

How, then, does this pervasive anxiety about risk impact on the development of child protection policy? This is one of the central questions explored in this book, and the answer largely depends on how risk is understood. If policy were to be informed by artefact approaches to risk, the emphasis can be placed on identifying the risk in question, what leads to it, and taking action designed to reduce the danger that it poses through strategies designed to eliminate that risk, such as by incapacitating a potential source of risk. This was largely the approach taken in simple modernity. Constructivist approaches, on the other hand, would place some emphasis on understanding what turns a social phenomenon into a risk. The real difference between artefact and constructivist approaches from a policy perspective, therefore, lies in the question of the extent to which risk can be tamed. Constructivist approaches demand that risks are experienced as risks. I argue that child protection law and policy reflect an awareness that uncertainty over risk cannot be converted into definitive knowledge and therefore it must be accepted that the risk cannot be entirely eliminated, only managed. In embracing the view that risk is partially constructed, this book accepts Giddens' view on the impossibility of eradicating risk, as it is impossible to identify and take preventative action against all forms of danger. It does recognise, however, that certain risks can be managed through various reduction strategies, such as prevention and early intervention services, pre-employment screening and mandatory reporting systems. It also accepts that understanding the forces shaping the risk are as important as the risk itself. Therefore, this book will attempt to understand the framing of risks while also addressing the type of risk management procedures adopted in Irish child protection throughout its historical development, highlighting who were regarded as sources of risk and who were regarded as legitimate bearers of those risks.

46 Gillian Ruch, Amanda Lees and Jane Pritchard, 'Getting Beneath the Surface: Scapegoating and the Systems Approach in a Post-Munro World' (2014) 28(3) *Journal of Social Work Practice* 313.

47 Indeed, it has been argued that this is exactly the approach currently being adopted by Ireland's statutory child protection agency in its Parenting, Prevention and Family Support programme and the adoption of the Signs of Safety Model – see Caroline McGregor and Carmel Devaney, 'Protective support and supportive protection for families "in the middle": Learning from the Irish context' (2019) *Child and Family Social Work* 1 and Kenneth Burns and Caroline McGregor, 'Child Protection and Welfare Systems in Ireland: Continuities and Discontinuities of the Present' in Lisa Merkel-Holguin, John D Fulke and Richard Krugman (eds), *National Systems of Child Protection: Understanding the International Variability and Context for Developing Policy and Practice* (Springer 2019).

Agency and childhood

International and domestic law usually define a child as a person under the age of 18.[48] However, contemporary attitudes to childhood and the idea that childhood lasts this long would likely be unrecognisable to our historical forebears. Certain aspects of childhood may be claimed as natural; for instance, children's dependency, their lack of capacity, their innocence and their position relative to both their families and wider society. While it is clearly the case there may be physical or developmental stages associated with childhood which can claim near-universality, there is an important distinction to be drawn between biological childhood and social childhood, the latter being merely a construct, an artefact.[49]

Ariès was the first to argue in favour of a social constructionist perspective on childhood.[50] In *Centuries of Childhood*, he argued that childhood as currently conceived did not exist until the seventeenth century. This inspired other writers to examine childhood from the perspective of how society felt about children, the emotional meaning invested in them, and how they were valued for what they represented.[51] This view has not achieved universal consensus, with Pollack, in particular, highlighting significant flaws in aspects of Ariès' approach.[52] Nonetheless, this focus on childhood as a construct leads to two important propositions: first, that childhood cannot be regarded as an unproblematic description of a natural biological phase, but should instead be regarded as a cultural phenomenon attaching to the early part of the life course, and second, that how we see children and the way we behave towards them shape children's experiences and their engagement with the adult world.[53] Indeed, it is possible to argue that while all societies have a concept of childhood, comprised of beings thought of as children, different societies at different historical moments will have different conceptions of childhood.[54] Importantly, this conception of childhood will also change across generations – as James and James argue, "the childhood of the current generation of children will undoubtedly be different from that remembered by their parents."[55]

48 Age of Majority Act 1985, s 2, Child Care Act 1991, s 2, Convention on the Rights of the Child (adopted 20 November 1989, entered into force 2 September 1990) 1557 UNTS 3.
49 Neil Postman, *The Disappearance of Childhood* (Vintage 1994) and Michael Freeman, *The Rights and Wrongs of Children* (Frances Pinter, London 1983) 6.
50 Philippe Ariès, *Centuries of Childhood* (Jonathan Cape 1962).
51 Lawrence Stone, *The Family, Sex and Marriage in England, 1500–1800* (Weidenfeld 1977). Lloyd deMause (ed), *The History of Childhood: Untold Story of Child Abuse* (Souvenir Press 1976), Michael Anderson, *Approaches to the History of the Western Family 1500–1914* (Cambridge University Press 1980)
52 Linda Pollack, *Forgotten Children: Parent-child Relations from 1500 to 1900* (Cambridge University Press 1983).
53 Allison James and Adrian L James, *Constructing Childhood: Theory, Policy and Social Practice* (Palgrave Macmillan 2004) 12.
54 David Archard, *Children: Rights and Childhood* (Routledge 1993) 21–24.
55 James and James (n 53) 20. See also Jens Qvortrup, 'Childhood Matters: An Introduction' in Jens Qvortrup, Marjatta Bardy, Giovanni Sgritta and Helmut Wintersburger (eds), *Childhood Matters: Social Theory, Practice and Politics* (Avebury 1994).

One of the most important aspects of this process of social construction is bound up with the extent to which we regard children as individuals who are capable of acting or participating in their own right; in short, the question of whether we regard them as possessing agency. Agency is ordinarily seen as the ability to exert choice for, and to influence the world around, oneself.[56] Having been disentangled from traditional power structures, been granted control over one's biography and with conceptions of expertise radically altered, agents in late modernity are seen to possess significant power over their destinies. However, agency is differentially distributed across society due to a range of factors, one of which is age. Children have traditionally been regarded not as agents, but as passive presences in an adult world, without the capacity for reason.[57] Children have traditionally been thought of as "becoming" rather than "being". Durkheim posited that childhood is "a period in which the individual, in both the physical and moral sense, does not yet exist".[58] While adulthood is regarded as a stage of full development, during childhood the person is merely becoming themselves.

However, later sociologists attempted to turn this idea on its head, arguing that children were indeed "beings" in a full sense. According to James, Jenks and Prout, the child is a social actor, who does not have to suffer from a "shortfall of competence, reason or significance."[59] Prout later posited that children can be seen as "participants shaping, as well as being shaped by, society".[60] This is because while the immaturity of children is a biological fact, the ways in which this immaturity is understood is a fact of culture.[61] Not only are children capable of being participants in social processes, such as decision-making, they also participate in the act of constructing the world around them.[62] Corsaro has written of children not as passive recipients of knowledge and values, but as agents who actively interpret the adult world, using it to shape their own moral frameworks.[63]

As attested to both by Oswell,[64] and King,[65] the literature on children's agency owes an enormous debt to the work of Giddens who began to conceive of a more complex relationship between agency and structure than had previously been achieved. He turned away from a clear distinction between structure and agency,

56 Mustafa Emirbayer and Ann Mische, 'What is Agency? (1998) 103(4) *American Journal of Sociology* 962.

57 John Stuart Mill, *On Liberty* (1859, 2nd edn, Oxford University Press 2015) 13.

58 Émile Durkheim, 'Childhood' in WFS Pickering (ed), *Selected Writings on Education: Volume I: Durkheim: Essays on Morals and Education* (Routledge 1979) 150.

59 Alison James, Chris Jenks and James Prout, *Theorizing Childhood* (Polity Press 1998) 207.

60 Alan Prout, *The Body, Childhood and Society* (Macmillan 2000) 2.

61 Allison James and Alan Prout, *Constructing and Reconstructing Childhood: Contemporary Issues in the Sociological Study of Childhood* (Routledge 1990) 7.

62 Michael Wyness, *Childhood and Society: An Introduction to the Sociology of Childhood* (Palgrave Macmillan 2006).

63 William Carsaro, *The Sociology of Childhood* (2nd edn, Pine Forge Press 2005).

64 David Oswell, *The Agency of Children: From Family to Global Human Rights* (Cambridge University Press 2013) 38.

65 Michael King, 'The Child, Childhood and Children's Rights within Sociology' (2004) 15(2) *King's Law Journal* 273, 291.

preferring instead the concept of structuration, whereby "systems, grounded in the knowledgeable activities of situated actors who draw upon rules and resources ... are produced and reproduced in interaction."[66] The role for agents in this context is not merely to act, but to "make a difference".[67] This leads to the question of quite what difference children can make to the institutions around them. In order to deal with this question, it is necessary to have recourse to the idea of children's agency being regarded as a collectivity. Children are commonly spoken of as belonging to a single sociological category or class based on their generation.[68] It is important to question whether this risks totalising the experiences of the different children within that collectivity – "even within one generation of children, in any one society, each child's experiences of 'childhood' will nonetheless be tempered by the particularities of their social circumstances".[69] With this goes the idea that it may not make sense to speak of "children" as possessing agency, but rather of individual children being capable of doing so. Yet not all children will be in the position to exert the kind of influence on their surrounding social structures, or even control over their own biographies, seemingly demanded of agents living in conditions of reflexive modernity; indeed, precious few may be able to do so to even a limited extent.

Oswell highlights how this criticism may be dealt with by the idea of collectivity. This approach to agency does not reduce all children to a single sign or measure, but accounts for the fact that children "as a collectivity comprise a multitude of experiences and positionalities".[70] In this way of seeing agency as comprised of multiple experiences, children can have different effects on different parts of the infrastructure which surround them. He uses the analogy of a children's ophthalmic clinic to demonstrate the point. In such a clinic, children with no knowledge of each other or commonalities except for being children are continually subdivided and aggregated in order to design and administer tests and strategies for the rectification of eye problems. Using Foucault's language of conditions of possibility, Oswell makes the point that once such conditions are created by the clinic, children can then begin to act in and upon the world around them – "capacity to see is enhanced through the spectacles; their capacity to act in the world is enhanced by the facilitatory technology of lens and metal frame."[71] Agency is thought of relationally, not as a binary property that one has or does not have. As indicated above, the book will deploy this collectivist approach to agency when discussing how children came to play a role in the development

66 Giddens, *The Constitution of Society* (n 4) 25.
67 Ibid 14.
68 For the emerging development of a more relational approach to agency incorporating these concepts, see generally, Florian Esser, Meike S Baader, Tanja Betz and Beatrice Hungerland, *Reconceptualising Agency and Childhood: New Perspectives in Childhood Studies* (Routledge 2016).
69 James and James (n 53) 22.
70 Oswell (n 64) 77.
71 Ibid 78.

of the current system; in doing so, it allows us to highlight the ways in which children were able to exert change not only through direct participation but also through being considered individuals with interests and rights.[72]

The role of law

It remains to explain the role that law will play in this book. Briefly, the nature and content of various legal rules will be outlined and explained, but this exposition is not an end in itself. Rather, the primary purpose of this legal analysis is to demonstrate how the law has been used not just to further certain policy aims, such as more effective child protection, but to express and embody certain ideas about childhood and the nature of child protection work. As the law extended its scope, it regulated previously ungoverned aspects of social life, and finally, it imposed regulations to help manage the risks associated with child protection in late modernity.

Law is often thought of as reflecting broader social or moral attitudes to social phenomena. This is, for example, one of the common themes found in literature positing that law ought in some way to reflect universal moral principles.[73] Alternatively, it may be argued that law's main purpose is the maintenance of a peaceful social order,[74] or that law may be used to facilitate social change.[75] A broader understanding of the way in which law expresses and communicates social ideas is found in the work of a range of scholars. Elizabeth Anderson and Richard Pildes, for example, argue for an expressivist account of law,[76] which allows us to see the creation or reform of legal rules as expressing "official state beliefs and attitudes".[77] Expression of a particular view in law can, therefore, act as a form of official rubber stamp approving of that view. This way of conceptualising law is similar, but not identical, to the view held by theorists such as Michael King who focus less on the messages that law expresses, and more on what lies behind those messages. The difference between these ideas lies in the emphasis that they place on the intention of lawmakers. King posits that when lawmakers designate certain acts to be unlawful, or grant rights to certain individuals, this

72 For a consideration of the more direct ways in which children can participate in the democratic process, see both Aoife Nolan, 'The Child as 'Democratic Citizen' – Challenging the "Participation Gap"' [2010] *Public Law* 767 and Gerison Lansdown, *Promoting Children's Participation in Democratic Decision-Making* (Innocent Research Centre 2001).

73 See, for example, John Finnis, *Natural Law and Natural Rights* (Clarendon Press 1980).

74 See, for example, Garrett Barden and Tim Murphy, *Law and Justice in the Community* (Oxford University Press 2010) 19–40.

75 See generally, Sharyn L Roach Anleu, *Law and Social Change* (2nd edn, Sage 2010).

76 Elizabeth S Anderson and Richard H Pildes, 'Expressive Theories of Law: A General Restatement' (2000) 148 *University of Pennsylvania Law Review* 1503. See also Cass R Sunstein, 'On the Expressive Function of Law' (1996) 144(5) *University of Pennsylvania Law Review* 2021, and Patricia Funk, 'Is There an Expressive Function of Law? An Empirical Analysis of Voting Laws with Symbolic Fines' (2007) 9(1) *American Law and Economics Review* 135.

77 Anderson and Pildes, ibid, 1506.

acts as a shorthand that is "immediately accessible to popular culture through the media of mass communicators such as politicians, broadcasters, journalists and the charismatic leaders of pressure groups".[78] This communicates a desire that an individual or group is to be thought of in a certain way.

Using the approach that laws can communicate or express certain values or messages, we can begin to unpack the different ways of ideas of childhood and risk which have been present throughout both traditional and late modernity. This is especially so when the law expands into territory where there was previously no legal regulation which are seen to be in need of better regulation. This process is known as juridification, which Habermas explains as

> the tendency toward an increase in formal (or positive, written) law that can be observed in modern society. We can distinguish here between the expansion of law, that is the legal regulation of new, hitherto informally regulated social matters, from the increasing density of law, that is, the specialized breakdown of global statements of the legally relevant facts into more detailed statements.[79]

Juridification, therefore, refers both to the increased territory that law seeks to govern, and to the elaboration of more detailed standards of acceptable behaviour.[80]

It will become evident as this book progresses that the social space which children inhabit – and this is especially so for children experiencing high levels of risk – has become increasingly regulated and juridified.[81] This is true both of Ireland and beyond. Childhood was described as "the most intensively governed sector of personal existence".[82] It was not always so. The period between the late nineteenth century and the present day has seen an exponential increase in the level of legal regulation of children and childhood. Later chapters will detail the development of a highly complex series of legal rules, ranging from constitutional

78 Michael King, 'Children's Rights as Communication: Reflections on Autopoietic Theory and the United Nations Convention' (1994) 57(3) *Modern Law Review* 385, 391. See also Michael King and Christine Piper, *How the Law Thinks about Children* (2nd edn, Ashgate 1995).

79 Jürgen Habermas, *The Theory of Communicative Action – Volume 2: Lifeworld and System* (Polity Press 1987) 357.

80 Gunther Teubner, 'Juridification: Concepts, Aspects, Limits, Solutions' in Gunther Teubner (ed) *Juridification of Social Spheres* (De Gruyter 1987).

81 See generally, Michael King, *A Better World for Children? Explorations in Morality and Authority* (Routledge 1997) 58–84 and Samantha Ashenden, *Governing Child Sexual Abuse: Negotiating the Boundaries between Public and Private, Law and Science* (Routledge 2003) 59–89. See also Neil Gilbert, Nigel Parton and Marit Skivene, *Child Protection Systems: International Trends and Orientations* (Oxford University Press 2011) and Neil Gilbert, 'A comparative study of child welfare systems: abstract orientations and concrete results' (2012) 34 *Child and Youth Services Review* 532.

82 Nikolas Rose, *Governing the Soul* (Routledge 1989) 121.

provisions to statutory regulations, governing responses to one particular area of children's lives. Little or nothing will be said of other areas affecting children such as education, healthcare, employment, immigration, financial support or private law responses to parental separation, all of which have themselves developed an elaborate legal framework. It must be recognised that all of these issues do have a bearing on child protection law and its exercise because of the impact of structural and social inequalities on legal interventions to protect children.[83] That childhood has become juridified seems beyond question; later chapters will demonstrate what that process of juridification in the specific context of child protection tells us about the changes in how childhood has been thought about.

Perhaps the most fundamental legal change for children over the past few decades has been the recognition that children have rights. Rights have played a significant role in the development of all child protection systems, given the interplay between children's and parents' rights. While an extensive examination of children's rights lies outside the scope of this work, it is important to highlight in particular the link between rights and agency. Once a person is recognised as having the capacity for agency, this leads to them having "a right, in the sense of a moral claim, to be recognized by others as a 'rights-bearing person,' entitled to a legally instituted schedule of rights."[84] These rights may occur at different levels, from a grand level of theoretical abstraction to a more grounded rights discourse dealing with the application of statutory rights,[85] but they ultimately convert moral claims into judicialised and legally concretised rights.[86] As Freeman explained, rights

> are important because those who have them can exercise agency … As agents, rights-bearers can participate. They can make their own lives, rather than having their lives made for them. And participation is a fundamental human right. It enables us to demand rights.[87]

Yet the use of agency as a basis for rights poses some significant problems in the context of children's rights, as it brings into sharp focus the distinction between the will and interest theories of rights. The will theory, as outlined by Hart,[88] posits that it is essential to be able to exercise power over a particular claim, in the

83 Paul Bywaters et al, 'Child Welfare Inequalities in the Four Nations of the UK' (2018) *Journal of Social Work* (online).
84 Seyla Benhabib, 'Reason-bearing and Rights-giving: Constructing the subject of rights' (2013) 20(1) *Constellations* 38.
85 On which, see James W Nickel, *Making Sense of Human Rights. Philosophical Reflections on the Universal Declaration of Human Rights* (University of California Press 1987) 44.
86 Benhabib (n 84) 47.
87 Michael Freeman, 'Why It Remains Important to Take Children's Rights Seriously' (2007) 15 *International Journal of Children's Rights* 5, 8.
88 HLA Hart, *Essays on Bentham: Jurisprudence and Political Theory* (Oxford University Press 1982) 183.

form of choosing to exercise it or to waive it, in order to establish it as a right. Interest theorists, on the other hand, emphasise that there are some interests that cannot be waived, such as the interest in not being enslaved.[89] As such, the will theory effectively regards agency as a prerequisite for holding legal rights, and if children are denied the status of agent, they are denied the status of rights-holder. Griffin argues that infants cannot be recognised as having rights, as they are not normative agents, only potential agents.[90] Moreover, he argues that the justification of adults having obligations towards children cannot be run together with the justification of children having rights where children's status as agents is in doubt.[91] Tobin posits that this is problematic if we see part of the purpose of rights as being to influence the exercise of power.[92]

Yet there are powerful objections to this approach. First, Freeman convincingly established that if one were to undertake a Rawlsian thought-experiment, the preference for an interest-based theory of rights, and the legal recognition of those rights, would be convincing.[93] Secondly, children are now more commonly regarded as "beings" rather than "becomings",[94] and are capable of claiming many the same kinds of interests as adults. This is a powerful objection when allied with Oswell's concept of agency, outlined earlier in this chapter. By recognising children as members of the moral community, whose interests not only need to be taken into account, but can influence policy without them having to express their will, the approach to agency-based rights adopted by Griffin is undermined. Griffin's approach to agency is also based on an older version of agency/structure distinction, whereby the ability to exercise free will and structuring nature of social forces existed as opposites. Such a clear distinction now seems unreal, as sociological theory has pointed to ways in which agency and structure can feed off each other.[95] It neglects the more dialectical approach found in Gidden's structuration theory whereby the two feed each other. If agency is construed in the more collective way used by Oswell in his ophthalmic clinic analogy, then even young infants lacking the cognitive skill traditionally demanded of normative agents will be regarded as capable of helping to shape the structural environment in which they live. In this way, the recognition of children as citizens with legal rights and the ability to influence policy-making does not have to depend on the exercise of direct participation rights, while also not falling foul of the perils of paternalism.

89 Neil MacCormick, 'Children's Rights: A Test-Case for Theories of Rights' (1976) 62(3) *Archiv für Rechts und Sozialphilosophie* 305, Joseph Raz, *The Morality of Freedom* (Oxford University Press 1986).
90 James Griffin, *On Human Rights* (Oxford University Press 2008) 83.
91 Ibid 85.
92 John Tobin, 'Justifying Children's Rights' (2013) 21(3) *International Journal of Children's Rights* 395, drawing on Katherine Hunt Federle, 'Rights Flow Downhill' (1994) 2 *International Journal of Children's Rights* 343.
93 Michael Freeman, *The Rights and Wrongs of Children* (Continuum 1983) chapter 2.
94 Qvortrup (n 55).
95 Giddens, *The Constitution of Society* (n 4).

This more flexible approach to agency allows all children to be recognised as agents and the debate on will and interest theories of children's rights identified by Tobin and others to be circumvented.[96] Instead, the focus will be on the ways in which the accrual of legal rights by children tell us something about how children are perceived within the child protection system. For Tobin, rights are thought of primarily as a cultural system, "that produces and constructs rather than discovers some metaphysical vision of the rights to which children are entitled."[97] Thus, the accrual of each new legal right represents something more than a new legal entitlement – it represents another act of recognition that children can and ought to be regarded as capable of shaping their own lives and their structures they inhabit.

As a result, the book will not engage in a sustained examination of the nature and extent of children's rights (in terms of either international or domestic human rights law), or a comparison of children's rights in Irish law with international standards. To do so would not assist in engaging with the central focus of this research, which looks at the construction of children and childhood through simple and late modernity and the construction of risk in child protection law, rather than the precise extent of legal rights or obligations. The development of rights language, it is argued, demonstrates that law is communicating the idea that children have become increasingly morally relevant. Secondly, the granting of legal rights to children in Ireland will be seen as a way of facilitating the advancement of children's interests where previously the state showed little concern for these. For instance, the development of legal mechanisms to remove children from dangerous situations in their family homes represented not only a juridification of the parent–child relationship, but eventually a site of dispute over the priority of parents' or children's rights that resulted in new standards of acceptable parental behaviour being imposed in furtherance of children's rights. Finally, the recognition that children do have rights serves to indicate that they have not just become a different kind of object, one we are concerned for rather than one that we impose discipline upon, but have instead become legal subjects.

A further aspect of juridification as a means of expressing certain ideas through law can be seen in how the law handles risk. It has been argued that risk has not figured prominently in legal theory.[98] However, since that claim was made, several attempts have been made to theorise the links between risk and law, in particular by Jenny Steele and Elizabeth Fisher. Steele argues that legal theorists have been selective in their use of ideas associated with risk, ignoring questions of statistical probability in favour of questions of luck and chance. Everything was focussed on outcomes, "those aspects of decision-making method which make a link between individual autonomy and preference on the one hand, and objective or universal standards for responsibility on the other."[99] Yet there is also, she argues, a complex relationship between law, risk, autonomy and the welfare

96 Tobin (n 92) and MacCormick (n 89).
97 Tobin ibid 433.
98 Anthony Giddens, 'Risk and Responsibility' (1999) 62 *Modern Law Review* 1.
99 Jenny Steele, *Risk and Legal Theory* (Hart Publishing 2004) 12.

state,[100] as individuals were thought of as taking responsibility for the risks generated by their own choices. In a phrase reminiscent of reflexivity theorists, she describes people as having "responsibility for planning their life in the context of numerous uncertainties".[101] This is made particularly clear when she considers the relationship between individuals and public agencies.[102] For Steele, public agencies are increasingly employed in presenting information about risks, information which is conceded to be inconclusive. Decisions on dangerous activity are thereby delegated to individuals who possess greater agency, and responsibility for self-government, than at any previous point in history, but who may not be fully capable of making the right decision for themselves nor of handling the ontologically troubling continual exposure to hazard. To combat this, decision-making seems to require analysis in terms of risk, leading to what she calls "problem closure", but this can only ever be hoped to be a temporary solution, given the increasingly ubiquitous nature of risk.

Fisher elaborates on the role of legal disputes about risk appraisal in this context. She describes these disputes as "essentially disputes about what is, and should be, the role and nature of 'good' public administration in risk regulation."[103] Public administration, for Fisher, is the institutional context for the risk evaluation process.[104] She argues that traditional approaches to risk in public administration are based on a dichotomy between science and democracy, with a more scientific approach to risk resembling the artefact approach associated with simple modernity, whereas the democratic approach requires greater cognisance of the socially constructed aspects of any given risk. In seeking to move beyond what she sees as the false dichotomies involved in traditional thinking about the legal regulation of risk, she argues that law "is not just a tool for ensuring more science or more democracy but is an influential discourse that actually constructs these concepts."[105] Therefore, not only do risks shape law and legal responses to risks, but the law can also shape risks and how they are dealt with by other fields of expertise.

Historically, the more scientific approach was preferred; legislatures set mandates for administrative bodies designed to reflect a public preference for how a particular risk should be managed while also restraining the discretion of the decision-maker. In this way, it represents a view of risk and of a role for law which has much in common with simple modernity. When the ways in which the risks to children were regulated in this period are discussed in later chapters, the idea that risk was governed instrumentally in simple modernity will become clear. When the early decades of the child protection system are covered in later

100 Ibid 38–50 and chapter 4.
101 Ibid 204.
102 Ibid, especially chapter 5.
103 Elizabeth Fisher, *Risk Regulation and Administrative Constitutionalism* (Hart Publishing 2007) 3.
104 Ibid 18–16.
105 Ibid 17.

chapters, it will become evident that attempts were made to deal with risk in this fashion. The more constructivist, late modern approach, however, sees law taking a more flexible approach. Decision-making bodies are not bound by a set of legislative imperatives but are granted discretion to resolve disputes over risks in line with general principles and within broad parameters. The positivist methodologies adopted for dispute resolution in the former model give way to the need to accommodate different perspectives on knowledge, and the decision-maker must now engage in a deliberative process. Examples of this will be seen in chapters dealing with the reforms initiated from the 1990s onwards when the processes of risk-based decision-making provided for in contemporary child protection law are outlined.

Conclusion

This chapter has sought to outline the key concepts that will inform the analysis that follows in subsequent chapters. In particular, it has sought to explain how the ideas of late modernity, reflexive modernity and risk society will be used in explaining the historic and contemporary nature of the child protection framework. The legal framework was theorised, utilising the concept of juridification as a way of understanding not only the proliferation of law but also how it mirrors and expresses the concerns of late modernity. Each of these themes will be further explored in subsequent chapters.

References

Adams M, 'The Reflexive Self and Culture: A Critique' (2003) 54(2) *British Journal of Sociology* 221.

Anderson ES and Pildes RH, 'Expressive Theories of Law: A General Restatement' (2000) 148 *University of Pennsylvania Law Review* 1503.

Anderson M, *Approaches to the History of the Western Family 1500–1914* (Cambridge University Press 1980).

Archard D, *Children: Rights and Childhood* (Routledge 1993).

Archer M, *The Reflexive Imperative in Late Modernity* (Cambridge University Press 2012).

Ariès P, *Centuries of Childhood* (Jonathan Cape, London 1962).

Ashenden S, *Governing Child Sexual Abuse: Negotiating the Boundaries between Public and Private, Law and Science* (Routledge 2003).

Atkinson A, *Class, Individualization and Late Modernity: In Search of the Reflexive Worker* (Palgrave Macmillan 2010).

Barden G and Murphy T, *Law and Justice in the Community* (Oxford University Press 2010).

Beck U, *Risk Society: Towards A New Modernity* (Sage 1992) 10.

Beck U, 'Risk Society and the Provident State' in Scott Lash, Bronislaw Szerszynski and Brian Wynne (eds), *Risk, Environment and Modernity: Towards a New Ecology* (Sage 1996).

Beck U, *The Reinvention of Politics: Rethinking Modernity in the Global Social Order* (Polity Press 1997).

Beck U, *World Risk Society* (Wiley Blackwell 1999).
Beck, Bonss W and Lau C, 'The Theory of Reflexive Modernization: Problematic, Hypotheses and Research Programme' (2003) 20(2) *Theory, Culture & Society* 1.
Benhabib S, 'Reason-Bearing and Rights-Giving: Constructing the Subject of Rights' (2013) 20(1) *Constellations* 38.
Burns K and McGregor C, 'Child Protection and Welfare Systems in Ireland: Continuities and Discontinuities of the Present' in Lisa Merkel-Holguin, John D Fulke and Richard Krugman (eds), *National Systems of Child Protection: Understanding the International Variability and Context for Developing Policy and Practice* (Springer 2019).
Bywaters P, 'Child Welfare Inequalities in the Four Nations of the UK' (2018) *Journal of Social Work*, doi.org/10.1177/1468017318793479.
Carsaro W, *The Sociology of Childhood* (2nd edn, Pine Forge Press 2005).
deMause L (ed), *The History of Childhood: Untold Story of Child Abuse* (Souvenir Press 1976).
Douglas M, *Risk Acceptability According to the Social Sciences* (Routledge 1986).
Douglas M, *Risk and Blame* (Routledge 1992).
Durkheim É, 'Childhood' in WFS Pickering (ed), *Selected Writings on Education: Volume I: Durkheim: Essays on Morals and Education* (Routledge 1979).
Emirbayer M and Mische A, 'What is Agency? (1998) 103(4) *American Journal of Sociology* 962.
Esser F, Baader MS, Betz T and Beatrice Hungerland B, *Reconceptualising Agency and Childhood: New Perspective in Childhood Studies* (Routledge 2016).
Farrugia D, 'Addressing the Problem of Reflexivity in Theories of Reflexive Modernisation: Subjectivity and Structural Contradiction' (2015) 51(4) *Journal of Sociology* 872.
Ferguson H, *Protecting Children In time: Child Abuse, Child Protection and the of Modernity* (Palgrave Macmillan 2004).
Finnis J, *Natural Law and Natural Rights* (Clarendon Press 1980).
Fisher E, *Risk Regulation and Administrative Constitutionalism* (Hart Publishing 2007) 3.
Freeman M, *The Rights and Wrongs of Children* (Continuum 1983)
Freeman M, 'Why it Remains Important to Take Children's Rights Seriously' (2007) 15 *International Journal of Children's Rights* 5.
Freudendal-Pedersen M, *Mobility in Daily Life: Between Freedom and Unfreedom* (Routledge 2009).
Funk P, 'Is There an Expressive Function of Law? An Empirical Analysis of Voting Laws with Symbolic Fines' (2007) 9(1) *American Law and Economics Review* 135.
Giddens A, *New Rules of Sociological Method* (Hutchinson 1976)
Giddens A, *The Constitution of Society: Outline of the Theory of Structuration* (Polity Press 1984).
Giddens A, *The Consequences of Modernity* (Polity Press 1990).
Giddens A, *Modernity and Self-Identity: Self and Society in the Late Modern Age* (Polity Press 1991).
Giddens A, *The Transformation of Intimacy: Love, Sexuality and Eroticism in Modern Societies* (Polity Press 1993).
Giddens A, 'Risk and Responsibility' (1999) 62 *Modern Law Review* 1.
Giddens A and Pierson C, *Conversations with Anthony Giddens: Making Sense of Modernity* (Stanford University Press 1998).

Gilbert N, 'A Comparative Study of Child Welfare Systems: Abstract Orientations and Concrete Results' (2012) 34 *Child and Youth Services Review* 532.

Gilbert N, Parton P and Skivene M, *Child Protection Systems: International Trends and Orientations* (Oxford University Press 2011).

Green J, *Risk and Misfortune: The Social Construction of Accidents* (Routledge 1997).

Habermas J, *The Philosophical Discourse of Modernity* (MIT Press 1987).

Habermas J, *The Theory of Communicative Action – Volume 2: Lifeworld and System* (Polity Press 1987) 357.

Hart HLA, *Essays on Bentham: Jurisprudence and Political Theory* (Oxford University Press 1982) 183.

Harvey D, *The Condition of Postmodernity: An Enquiry into the Origins of Cultural Change* (Wiley-Blackwell 1989).

Holzer B and P Sorensen MP, 'Rethinking Subpolitics: Beyond the Iron Cage of Modern Politics' (2003) 20(2) *Theory, Culture and Society* 79.

Horlick-Jones T, 'Meaning and Contextualisation in Risk Assessment' (1998) 5 *Reliability Engineering and System Safety* 79.

Hunt Federle K, 'Rights Flow Downhill' (1994) 2 *International Journal of Children's Rights* 343.

James A and Prout A, *Constructing and Reconstructing Childhood: Contemporary Issues in the Sociological Study of Childhood* (Routledge 1990).

James A and James AL, *Constructing Childhood: Theory, Policy and Social Practice* (Palgrave Macmillan 2004) 12.

James A, Jenks C and Prout J, *Theorizing Childhood* (Polity Press 1998).

Jameson F, *Postmodernism: Or, The Cultural Logic of Late Capitalism* (Verso 1992).

Kemshall H, *Understanding Risk in Criminal Justice* (Open University Press 2003).

King M, *A Better World for Children? Explorations in Morality and Authority* (Routledge 1997).

King M, 'The Child, Childhood and Children's Rights within Sociology' (2004) 15(2) *King's Law Journal* 273.

King M and Piper C, *How the Law Thinks about Children* (2nd edn, Ashgate 1995).

L Roach Anleu SL, *Law and Social Change* (2nd edn, Sage 2010).

Lansdown G, *Promoting Children's Participation in Democratic Decision-Making* (Innocent Research Centre 2001).

Lemke T, 'The Birth of Bio-Politics: Michel Foucault's Lectures at the College de France on Neo-Liberal Governmentality' (2001) 30(2) *Economy and Society* 190.

Lupton D, *Risk* (Routledge 1999).

Lyotard JF, *The Postmodern Condition: A Report on Knowledge* (Manchester University Press 1984).

MacCormick N, 'Children's Rights: A Test-Case for Theories of Rights' (1976) 62(3) *Archiv für Rechts- und Sozialphilosophie* 305.

May C and Cooper A, 'Personal Identity and Social Change: Some Theoretical Considerations' (1995) 38(1) *Acta Sociologica* 75.

McGregor C and Devaney C, 'Protective Support and Supportive Protection for Families "in the Middle": Learning from the Irish Context' (2019) *Child and Family Social Work*, doi.org/10.1111/cfs.12683.

Mill JS, *On Liberty* (London 1859, 2nd end Oxford University Press 2015).

Nickel JW, *Making Sense of Human Rights. Philosophical Reflections on the Universal Declaration of Human Rights* (University of California Press 1987) 44.

Nolan A, 'The Child as 'Democratic Citizen' – Challenging the "Participation Gap"' [2010] *Public Law* 767.
Oswell D, *The Agency of Children: From Family to Global Human Rights* (Cambridge University Press 2013).
Pollack L, *Forgotten Children: Parent-child Relations from 1500 to 1900* (Cambridge University Press 1983).
Postman N, *The Disappearance of Childhood* (Vintage 1994).
Prout A, *The Body, Childhood and Society* (Macmillan 2000).
Qvortrup J, 'Childhood Matters: An Introduction' in Jens Qvortrup, Marjatta Bardy, Giovanni Sgritta and Helmut Wintersburger (eds), *Childhood Matters: Social Theory, Practice and Politics* (Avebury 1994).
Rayner S, 'Cultural Theory and Risk Analysis' in Sheldon Krimsky and Dominic Golding (eds), *Social Theories of Risk* (Praeger 1992).
Raz J, *The Morality of Freedom* (Oxford University Press 1986).
Rhodes T, 'Risk Theory in Epidemic Times: Sex, Drugs and the Social Organisation of "Risk Behaviour"' (1997) 19(2) *Sociology of Health and Illness* 208.
Rose N, *Governing the Soul* (Routledge 1989).
Ruch G, Lees A and Pritchard J, 'Getting Beneath the Surface: Scapegoating and the Systems Approach in a Post-Munro World' (2014) 28(3) *Journal of Social Work Practice* 313.
Sparks R, 'Risk and Blame in Criminal Justice Controversies: British Press Coverage and Official Discourse on Prison Security' in Mark Brown and John Pratt (eds), *Dangerous Offenders: Punishment and the Social Order* (Routledge 2000).
Sparks R, 'Degrees of Estrangement: The Cultural Theory of Risk and Comparative Penology' (2001) 5(2) *Theoretical Criminology* 159.
Steele J, *Risk and Legal Theory* (Hart Publishing 2004).
Stone L, *The Family, Sex and Marriage in England, 1500–1800* (Weidenfeld 1977).
Sunstein CR, 'On the Expressive Function of Law' (1996) 144(5) *University of Pennsylvania Law Review* 2021.
Teubner G, 'Juridification: Concepts, Aspects, Limits, Solutions' in Gunther Teubner (ed), *Juridification of Social Spheres* (De Gruyter 1987)
Thompson M and Wildavsky A, 'A Proposal to Create a Cultural Theory of Risk' in Howard Kunreuther and Eryl V Ley (eds), *The Risk Analysis Controversy: An Institutional Perspective* (Springer-Verlag 1982).
Tobin J, 'Justifying Children's Rights' (2013) 21(3) *International Journal of Children's Rights* 395
Wagner P, *A Sociology of Modernity: Liberty and Discipline* (Routledge 1994).
Wyness M, *Childhood and Society: An Introduction to the Sociology of Childhood* (Palgrave Macmillan 2006).
Wynne B, *Rationality and Ritual: Participation and Exclusion in Nuclear Decision-making* (Routledge 1982).

2 Threats, victims and agents

Victorian law reform and the beginning of modern child protection

Introduction

This chapter traces the changing conceptions of childhood which can be seen during the development of child protection legislation in the late nineteenth and early twentieth centuries. In particular, it will ask how selected civil and criminal law statutes represented children and the risks they faced, and in doing so, it will seek to add complexity to our traditional understanding of how children, risk and the role of the state were thought about at this time. This was the period in which child abuse came to public attention, new criminal offences targeting sexual offenders were created and welfare-based interventions were also given a clear statutory basis. The reforms undertaken in five pieces of legislation will be examined – the Criminal Law (Amendment) Act 1885 (the "1885 Act"), the Prevention of Cruelty to Children Acts 1889 and 1894, the Children Act 1908 and the Punishment of Incest Act 1908. These Acts are chosen because of the significance of the legal reforms they brought about. The 1885 Act is best known for the raising of the age of consent, the 1889 Act for the creation of a criminal offence relating to child abuse and neglect, the 1894 Act for reform of the law of evidence, the incest legislation for transferring incest cases from the ecclesiastical courts, and the Children Act 1908 for being the most important consolidation of the law relating to child welfare to date. However, the legislative histories of these Acts engaged with a range of issues that are far more rich and diverse than the creation, amendment and consolidation of legal rules. They also demonstrate new ways of thinking about childhood and the ways in which lawmakers attempted to rationalise the developing relationship between children, their parents and the state in light of the heightened social regulation of parenting.

One of the most important concepts in the literature on the legislative reforms affecting children during this period is the idea that the state regarded children in a binary way, as being simultaneously both victims and threats. This idea underpins Hendrick's historical accounts of child welfare,[1] and has also been applied

1 Harry Hendrick, *Child Welfare: Historical Dimensions, Contemporary Debate* (Polity Press 2003).

in more recent scholarship.[2] This approach ignores many important references to children, childhood and risk in parliamentary debates which demonstrates a more nuanced approach is required. Specifically, I argue, there is clear evidence that while it is possible to detect a duality in the 1885 Act, it rapidly gave way to a new discourse which was predicated on more protective impulses. Additionally, and most problematically for our current understanding of the development of child protection laws, an early recognition of the possibility of childhood agency can also be glimpsed. This significantly complicates our understanding of how lawmakers approached children's issues. Children were also seen inconsistently, with this perception largely dependent on the nature of the legal reform in question. These claims should not be overstated. I do not make the case that legal reform was approached from a children's rights perspective in a modern sense or that legal institutions treated children as equal citizens; merely that during this period, children were beginning to be seen as capable of being active participants within the legal system and that they were granted a new set of legal entitlements which exceeded significantly those which they had previously.

The first part of this chapter will focus on the 1885 Act. This is an extraordinarily important law in the development of child protection, as it deals with substantive criminal law reforms relating to the age of consent, the punishment of offenders and the consequences for family autonomy when children had been victimised. Drafted in the glare of significant media attention and major public controversy over the publication of stories about the sexual exploitation of young girls, it was extensively debated in both Houses of Parliament and consequentially it provides us with a rich insight into what could have been the developing fault lines in social policy debates involving children – the idea of children as victims on the one hand, and children as threats to the existing social order on the other. As the chapter progresses, the argument will be made that this fault line did not subsequently appear. Rather, the idea of children as threats largely recedes from view, so that legislation involving the relationship between families and the state passed in 1889 and 1908 is instead framed on the understanding that children were victims, and victims only. Legislation dealing exclusively with criminal law issues such as incest and the giving of evidence will then be examined. This not only confirms the absence of the image of children as threats but introduces a new concept – the child with a story to tell and which could be heard, allowing that child to influence the world around it.

Children as threats and victims in criminal law reform

Children, consent and coercion

The prohibition of sexual contact with minors has been a constant in legal history; the age at which young people were deemed able to give consent has not.

2 Sarah-Anne Buckley, *The Cruelty Man: Child Welfare, the NSPCC and the State in Ireland, 1889–1956* (Manchester University Press 2015)

Traditional Irish laws are unclear on the exact age of consent,[3] although children under the age of seven appear to have been more highly valued that older children, in that attacks upon them received harsher penalties.[4] Under English law, it was a criminal act to engage in sexual activity with girls, especially prior to puberty. The First Statute of Westminster of 1275 stated that it was an offence to ravish a "maiden within age" (i.e., under 12 years of age) with or without her consent.[5] Several other legislative interventions clarified that carnal knowledge of girls under ten was a felony.[6] In 1861, the Offences against the Person Act introduced several important reforms. First, it raised the age of consent to 12,[7] and created a separate offence for the unlawful carnal knowledge of a girl under 10,[8] with the difference between the two provisions being the length of sentence a convicted man was liable to receive. Additionally, the 1861 Act also created a new offence of indecent assault,[9] thereby extending the ambit of the criminal law to cover sexualised conduct towards a child other than penetrative intercourse, and, until the decision in *R v J*, provided a means by which penetrative intercourse could be prosecuted where a complaint was not made soon after the incident.[10] The age at which it became criminal to have sex with a girl was raised from 12 to 13 in 1875.[11]

The Criminal Law Amendment Act 1885 sought, according to its long title, to be an "Act to make further provision for the Protection of Women and Girls", and grew out of the campaign against prostitution, especially juvenile prostitution. Among its most important reforms was the raising of the age of consent to 16,[12] as well as a variety of measures designed to tackle child prostitution. The campaigns leading up to the introduction to the 1885 Act are well-known, given the massive publicity they engendered at the time. WT Stead's articles for the *Pall Mall Gazette* tapped into a mood of public concern for children who were entering what was seen as a "white slave trade"; prominent public figures like George Bernard Shaw lent their support to distribute the newspaper when newsagents refuses to stock it; a public demonstration of around 250,000 people gathered in

3 See the comment by the Law Reform Commission that a fixed age of maturity was unknown – Law Reform Commission, *Report Relating to Age of Majority* (LRC 5-1983) 1983, 3.

4 John Biggins, 'Children of the Fíne and Children of the Family: Reformulating Children's Best Interests and Social Parenting in the Spirit of the Brehon Laws' (2010) 9 *Hibernian Law Journal* 155, 164–165 and Colin Smith and James Gallen, 'Cáin Adomnáin and the Laws of War' (2014) 16 *Journal of the History of International Law* 63, 77–80.

5 3 Edw 1 stat 1 c 13.

6 Benefit of Clergy Act 1575 (18 Eliz 1 cap 7), s 4; Offences against the Person Act 1828 (9 Geo IV c 31), ss 16 and 17. For subtly differing accounts of this reform process, see the judgments of Lord Bingham and Lady Hale in *R v J* [2004] UKHL 42 at [6] and [73], respectively.

7 Section 51.

8 Section 50.

9 Section 52.

10 *R v J* (n 6).

11 Offences against the Person Act 1875 (38 & 39 Vict c 94), ss 3 and 4.

12 Criminal Law Amendment Act 1885 (48 & 49 Vict c 69), s 5.

Hyde Park as moral purity campaigners focused on images of sexual innocence betrayed. The social desire to see the young women and girls involved in the sex trade as sexually innocent and as having been individually brought to sin was therefore central to the 1885 Act's final form; indeed, Stead wrote his articles in part to try to exert pressure to ensure the passage of the legislation. Both Jeffrey Weeks and Deborah Gorham have argued that this image of girlhood presented a more palatable vision for late Victorian society than that which would have been presented if it had been recognised that prostitution was seen as a way out of poverty by young women with no other real alternatives.[13] It also ignored the reality that children were sexualised from a relatively young age due to factors such as living conditions, whereby children shared bedrooms with their parents, and that teenagers sometimes acted out of sexual desire.[14] Scholarship examining this legislation has therefore tended to highlight the confluence of sexual discourses which came together in the late nineteenth century,[15] and the role that Christian economy played among reform advocates outside Parliament.[16]

Hendrick has posited that there was a victim/threat duality that characterised how Victorian social reformers thought about children and that it was central to the 1885 Act.[17] One of the most important concepts in the literature on the legislative reforms affecting children during this period, it has underpinned Hendrick's historical accounts of child welfare as well as the work of other scholars.[18] The idea of the duality posits that ostensibly protective legislation was often predicated on the idea that children and young people were victims, but also simultaneously presented them as a threat to the established social and moral order. As Hendrick argues, it is necessary when discussing social policy reform of this period to understand just how much of the "so-called protective legislation [was] concerned with their presence as threats rather than their suffering as victims. Indeed, more often than not, the image of young people as threats has undermined their reality as victim."[19]

The existence of this duality is most frequently said to be evidenced by the controversies over the raising of the age of consent. The Government initially suggested an age of consent of 15 to ensure the smooth passage of the

13 See Jeffrey Weeks, *Sex, Politics and Society: The Regulation of Sexuality since 1800* (2nd edn, Longman, London 1989) and Deborah Gorham, "The 'Maiden Tribute of Modern Babylon' Re-examined: Child Prostitution in Late-Victorian England" (1978) 21(3) *Victorian Studies* 353.

14 This does not apply so much to child prostitutes but to working-class young people more generally. As an example, see evidence given by CE Howard Vincent on 19 July 1881 *(Report from the Select Committee (H.L.) on the Law Relating to the Protection of Young Girls* (1881) 70 quoted in Gorham, ibid 365.

15 See Weeks (n 13)

16 Louise A Jackson, *Child Sexual Abuse in Victorian England* (Routledge 2000).

17 Harry Hendrick, *Child Welfare 1872–1989* (Routledge 1994); Hendrick (n 1).

18 For example, Lucinda Platt, *Discovering Child Poverty: The Creation of a Policy Agenda from 1800 to the Present* (Policy Press 2005).

19 Harry Hendrick, *Children, Childhood and English Society 1880–1990* (Cambridge University Press 1997) 7.

legislation,[20] while Lord Bramwell thought that 14 may be a suitable age limit.[21] One MP stated that "it should be clearly understood that this was not a Bill for penal legislation directed against the poor helpless girls in question, but for their protection."[22] Offences against young girls were described as "horrible",[23] as among "the most brutal offences in the world",[24] as "most horrible and revolting barbarities".[25] The debates demonstrate early, striking examples of the idea that legislation dealing with child protection matters ought to be cognisant of the risks posed by people who may seek to exploit a young person's vulnerability. On the other hand, it was argued that

> the only objection that had been raised to the measure [raising the age of consent] was that men might be induced to yield to the temptations of these poor children, who might use the powers of this Bill for the purpose of obtaining money. Well, let men take that risk.[26]

The implication that children would pose a real risk of temptation for men, or that children would pose as older teenagers in an organised blackmail operation, was a common theme among those parliamentarians who saw girls and young women as objects for discipline and control, a theme that was present from the earliest stages of debate. Underpinning all of this was the belief that amid the "strong language of abuse ... a man might be more sinned against than sinning".[27] On the Bill's introduction in the House of Lords, one of the first statements made was that "[t]he danger to be guarded against was ... that of unfounded charge".[28] Similarly, a defeated proposal to introduce a provision that would effectively provide a defence to a charge under the Act if a girl under 16 was a "common prostitute or of known immoral character" was based on the fear that a man might be "inveigled, or enticed, or decoyed by a woman who was a woman of the town" who happened to be under 16.[29]

Charles Henry Hopwood MP, who would go on to oppose many of the proposed reforms, stated bluntly when responding to the introduction of the Bill in the House of Commons that "[t]he provisions of this Bill ... would place young men and boys in the power of designing girls, and would be a most powerful weapon for extortion."[30] Taking the theme further, he later argued that if the age of consent were raised there would be

20 HL Deb 13 April 1885, vol 296, col 1439, Earl of Dalhouse.
21 HL Deb 28 April 1885, vol 299, col 947, Lord Bramwell.
22 HC Deb 09 July 1885, vol 299, col 208, Samuel Smith MP.
23 HC Deb 31 July 1885, vol 300, col 731, Arthur Arnold MP.
24 HC Deb 31 July 1885, vol 300, col 733, George Hastings MP.
25 HL Deb 28 April 1885, vol 297, col 941, Earl of Milltown.
26 HC Deb 09 July 1885, vol 299, col 208, William E Forster MP.
27 HC Deb 31 July 1885, vol 300, col 747, Sir Thomas Chambers MP.
28 HL Deb 13 April 1885, vol 296, col 1441, Earl of Milltown.
29 HC Deb 31 July 1885, vol 300, col 775, Charles Hopwood MP.
30 HC Deb 09 July 1885, vol 299, col 200, Charles Hopwood MP.

> practically be no protection for youths and the sons of persons of position. There were cases in which girls were steeped in depravity at the ages of 13 to 16 years; and he believed that if the Bill were allowed to pass there would be great danger of young men and even boys being betrayed by designing creatures, whose object was to levy 'blackmail'.[31]

Objections to the legislation such as these were almost always expressed in class-based terms, underscoring the potential for young people to threaten the established order of social relations. The trope of working-class girls seducing wealthier men was repeated constantly in the debates. The quotation above speaks of the need to protect young men of position from extortion, with no heed taken of the young girl in question. Another opponent of the legislation, while stating that proper protection must be afforded to young women, claimed the real purpose of the "promoters of the Bill—ill-conditioned Democrats and Salvationist sentimentalists—was to set class against class."[32] This was not an isolated expression of the idea that those promoting the legislation were doing little more than causing trouble for class relations. Another opponent of the legislation directed his ire at the child protection societies, many of whom supported the raising of the age of consent to 16. He claimed that prosecutions undertaken by these groups were "got up by Societies pretending to be formed for the protection of young girls" and that no man, "however innocent and respectable, was safe from such organizations."[33] Child abuse was, therefore, not recognised as a real phenomenon but was seen as the product of a conspiracy bent on promoting class war, a view emphasised when potential sentencing regimes were discussed. In these contributions, the construction of children as the source of threats to the social order could even be extended to those who advocated on their behalf, so that their attempts to reform and enforce the law would be resisted.

It has also been argued that the legislation was partly designed to protect a guardian's right to control a girl's sexuality, rather than prevent harm to the girl.[34] This can be said to be particularly true of the offences relating the procuring of girls under 21,[35] and the abduction of girls under 16.[36] This mixture of regulatory impulses with some elements of protective intent may have arisen from "an uncertainty about the nature of childhood and the proper relationship of children

31 HC Deb 30 July 1885, vol 300, col 582, Charles Hopwood MP.
32 HC Deb 30 July 1885, vol 300, col 587, Charles Warton MP.
33 HC Deb 09 July 1885, vol 299, col 206, Charles Warton MP.
34 Gorham (n 13) 363–336. However, at 368, Gorham draws attention to competing views among the social purity movement such as the view expressed in the *Journal of the Vigilance Association of the Defence of Personal Rights* that law reform should not "girls to an amount of espionage and control damaging … to their self respect and strength of character."
35 Section 49.
36 Section 55.

to the structure of the family and the wider society",[37] and continued to be present during the drafting the of 1885 Act. While social reformers saw children as exploited, and so as victims, those same reformers' concern with a highly gendered understanding of moral purity meant that victims could be simultaneously constructed as social threats. This facilitated a disciplinary and regulatory approach to law reform. It is certainly the case that some provisions designed to facilitate the greater protection of children themselves were strongly opposed during its passage through Parliament. Even where protective measures were not seriously opposed, the reality was that many of the provisions relating to the age of consent were passed with the aim of protecting girls, sometimes from themselves.[38]

The material just outlined certainly demonstrates something approaching Hendrick's duality – the simultaneous discursive construction of children as both innocent and dangerous. However, debates about other aspects of the 1885 Act indicate less of an impulse to regard young people, and young women in particular, as sites of social threat. These parts of the legislative debate show a more overwhelmingly protective attitude, demonstrating real concern for the welfare of young or vulnerable women. A successful proposal was made to extend the zone of protection afforded to women who lacked the capacity to fully consent to sex. Section 5(2) of the 1885 Act states that it shall be an offence to have, or attempt to have, unlawful carnal knowledge of any

> female idiot or imbecile woman or girl, under circumstances which do not amount to rape, but which prove that the offender knew at the time of the commission of the offence that the woman or girl was an idiot or imbecile.

In the original draft of the legislation, the phrase "idiot" alone was used. At the time, this meant a person who was deemed to lack all capacity, or at the very least those with profound or severe disabilities.[39] In proposing the amendment which extended the application of the provision to include "imbeciles", Denzil Onslow MP highlighted that the law ought to protect many more women and girls than the original draft allowed for, showing concern that it was the vulnerable condition of these women that promoted his desire to alter the draft.[40] Interestingly, there was no opposition to the introduction of this amendment. This would

37 Gorham (n 13) 355. See also Heather Keating, 'When the kissing has to stop: children, sexual behaviour, and the criminal law' in Michael Freeman (ed), *Law and Childhood Studies* (Oxford University Press 2012).

38 Criminal Law Revision Committee, *Fifteenth Report on Sexual Offences* (Cmnd 9213, 1984) [5.22]. On this generally, see Weeks (n 13).

39 However, for an argument that the common law understood the term in a much wider sense, see Michael Clemente, "A Reassessment of Common Law Protections for 'Idiots'" (2014–2015) 124 (8) *Yale Law Journal* 2680. See also the Idiots Act 1886, which drew a distinction between "idiots" and "imbeciles", the latter of which were deemed to have slightly greater capacity than the former, but which did not equate to the capacity enjoyed by the rest of the population.

40 HC Deb 31 July 1885, vol 300, col 788, Denzil Onslow MP.

indicate that there was certainly strong protective ethos underlying the legislation, and that this extended to those women who were in a position of particular vulnerability, and that this was shared across Parliament. Additionally, no attempt was made to narrow its application through parsing the meaning of "imbecile", or through the introduction of an upper age limit.

Furthermore, a proposal was made which shows a quite far-sighted approach to what we would now call sexual exploitation. An amendment tabled in the House of Lords proposed to insert a clause which stated that if any master (effectively an employer) or guardian assaulted a girl under the age of 18, they would be guilty of an offence and liable to imprisonment for up to two years with hard labour.[41] In putting forward this amendment, Lord Mount-Temple recognised that employers or guardians were in a "position of trust" and that "abuses of power by masters ... were common and by guardians ... were not rare".[42] The amendment was rejected, but the fact that it was put forward, almost 120 years before modern abuse of trust provisions became commonplace in sexual offences legislation is striking.[43] A further noteworthy feature of this is that the age at which a woman would be classified as a victim for the purposes of this provision was substantially higher (18 years) than the age of consent found in the final version of the legislation. The realization that sex in these kinds of circumstances was not only common but resulted from an abuse of a position of trust and power demonstrates a clear concern that only novel legal protections could address.

Sentencing and the complexities of abuse

In addition to changing the substantive criminal law relating to sexual abuse of children, the 1885 Act also amended the penalties applicable to such crimes. As with the reforms relating to consent, there was a range of views based on the competing ideas of children as threats or as victims. Some contributors seemed to perceive children, and girls in particular, as dangerous and in need of discipline even when criminal acts had been committed against them. Others saw perpetrators as potentially deserving execution. Sentencing policy can, therefore, tell us a great deal about how children and the risks they faced were thought about. A survey of the actual punishments handed down by courts lies outside the scope of the present work, but what follows highlights the approach taken in Parliament and official documentation towards the treatment meted out to those involved in criminal behaviour. Nevertheless, an examination of the parliamentary record demonstrates that the idea of duality can at most only be regarded as an aggregate of views. Few contributions indicate that a single speaker held such

41 HL Deb 28 April 1885, vol 297, col 948, Lord Mount-Temple.

42 Ibid.

43 In the UK, the offence of "having sexual intercourse or engaging in any other sexual activity with a person under 18 if in a position of trust in relation to that person" was introduced for the first time by section 3 of the Sexual Offences (Amendment) Act 2000.

a simultaneously split view of children affected by the legislation in mind. Instead, such children were regarded as either victims or threats, a view which would often be influenced by issues such as class and gender.

Perpetrators of sexual crimes against children were said to be savages,[44] and wretches who escaped adequate punishment.[45] Harsh punishments were advocated for offenders; capital punishment and flogging were spoken of as possible sentencing options.[46] Yet the idea that philanthropic agencies might be behind many of the claims of abuse was used as a justification against introducing capital punishment for persons convicted under the 1885 Act. While it was said "society might be all the better if they hanged", society would be harmed by the introduction of such measures because there was the possibility that "a great many of the philanthropists would develop into a most bloodthirsty class".[47] On the other hand, Samuel Smith MP cautioned that if more severe punishment were not meted out to the men who committed such crimes, England

> would see the application of the lynch law to the monsters whose whole lives were devoted to this detestable occupation. … in no country except England would such men be allowed to go about unharmed; certainly in the United States brutes like those would soon receive a taste of the lynch law.[48]

While these quotations outline an approach which could be said to be protective of children and punitive towards perpetrators, other measures seemed to regard children more negatively. In particular, female victims or potential victims were regarded by some as threats to be controlled, as were young male offenders, who were thought of differently from older perpetrators, and so requiring a different form of punishment and control, harsher than that meted out to the general population. The evidence, therefore, points to a more complex discursive construction of childhood heavily influenced by sociological factors other than age.

Gender was one such factor. As outlined earlier in this chapter, MPs opposed to raising the age of consent often sought to portray women and girls who were exploited and abused as temptresses leading often richer men astray, sometimes for financial gain, thereby also bringing class into the discussion. A proposal was made which, if successful, would have resulted in a female victim potentially being committed to a reform school for two years, even though a man had been convicted of abusing her. Specifically, it was proposed that where a man was convicted of defiling a girl between 13 and 16, the judge would have to inquire of the jury whether the girl had in fact consented.[49] If the jury found that she had, the judge would have to commit her to a reformatory school for a period not

44 HC Deb 31 July 1885, vol 300, col 717, John Serjeant Simon MP.
45 HL Deb 28 April 1885, vol 297, col 941, Earl of Milltown.
46 HC Deb 31 July 1885, vol 300, col 724, Henry H Fowler MP.
47 HC Deb 31 July 1885, vol 300, col 744, Lyulph Stanley MP.
48 HC Deb 31 July 1885, vol 300, col 734, Samuel Smith MP.
49 HC Deb 06 August 1885, vol 300, col 1391, Alexander Staveley Hill MP.

exceeding two years.[50] The MP proposing this measure claimed that the number of false reports would be significantly lessened.[51] Despite the fact that this would have led to the incarceration of a girl who had committed no offence, it was argued that "cases … constantly occurred in which girls under 16 were a hundred times more culpable than the youths whom, in reality, they seduced—cases where the girls were more advanced and matured, both in body and mind".[52] This argument proved unsuccessful, leading the amendment to be defeated.

Gender and age again interacted in a complex way when legislators attempted to determine how male offenders would be punished. Distinctions which were drawn between older and younger perpetrators did not necessarily favour the latter group, meaning that more severe punishments could be imposed on boys than on men. In respect of adult perpetrators, the 1885 Act stated that a person who was guilty of an offence under section 5 – defilement of a girl between 13 and 16, or of a woman lacking capacity – would be liable for imprisonment of up to 2 years, with or without hard labour. With respect to offences under section 4 – defilement of a girl under 13 – the maximum available punishments were penal servitude for a period of 5 years to life, or imprisonment of up to 2 years. If the offender was under 16, however, the offender could be whipped and additionally be sent to a reform school for a period of between 2 and 5 years. This special form of punishment for young men, available where an offence had been committed against a girl under 13, is of particular importance when thinking about the view taken of children in the legislation. As indicated above, there was some discussion of introducing extreme penalties for adult offenders, including capital punishment, although more attention was paid to the possible introduction of flogging. In support of this, MPs argued that not only would flogging constitute a proper punishment, but that it would have a deterrent effect,[53] which was seen as important given the evidence that offences of this nature were increasing.[54] However, there was also opposition to the introduction of flogging for reasons ranging from the practical to the humanitarian. Crucially, the idea that "[i]n the case of boys, whipping was the proper punishment, and nothing but it" held significant sway.[55] While section 4 retained whipping as a punishment for boys under 16 who had been convicted, the proposal to permit the flogging of adult men was defeated by 91 to 125,[56] whereas the amendment which led to the inclusion of the whipping of boys was supported by a margin of 204 to 24.[57]

The attitudes of the senior judiciary and the Home Office also demonstrate an unclear and inconsistent approach to the question of sentencing. Legislation will

50 Ibid.
51 Ibid.
52 HC Deb 06 August 1885, vol 300, col 1394, Charles Hopwood MP.
53 HC Deb 31 July 1885, vol 300, col 724, Henry H Fowler MP.
54 HC Deb 31 July 1885, vol 300, col 732, George Hastings MP.
55 HC Deb 31 July 1885, vol 300, col 726, Sampson Lloyd MP.
56 HC Deb 31 July 1885, vol 300, col 747.
57 HC Deb 31 July 1885, vol 300, col 766.

usually stipulate a maximum sentence which may be imposed, and will sometimes impose a minimum sentence, but the exact sentence imposed in an individual case is determined by the judge hearing it, taking into account aggravating and mitigating factors, as well as the prevailing understanding of the seriousness of the crime concerned. In 1901, a memorandum outlining the normal expected range of punishment was adopted by a committee of the English judiciary chaired by Lord Alverstone.[58] This outlined that the accepted normal sentence where rape was committed against a woman over 13 years age was penal servitude for between 5 and 7 years, although this could have been increased if the perpetrator were the woman's employer.[59] For offences against children under 13 years of age, the judges made provision for the "consent in fact" of girls under 13, the idea being that despite being legally incapable of giving consent to any sexual contact, even the youngest of victims were seen as possibly bearing some element of culpability for the offence. Therefore, while Parliament has expressly refused to adopt a "consent in fact" measure when it came to the question of potentially incarcerating young women over the age of 13, judges were using the same idea of consent by a victim to lessen the severity of sentence imposed on an offender. Yet the Alverstone memorandum also sought to punish those who exploited a position of trust, such as family members, more harshly than strangers. Given the variety of categories of offender and the qualifications adopted, it is worth quoting from the memorandum extensively:

> If by a parent, in the absence of exceptional brutality or intimidation or cruelty, penal servitude, 10 years.
> If by an adult stranger, penal servitude for 7 years.
> If by a youth under 18, and upon a child nearly 13 years of age, and with consent in fact, imprisonment from 3 to 12 months.
> If by a youth over 18 years of age, under the same circumstances, imprisonment from 12 to 18 months.[60]

An alternative series of tariffs was proposed by one judge sitting on the committee, who proposed that offences committed by fathers upon their children be subject to "12 to 16 years penal servitude as a normal standard of punishment; and where helpless children have been forced by strangers" a tariff of between 10 and 15 years was deemed suitable.[61] Additionally, a conviction for sodomy was to attract a maximum sentence of ten years if the offence had been committed

58 'The Alverstone Memorandum 1901: Memorandum on Normal Punishments in Certain Kinds of Crime', reproduced in Advisory Council on the Penal System, *Sentences of Imprisonment: A Review of Maximum Penalties, Report of the Advisory Council on the Penal System* (HMSO 1978) Appendix E. It should also be noted that Alverstone was none other than Richard Webster, who had been Attorney General during the passage of the 1889 Act.

59 Ibid 194.

60 Ibid 195.

61 Ibid.

against a youthful and unwilling victim, although three judges felt that this was too low. Interestingly, it has been pointed out that when civil servants reviewed the memorandum, they felt that the model sentences proposed by the judges were too low, in part because they felt that the public would demand more severe sentences.[62] A further memorandum, prepared by Winston Churchill in 1910 during his tenure as Home Secretary, felt that offences against minors and incest were to be considered as offences against morals, and hence should be treated less severely by the courts than other offences against the person, and also less seriously than property offences, such as fraud and blackmail.[63] Throughout his time in this office, he reduced the sentences of sexual offenders and also argued that a standard sentence of seven years should be borne in mind when dealing with rape or unlawful carnal knowledge, though circumstances of particular aggravation could warrant a sentence of over ten years.[64]

The political and judicial debates over sentencing show how deeply divisive these issues were. It seems improbable that a proposal for the incarceration of young female victims was tabled only a matter of months after the proposal to criminalise sexual relationships between young people and employers which were grounded in exploitation. It also feels improbable that a member of the government would seek to reduce what they saw as the overly harsh sentences imposed on sexual offenders. The difficulty in arriving at an internally consistent position on how children were thought about during these exchanges indicates not so much a duality but rather that legislators and others were attempting to address a newly recognised problem which society had not yet figured out how to deal with.

The one occasion on which children were indisputably constructed as victims can be seen in the debates leading the passage of section 12 of the 1885 Act. This provides that where it is proved that the seduction or prostitution of any girl under 16 was "caused, encouraged, or favoured by her father, mother, guardian, master or mistress", it would be within the power of the court to divest that person of all authority over the child, and to appoint another guardian until the child reached 21 or such other age as the court may direct. This provided an early example of what would now be considered something similar to a care order and was designed to ensure that a child who had been sexually exploited with the connivance of a person charged with their care would not be placed back under that person's authority.

This represented a significant incursion on parental rights and a major innovation in that it was welfare-based; it provided clear statutory authority for the removal of children from their parents for purely welfare-related reasons for the first time. Parents were now regarded as a potential source of danger to children,

62 See Leon Radzinowicz and Roger Hood, *A History of English Criminal Law in England and its Administration, Volume V: The Emergence of Penal Policy in Victorian and Edwardian England* (Clarendon Press 1990) 1324.

63 'The Churchill Scale of Offences 1910', in Advisory Council (n 58) Appendix F.

64 On both of these points, see Radzinowicz and Hood (n 62) 1342.

with one MP stating "[i]t must, unfortunately, be admitted that in many cases the parents of a child were its worst guardians."[65] Section 12 attracted a wide consensus, with not a single MP objecting to it on normative grounds. There was sustained discussion as to how to amend the clause, and how it would work in practice.[66] Yet not a single speaker objected to the clause on principle as a violation of parental rights, or as a legal innovation without precedent. To allow a parent to resume charge of a child in such circumstances was described as a "most monstrous thing",[67] and it was believed that the "the only chance of rescuing girls in the position described was to take them away from their natural guardians who had violated their trust."[68] It was argued from a moral standpoint "that parental rights should cease when they were neglected or violated in the manner described in the clause" as "[i]t was perfectly well known that there were a number of wretches in the country who would commit outrages on their own children, and then insist on their parental rights."[69] Parents such as these were described as "human beings only in name".[70]

It is also worth noting, however, the limitations of section 12. It only applied to girls against whom offences relating to seduction or prostitution had been committed. It provided no protection for boys, or for the sisters of girls who had been sexually exploited. It also did not seem to provide for the transfer of parental rights where the girl had been sexually abused by her parents, but only where the parent had encouraged or facilitated others in abusing them, and so it targeted sexual exploitation rather than sexual abuse itself. Finally, the language of the section meant that it was at the court's discretion whether to transfer legal rights, rather than this being the automatic consequence of a conviction. At best, section 12 can be seen as a partial recognition that a child who had been victimised was entitled to have their need for future protection considered by a court. Such a partial recognition was, in itself, a novel provision which conceded the principle that children's independent interests could be considered separately from those of the family as a unit, a position which had invariably meant the marginalization of children.

Childhood, victimhood and incest

The idea that childhood had become synonymous with victimhood in the late nineteenth century is reinforced when the issue of the criminalization of incest is

65 HC Deb 03 August 1885, vol 300, col 854.

66 One MP went as far as saying that he "was always alarmed when the occupants of the two Front Benches united in saying that a clause which was sound in principle was unworkable in practice." See HC Deb 06 August 1885, vol 300, col 1402, James Edwin Thorold Rogers MP.

67 HC Deb 06 August 1885, vol 300, col 1398, Henry Labouchere MP.

68 HC Deb 06 August 1885, vol 300, cols 1401–1402, Lewis Dillwyn MP.

69 HC Deb 06 August 1885, vol 300, col 1402, ibid.

70 HC Deb 06 August 1885, vol 300, col 1403 Alexander McArthur MP.

examined. This issue attracted significant attention from London-based child protection societies, moral purity campaigners, and in the Westminster Parliament. Traditionally, incest had been regulated by the law governing capacity to marry.[71] It became a concern for the criminal law when it was declared to be a felony punishable by death in 1650.[72] However, that legislation has been described as a "dead letter",[73] as the matter was largely regarded as within the proper remit of ecclesiastical courts administering the law on marriage, rather than a criminal law concern. In order to address this, incest bills were introduced in 1899, 1903 and 1907, but failed to pass each time. As a result, incest was not properly regulated by the criminal law until the passage of the Punishment of Incest Act 1908.[74] Much like the 1885 Act, this owed much to the efforts of social reform organizations such as the National Vigilance Association and the National Society for the Prevention of Cruelty to Children, who engaged in sustained campaigning with the aim of bringing incest within the ambit of the criminal law.[75] The main provisions of the 1908 Act are outlined in section 1 which makes it an offence for any man to carnally know his grand-daughter, daughter, sister or mother. On conviction for this offence, the man was liable to penal servitude of between three and seven years, or imprisonment for a maximum of two years with or without hard labour.[76] If the female victim was under thirteen years of age, a harsher sen-

71 See Maebh Harding, '"To Affinity and Beyond": A Critical Analysis of the Law on Marriage within Prohibited Degrees of Relationship" in Katharina Boele-Woelki and Tone Sverdrup (eds), *European challenges in contemporary family law* (Intersentia 2008); Maebh Harding, 'The Curious Incident of the Marriage (No 2) Act 1537 and the Irish Statute Book' (2012) 32(1) *Legal Studies* 78; Sybil Wolfram, *In-laws and Outlaws: Kinship and Marriage in England* (Palgrave Macmillan 1987).

72 An Act for suppressing the detestable sins of Incest, Adultery and Fornication 1650.

73 Victor Bailey and Sheila Blackburn, 'The Punishment of Incest Act 1908: A Case Study in Law Creation' [1979] *Criminal Law Review* 708.

74 One reason offered for the failure to pass the legislation in 1903 was that the definition of incest would have included affinal relatives, that is relatives through marriage rather than blood. This was a matter of significant legislative concern at the time in its own right – incestuous adultery was one of the few grounds on which a woman could obtain a divorce when it became a civil matter with the Matrimonial Causes Act 1857; it was not until 1907 that a man could marry his dead wife's sister (Deceased Wife's Sister's Marriage Act 1907) and even after this, marriage law regarded a relationship between a man and his living wife's sister as incestuous. These ongoing concerns over the "other" meaning of incest would likely have delayed criminal legislation – see Sybil Wolfram, 'Eugenics and the Punishment of Incest Act 1908' [1983] *Criminal Law Review* 308.

75 It has been claimed by Nigel Walker, 'Morality and the Criminal Law' (1964) 11 *Howard Journal* 209 that the legislation was the result of pressure from the Church of England. While clergymen did play a role, the archival evidence amassed by Bailey and Blackburn (n 73) would indicate that that it was the National Vigilance Association and the National Society for the Protection of Cruelty to Children which were at the forefront of lobby efforts. See also Royal Commission on the Housing of the Working Classes, *Minutes of the Evidence of the First Report* (Cmnd 4402-1, 1885). See Buckley (n 2) for a discussion of the view that incest was predominately thought of as a working-class crime.

76 Section 1(1).

tencing regime would apply.[77] In all cases, the consent of the woman provided no defence.[78] Consent was only relevant if the woman was over 16, in which case she too would be guilty of an offence.[79] All proceedings under the 1908 Act were to be held *in camera*.[80]

One of the striking features of this legislation is that children were never really presented as potential direct threats during its passage; rather, they seemed to be thought of exclusively as victims. Opposition to the legislation instead centred on three grounds, the first two of which were the belief that offences against morals should not be made matters of concern for criminal law, and that there was little need for the legislation. Yet the Home Office was aware of problems with the operation of the law as it stood; the existing child protection legislation did not protect victims over the age of 16, and the courts were circumspect in their attitudes to charges brought under the 1885 Act,[81] highlighting a real need for legislative action. The idea that there was already enough criminal law, and that offences could be prosecuted under other legislation such as the 1885 Act has no real bearing on the changing social construction of children themselves, and so will not be assessed further.

The final ground of opposition, that blackmail by neighbours would be a possibility, does have some bearing on the matter, however. As already discussed, much of the opposition to the 1885 Act centred on the possibility that girls and their families would pose as victims, or entice a man to commit an offence, and use the legislation to extort money from wealthy families. However, blackmail was construed entirely differently in the debates about incest. Blackmail, it was feared, would not emanate from children telling "false" abuse stories, but from neighbours seeking to cast aspersions on other families, such as where a brother and a half-sister lived together.[82] At no point in the debates was the spectre of false accusations emanating from children raised, a radical shift from the discourse surrounding earlier legislation, and important in recognising children as innocent victims of sexual offences, rather than as justifiable targets or as a threat in their own right.

The view of children as victims, and especially as victims the protection of whose interests required legislative action, was crystallised in the discussions about the frequency of incest. Some public figures argued that there was no real need for the legislation due to the rarity of the offence; Bailey and Blackburn cite the opposition Lord Chancellor in 1899 when he stated that "the evil, though shocking, is of rare occurrence".[83] Even during the later debates, some MPs

77 Ibid, where it states that same punishment as applicable under section 4 of the Criminal Law Amendment Act 1885 would apply.
78 Section 1(2).
79 Section 2.
80 Section 5.
81 Bailey and Blackburn (n 73) 712.
82 HC Deb 26 June 1908, vol 191, cols 279–280, John Rawlinson MP.
83 PRO, HO 45/B29425/2, cited in Bailey and Blackburn (n 73) 714.

felt that the incidence of incest was on the decline; one particularly noteworthy contribution came from Charles Hemphill, MP for North Tyrone in 1903, who stated that "this crime had never been heard of in Ireland … [i]n ancient times there were certain offences so bad that no law was made against them because it was inconceivable that such offences could be committed."[84] This contribution is important from an Irish perspective. As I will argue later in the book there existed a culture of denial when it came to issues such as sexual abuse, at least until recent decades. This comment was one of the few made on the legislation by an Irish MP, making it difficult to determine whether this view was more widely held. However, arguments of this kind were consistently rebutted by those seeking to criminalise incest during the 1908 debates, by reference to personal experience derived from practice in the criminal courts,[85] information provided by the NSPCC and information held by the Home Office.[86] Indeed, the Lord Chief Justice, unable to attend the debates in person, sent a telegram which was read out stating that incest had to be criminalised due to the frequency of assaults by fathers on their daughters.[87] This makes Hemphill's earlier contribution even more noteworthy – as an experienced barrister and former Solicitor General for Ireland, he may not have had detailed knowledge of the caseload of local criminal courts, but the refusal to accept the evidence of those more familiar with such matters speaks volumes about the strength of his refusal to see child abuse as a significant problem.

Child welfare, children's interests and the state

Cruelty to children and the limitation of parental rights

The attitudes to children evident in the parliamentary debates about the 1885 Act changed radically within a few years; the passage of the Prevention of Cruelty to Children Act 1889 showed that lawmakers had come to see children as victims of circumstance, and the image of children as threats virtually disappeared from the parliamentary discourse. The 1889 Act introduced a new set of principles to the law and policy surrounding children whose welfare was endangered by parental behaviour, destitution, or other factors. Previously, children who lived in poverty were subjected to the Poor Law system of relief.[88] Further piecemeal reform had

84 HC Deb 26 June 1903, vol 124, col 704, Charles Hemphill MP.
85 See HC Deb 26 June 1908, vol 191, col 283, Donald McLean MP.
86 HO 45/A55202, HO 45/B29425/2, and HO 45/B29425/10 cited in Blackburn and Bailey (n 73) 713. On the latter two points, see HL Deb 02 December 1908, vol 197, col 1408, Lord Bishop of St Albans.
87 Ibid.
88 For a comprehensive overview of the right to relief, see Lorie Charlesworth, *Welfare's Forgotten Past: A Socio-Legal History of the Poor Law* (Routledge 2011) 35–73 and Nick Wikeley, *Child Support: Law and Policy* (Hart Publishing 2006). See also Nigel Parton, *The Politics of Child Abuse* (Palgrave 1985) 26, where he describes the Poor Law system as "punitive". The Poor Law did not apply in Ireland until 1838, leading Kearney and Skehill to describe the

seen the introduction of legislation which imposed limitations on the employment of children,[89] and minimum educational attendance requirements.[90] The 1889 Act, by contrast, saw the adoption of an expanded understanding of welfare and assigned responsibilities to different parts of the state's apparatus designed to safeguard welfare when it was endangered. The 1889 Act criminalised abuse and neglect and permitted children to be taken into care. What is remarkable in all of this is that the debates in Parliament were not debates about principle, much as the debates about the 1885 Act were. As a result, we can detect a recognition of the fact that children had entitlements, and that there was a need to balance the interests of parents and children.

Care must be taken not to take the idea of legal entitlements too far; the 1889 Act was not the birth of a children's rights consciousness in the modern sense. It was made clear that care must be taken not to "interfere with the legitimate conduct of parents".[91] In one of the early comments on the Bill's passage through Parliament, it was stated that

> [c]hildren have very few rights in England, and by this Bill I am really only anxious that we should give them almost the same protection that we give under the Cruelty to Animals Act and the Contagious Diseases Act for domestic animals.[92]

Nonetheless, it was recognised in the House of Lords that a parent who mistreated a child "shows himself or herself to be unfit for guardianship, and it is in the public interest that the child should be removed from such a parent."[93] The Lords also commented on, and commended, the speed at which the Bill passed,[94] highlighting that despite the legal novelty of some of its provisions, it commanded support across parties and across class, given the more aristocratic composition of the upper House.

Section 1 of the 1889 Act represents a crucial development in child protection law. It provided that any person over the age of 16 who had the custody, control or charge of a child who wilfully ill-treated, neglected or abandoned the

English system as comparatively generous – see Noreen Kearney and Caroline Skehill, *Social Work in Ireland: Historical Perspectives* (Institute of Public Administration 2005) introduction, 2, citing Helen Burke, *The People and The Poor Law in Nineteenth-Century Ireland* (Dublin Women's Education Bureau 1987).

89 Elizabeth Leigh Hutchins and Amy Harrison, *A History of Factory Legislation* (PS King 1903).

90 Elementary Education Act 1870.

91 HC Deb 19 June 1889, vol 337, col 228, Sir Richard Webster MP, Attorney General. One of the questions addressed in the debates was what constituted legitimate conduct. For instance, an amendment was introduced, but withdrawn, which sought to include intoxicated parents within the scope of section 1. See HC Deb 19 June 1889, vol 337, cols 234–236.

92 HC Deb 19 June 1889, vol 337, col 229, Anthony Mundella MP.

93 HL Deb 22 July 1889, vol 338, col 956.

94 Ibid cc 962.

child would be guilty of an offence. It was also an offence to expose a child to something that would cause unnecessary suffering or injury to its health.[95] This for the first time criminalises not only child abuse in the sense of causing deliberate harm to a child, but also neglect, and did so on pain of significant penalties. If a person were convicted on indictment, the maximum penalty was imprisonment with or without hard labour, and/or a fine of £100, a very significant sum for the day, equating to approximately £10,000 in today's terms. Should the person be convicted summarily, the lesser maxima of three months' imprisonment and/or a fine of £25 applied. Section 2 stipulates that where the offender had a known financial interest in the death of a child, the punishment would increase to £200. The child need not have died for this provision to be triggered; merely that the offender be prosecuted under section 1 and have the relevant financial interest.

The definition of a child to whom section 1 applies is worth noting, as it represents one of those practical compromises that helped to ensure the relatively smooth passage of the legislation when contrasted with that of the 1885 Act. The original version of the Bill stated that a child meant anyone under the age of 16. However, this was amended to cover boys under 14 and girls under 16. The rationale for the amendment was to protect parental rights.[96] It is evident from the speech of the Bill's sponsor, AJ Mundella MP, that significant compromises had to be made in order for the legislation to pass. He stated bluntly that "I do not think the House has the smallest conception of the appalling cruelties that are practised upon children, and the hardships they have to suffer" but that nonetheless that "[t]he Bill has been watered down."[97]

A further consequence flowing from a conviction under section 1 is found in section 5. This provides that the courts were empowered to remove the child from the custody of that person and place the child with a relative or with another fit person in three situations: where a person had been convicted under section 1, had been sent forward for trial for an offence under that section, or had been bound over to keep the peace towards a child.98 While this can be seen as a further penalty imposed on a parent, it is also possible to read it as a child protection measure. This was, it seems, the actual intention of Parliament. An earlier draft of the provision was described by one MP as providing a penalty, and as an extreme breach of parental rights.99 It was proposed that, given the extraordinary nature of the provisions it would only be possible to exercise the power where it was proven that the child had already suffered harm, as it was regarded as "too much to say that

95 Section 1 of the Prevention of Cruelty to Children Act 1894 (57 & 58 Vict c 41) extended this to include "mental derangement" within the meaning of injury to health.

96 HC Deb 19 June 1889 vol 337 col 228, Sir Richard Webster MP, Attorney General. The age at which the Act ceased to be applicable to boys was raised to 16 by virtue of section 1 of the Prevention of Cruelty to Children (Amendment) Act 1894 (57 & 58 Vict c 27).

97 HC Deb 19 June 1889, vol 337, col 229, Anthony Mundella MP.

98 Powers under section 5 would later be exercisable in respect of any offence involving bodily injury to a child – see Prevention of Cruelty to Children (Amendment) Act 1894, s 12.

99 HC Deb 19 June 1889, vol 337, col 232, Walter McLaren MP.

the child is to be taken away from the control of the parents, and given to some stranger, merely because some other person ... treated it in such a way as was likely to cause it unnecessary suffering."100 Several MPs opposed this amendment on the basis that it would defeat the purpose of the Bill, as "[t]he Bill contemplates prevention of crime, and surely our desire should be to prevent the improper treatment of children without first waiting to see if the child will be injured by that treatment."101 This is a hugely significant shift in attitudes towards children, and indeed towards risk. The ideas that children had an interest in not suffering ill-treatment, and the state had the right to take pre-emptive action to avoid the child coming to harm were now firmly embedded in legislation.

These provisions were built on by the Custody of Children Act 1891 which provided that where a child was living with someone other than their parents, the courts could refuse to allow the parents to commence legal proceedings to recover the child. Permission would be refused if the court was of opinion that the parents had abandoned or deserted the child, or that they had conducted themselves in such a way that the court should refuse to enforce the right to custody.[102] Where the court did allow the case to proceed, it was prevented from making an order for the child's return unless satisfied that the parent was a fit person to exercise custody rights, having regard to the welfare of the child.[103] These provisions, although only applicable in certain situations and with the courts given quite wide discretion, again represent a shift towards greater recognition that children were entitled to have their welfare considered as of right, and that parental conduct causing harm to a child could not be disregarded. When the clause was discussed in the House of Lords, it was recognised that, despite the highly novel nature of the provisions, the evidence presented to the Lords and the "general consensus" was that this was a necessary measure.[104] That consensus was that the necessity was borne out of the need to remove control of children's lives from "drunken fathers and profligate mothers [of] children who have been saved from misery, degradation, and ruin".[105] Opposition to the Bill in the Lords was described as fastidiousness.[106] Opposition in the Commons was virtually non-existent; its smooth passage summed up by the Attorney General's statement that "[j]udging from the representations received from all parts of the House, there appears to be a unanimous feeling that the Bill should be passed into law as soon as possible."[107]

100 Ibid.
101 HC Deb 19 June 1889, vol 337, col 233, Henry H Fowler MP.
102 Section 1.
103 Section 3.
104 HL Deb 06 February 1891, vol 350, col 113, Lord Morris.
105 HL Deb 06 February 1891, vol 350, cols 116–117, Lord Thring.
106 HL Deb 06 February 1891, vol 350, col 116, Lord Thring.
107 HC Deb 17 March 1891, vol 351, col 1259, Sir Richard Webster MP, Attorney General. There was some limited opposition however, from Irish MPs who initially refused to deal with the Bill – see HC Deb 12 August 1890, vol 348, col 723, Thomas Sexton MP. It appears that the problem was resolved outside the parliamentary record.

The Children Act 1908 and the expanding role of the state

As the range of statutes governing children's issues, including protection, education and employment matters, became ever more unwieldy, the opportunity to consolidate and update the law arose with the landslide election of a Liberal government in 1906. The resulting legislation, the Children Act 1908, was perhaps the most significant legislative initiative affecting children yet undertaken. While Cretney rightly points out that the Government was quick to compromise on controversial matters,[108] the following quotation from the Bill's second reading accurately sums up how the legislation was viewed:

> There was a time in the history of this House when a Bill of this kind would have been treated as a most revolutionary measure; and, half a century ago, if such a measure had been introduced it would have been said that the British Constitution was being undermined. Now a Bill of this kind finds itself in smooth water from the outset.[109]

With respect to those sections governing the relationship between children and parents, especially in the context of child protection, Cretney posits that there was a very clear emphasis "on the imposition of criminal sanctions as the means of protecting children's welfare",[110] pointing out the imposition of penalties for offences involving children injured or killed as a result of overlying by drunk parents or being left near open fires unsupervised. However, this view takes insufficient account of how the relationship between parent, child and state was thought about by legislators. A variety of positions have been taken in the literature on this point. Wasserstein describes it as a "landmark in the evolution of state acceptance of responsibility for children",[111] Heywood sees little new in the legislation, describing it as "derivative"[112] and Hendrick describes the 1908 Act as a continuation of the programme of investing in children as national assets.[113] However, the most accurate summation of the 1908 Act is provided by Stewart who says that the Act "sought to subtly redefine the relationship between children, parents and the state by creating a balance between a more explicit supervisory role for the state with the maintenance of parental obligation for the day to day raising of children."[114]

This view of the 1908 Act as carefully recalibrating the balance slightly in favour of a more child-centred approach within an overall framework of parental

108 Stephen Cretney, *Family Law in the Twentieth Century: A History* (Oxford University Press 2005) 643.
109 HC Deb 24 March 1908, vol 186, col 1252, Thomas Shaw MP, Lord Advocate.
110 Stephen Cretney (n 108) 644.
111 Bernard Wasserstein, *Herbert Samuel: A Political Life* (Oxford University Press 1992) 102.
112 Jean Heywood, *Children in Care* (Routledge 1978) 108.
113 Hendrick (n 17) 121–126.
114 John Stewart, 'Children, Parents and the State: The Children Act 1908' (1995) 9(1) *Children and Society* 90, 97.

rights is supported by comments made in Parliament. For instance, it was stated that "there is one principle of the Bill which I for one cordially endorse ... and that is the wider enforcement of parental authority."[115] It was recognised that "the State must step in and save the children of neglectful, ignorant, and criminal parents", but that "the State was a very blundering substitute for a parent".[116] There was a fear of creating "excessive interference" in people's private lives which might alienate public support for the legislation, as well as a fear of overburdening local authorities with new duties.[117]

Parliament attempted to balance these competing concerns largely through the juvenile court. This was usually a court of criminal jurisdiction but it was now given the power to exercise a more supervisory function over children's welfare. Section 58 of the 1908 Act permitted any person to bring a child under the age of 14 before the court where the child was found in a variety of problematic circumstances, including homelessness, being without adequate parental guardianship or having been the victim of a sexual offence. If one of the relevant circumstances was made out, then the court would commit the child to an industrial school, or to the care of a fit person, thereby removing the child from parental care.[118] Such a committal would be made if it was expedient, and not if the welfare of the child required. This compromise between the competing interests of children, parents and the state was the subject of sustained discussion in Parliament.[119] Clearly, the idea that the failure to be an adequate guardian was sufficient to justify removal represented a major curtailment of parental rights with potentially profound consequences. However, the determination that expediency rather than welfare ought to be the criterion for removal represents a challenge to the idea that the legislation was entirely welfare-orientated.[120]

Despite the state's ability to take children into care being limited to reasons of expediency rather than welfare, the role of the state in parenting did expand significantly. Not only was the range of criminal offences relating to problematic parenting increased, the relationship between families and the state was also significantly altered. One extremely important innovation was the introduction of the forerunner of the modern supervision order. Section 58(4) provides that where a parent proved that they were unable to control the child and that they desired the child to be sent to an industrial school, the court was empowered instead to place the child under the supervision of a probation officer, and deal with the child as if the child were subject to the Probation of Offenders Act 1907. This legislation was designed for use in criminal proceedings, and so there was a risk of criminalising children for breaching the terms imposed upon them.

115 HC Deb 24 March 1908, vol 186, col 1263, Arekas Akers-Douglas MP.
116 HC Deb 01 April 1908, vol 187, col 569, John Gulland MP.
117 HL Deb 28 October 1908, vol 195, col 233, Marquess of Lansdowne.
118 Cretney (n 108) 648 points out that fit person orders were rarely made.
119 See HL Deb 04 November 1908, vol 195, col 1162, Earl Beauchamp and col 1181, Lord Alverstone.
120 The operation of section 58 will be considered in greater depth in Chapter 4.

Nonetheless, this marks a real shift in thinking about the state's responsibilities where children could not be adequately cared for by their parents. Rather than removal from parental care being the only option available, children could now benefit from the supervision of a social work-orientated professional acting on behalf of the state. Although it is unclear how often the provision was used, the fact of its inclusion in the 1908 Act represents a radical innovation in how the state saw its own role in child welfare issues, while at the same time recognising that children's interests may not always be best served by removal from parental care.

Children, evidence and agency

Changes in the laws governing child cruelty and incest showed an understanding of children as victims – members of the moral community who had an interest in having their welfare protected by the state through the deployment of new regulatory measures. Recognition of the interests of children and the language of welfare allowed courts and other agencies to intervene, without conceding that the children being protected had rights. Yet in order to properly exercise these new criminal and supervisory jurisdictions, there had to be a wider recognition that children required new means of engagement with, and participation in, the legal process. In this admittedly rather limited sense, children could begin to be thought of as possessing some form of agency due to their ability to influence the processes which affected them. This should not be confused with what modern children's rights scholars would understand as a right of participation; rather that for the first time, legislation created the conditions of possibility for children to tell their stories in a way which accommodated their status as children.

This was first seen in the 1885 Act's reforms of the laws of evidence in cases involving young victims. Significant attention was paid to proposals for granting young victims the ability to give unsworn evidence. At common law, only evidence given under oath could be received in a criminal trial. In the case of children, this presented particular difficulties where the child was deemed incapable of understanding the nature of the oath, in terms of what it would mean in a religious sense to provide a false statement, and if they lacked an understanding of the importance of telling the truth more generally.[121] According to *R v Brasier*, this meant that the ability of the child to give evidence depended on the "sense and reason they entertain of the danger and impiety of falsehood" which was to be determined by a judge asking the child questions in the presence of the jury to determine their competence to give sworn evidence.[122] The net effect of this would have been to deny many young children, especially those from poorer

121 Peter Murphy, *Murphy on Evidence* (11th edn, Oxford University Press 2009) 531.

122 (1779) 1 Leach 199, 1 East PC 443, 168 ER 202. For a post-independence affirmation of this in Ireland, see *Attorney General v O'Sullivan* [1930] IR 522 (SC).

backgrounds who had not received significant formal religious instruction, the ability to participate in proceedings by giving evidence of the offences committed upon them.

The 1885 Act as passed did contain some significant reforms which increased the ability of children to participate as witnesses. Where an offence was charged under section 4, a child who did not understand the nature of the oath was permitted to give unsworn evidence where they were deemed to be of "sufficient intelligence to justify the reception of the evidence, and understands the duty of speaking the truth". This was subject to the caveat that such evidence had to be corroborated, and that the child could be prosecuted for perjury in the same way as an adult giving false testimony on oath. This provision significantly altered the common law, allowing for the first time a child victim to give unsworn evidence and so to speak in court as a witness with limited restrictions.

More radical proposals were put forward but rejected. Samuel Smith MP tabled an amendment to the Bill proposing that a clause be inserted providing that where a girl was too young to understand the oath, she would be permitted to give unsworn evidence, provided that no-one would be convicted in the absence of corroborating evidence.[123] Additionally, he proposed that an unsworn "statement made by her before the committing justice or magistrate, and taken down in writing at the time" could be admitted in evidence at the trial, as if she were giving sworn, *viva voce* evidence.[124] This radical change in the laws of evidence was withdrawn without attracting support. If introduced, it would have removed the need for a child to meet any capacity-based test of possessing "sufficient intelligence", and the need to even be present to give evidence, once a statement had been made to a court at an earlier stage in the criminal process. It was only with the passage of various measures in the 1990s that the law changed in a manner similar to the proposals made by Smith.[125]

Another defeated proposal also shows the early recognition that children could have a meaningful impact on the course of a trial. This sought to permit a girl who was too young to understand the nature of the oath to provide an unsworn statement "in corroboration or explanation of any other evidence which may be given in support of" a charge being brought.[126] While this was criticised as being too loose and informal a measure which ran the risk of putting words into a child's mouth,[127] the proposal attracted significant support given the nature of the crimes in question. One MP stated bluntly that he "could not understand this squeamishness about children giving evidence in cases where that evidence was absolutely necessary."[128] Others pointed out the necessity of including a measure

123 HC Deb 06 August 1885, vol 300, col 1390, Samuel Smith MP.
124 Ibid.
125 In the United Kingdom, see the changes relating to children's competence found in the Youth Justice and Criminal Evidence Act 1999.
126 HC Deb 31 July 1885, vol 300, col 754, Samuel Smith MP.
127 HC Deb 31 July 1885, vol 300, col 759, Charles Hopwood MP.
128 HC Deb 31 July 1885, vol 300, col 760, Albert Grey MP.

of this sort as there would otherwise be no point in passing the legislation as far as young children were concerned; unless the law was reformed to allow young children to give evidence in some manner, these crimes would continue to go unpunished.[129] Crucially, young children were spoken of as "the most truthful, oftentimes, of all witnesses, if only they were examined in a kindly manner."[130] This last point, about the manner in which children were examined by barristers, had been prompted by a discussion of how children were to be cross-examined, which highlighted that the ages of children needed to be taken into account so that their stories could be told.[131] The amendment was not, however, carried, being defeated by a narrow margin of 120 votes to 123.

Some of the defeated proposals were eventually to find their way onto the statute book. In 1894, the Prevention of Cruelty to Children (Amendment) Act and the Prevention of Cruelty to Children Act were passed.[132] By the end of that year, the judges were empowered to take a written deposition of a child's evidence on oath, if the judge was satisfied by the evidence of a registered medical practitioner that the attendance of the child in court would involve serious danger to its life or health.[133] This would apply in cases where the accused was charged with child cruelty, or any offence involving injury to a child.[134] Additionally, this deposition could now be admitted in evidence in court against an accused person, provided that the defendant was given the opportunity to cross-examine the child at the time the deposition was taken.[135] While it appears that this power was rarely, if ever, used,[136] it marks a significant advance in the ability of child victims to participate as witnesses in ways designed to accommodate them as children. These measures provoked some limited debate when introduced in Parliament. It seems that the main aim of the power to take and admit a written deposition was to ensure that the evidence of a dying child should form part of the prosecution case.[137] When clarification was sought on whether the clause would apply only to dying children, none was provided, save to say that dying depositions could not currently be tak-

129 HC Deb 31 July 1885, vol 300, col 762, James Picton MP.
130 Ibid.
131 HC Deb 31 July 1885, vol 300, col 761, James Picton MP.
132 Rather confusingly, the Amendment Act (57 & 58 Vict c 27) was passed in July, while the Prevention of Cruelty to Children Act (57 & 58 Vict c 41), which consolidated child protection law, was passed in August and repealed the Amendment Act. The provisions of the Amendment Act with respect to the laws of evidence were effectively re-enacted, but in a slightly expanded form.
133 Section 14 Amendment Act, section 13 Cruelty Act. The former provided that the power to take written depositions only applied to cruelty charge, while the latter extended the range of relevant offences considerably.
134 The earlier Amendment Act only applied in cases where the accused was charged with child cruelty, or any offence involving injury to a child.
135 Section 15 Amendment Act, section 14 Cruelty Act.
136 See Emily Henderson, 'Alternative Routes to Best Evidence' in JR Spencer and Michael E Lamb (eds), *Children and Cross-Examination: Time to Change the Rules* (Bloomsbury 2002) 47.
137 HC Deb 23 May 1894, vol 24, col 1120

en.[138] This was introduced as part of the earlier Prevention of Cruelty to Children (Amendment) Act, when the power only extended to prosecutions for cruelty. The subsequent extension of the provisions to cover any offence involving bodily injury so shortly after their initial introduction would indicate that the principle of accommodating children as witnesses was widely accepted.

A further important reform is found in section 15 of the Prevention of Cruelty to Children Act 1894. This provides that where a child is deemed not to understand the nature of an oath, the evidence of such child may nevertheless be introduced if the child is regarded as "possessed of sufficient intelligence to justify the reception of the evidence, and understands the duty of speaking the truth".[139] Further, the evidence of child "though not given on oath but otherwise taken and reduced into writing" was to be deemed to be a deposition and admissible in a trial on that basis.[140] Where evidence was admitted under this section, the accused was provided with certain safeguards. First, a person could not be convicted of the offence unless the child's unsworn testimony was "corroborated by some other material evidence in support thereof implicating the accused".[141] Additionally, any child who wilfully gave false evidence was themselves liable to prosecution. During the limited debate on these matters, it was simply stated that "[i]t had been the experience of the Judges that evidence given by children who were not sworn was perfectly trustworthy".[142]

Conclusion

The Victorian and Edwardian periods are rightly regarded as marking the beginning of the modern era of child protection. Given the extent of reforms undertaken in respect of the age of consent, the criminalization of cruelty to children and the expansion of the state's supervisory role over child welfare, it would be difficult to argue otherwise. However, it remains to be asked how children were thought about; while reforms were undertaken, understanding why this was done can help us to gain an insight into the social forces that not only gave the system its shape but impacted on its operation. While there has been significant attention paid to the idea of a duality whereby children were on the one hand presented as victims, while being simultaneously thought of as threats to be controlled, this chapter has outlined an alternative approach. The idea of children as a threat, prominent in the debate around the 1885 Act, largely disappears from the later parliamentary record. Later reforms seemed to proceed in earnest with an understanding that children were victims of abuse and exploitation. There was also the recognition that the state had a responsibility to intervene in order to remove children from the risk of further harm.

138 HC Deb 23 May 1894, vol 24, col 1121.
139 Section 15(1).
140 Ibid.
141 Section 15(1)(a).
142 HC Deb 23 May 1894, vol 24, col 1120, Sir Richard Webster MP.

Yet the most startling feature of this period is the emergence, in outline and in a limited sense, of the idea that children could have something to add to the legal process which affected them. Though the reform of evidence law on questions such as corroboration requirements cannot be used to argue that childhood agency was now an integral part of law's theoretical landscape, the advance that it represents should not be ignored. By recognising that children were capable of adding their own voices to trials, it showed that not only were those voices relevant but that they had a certain, limited, power. As such, one can see a crack emerging on the façade of the traditional social order. However, traditional modernity was a long way from finished. As a new independent Irish state emerged from the violence of the 1910s and 1920s, the solidity and stability of social relations reasserted themselves.

References

Bailey V and Blackburn S, 'The Punishment of Incest Act 1908: A Case Study in Law Creation' [1979] *Criminal Law Review* 708.

Biggins J, 'Children of the Fíne and Children of the Family: Reformulating Children's Best Interests and Social Parenting in the Spirit of the Brehon Laws' (2010) 9 *Hibernian Law Journal* 15.

Buckley SA, *The Cruelty Man: Child Welfare, the NSPCC and the State in Ireland, 1889–1956* (Manchester University Press 2015).

Burke H, *The People and The Poor Law in Nineteenth-Century Ireland* (Dublin Women's Education Bureau 1987).

Charlesworth L, *Welfare's Forgotten Past: A Socio-Legal History of the Poor Law* (Routledge 2011).

Clemente M, "A Reassessment of Common Law Protections for 'Idiots'" (2014–2015) 124(8) *Yale Law Journal* 2680.

Cretney S, *Family Law in the Twentieth Century: A History* (Oxford University Press 2005).

Criminal Law Revision Committee, 'Fifteenth Report on Sexual Offences' (Cmnd 9213, 1984).

Gorham D, "The 'Maiden Tribute of Modern Babylon' Re-examined: Child Prostitution in Late-Victorian England" (1978) 21(3) *Victorian Studies* 353.

Harding M, '"To Affinity and Beyond": A Critical Analysis of the Law on Marriage within Prohibited Degrees of Relationship' in Katharina Boele-Woelki and Tone Sverdrup (eds), *European Challenges in Contemporary Family Law* (Intersentia 2008).

Harding M, 'The Curious Incident of the Marriage (No 2) Act 1537 and the Irish Statute Book' (2012) 32(1) *Legal Studies* 78.

Henderson E, 'Alternative Routes to Best Evidence' in JR Spencer and Michael E Lamb (eds), *Children and Cross-Examination: Time to Change the Rules* (Bloomsbury 2002).

Hendrick H, *Child Welfare 1872–1989* (Routledge 1994).

Hendrick H, *Children, Childhood and English Society 1880–1990* (Cambridge University Press 1997).

Hendrick H, *Child Welfare: Historical Dimensions, Contemporary Debate* (Polity Press 2003).

Heywood J, *Children in Care* (Routledge 1978).
Hutchins EL and Harrison A, *A History of Factory Legislation* (PS King 1903).
Jackson LA, *Child Sexual Abuse in Victorian England* (Routledge 2000).
Kearney N and Skehill C, *Social Work in Ireland: Historical Perspectives* (Institute of Public Administration 2005).
Keating H, 'When the Kissing Has to Stop: Children, Sexual Behaviour, and the Criminal Law' in Michael Freeman (ed), *Law and Childhood Studies* (Oxford University Press 2012).
Law Reform Commission, *Report Relating to Age of Majority* (LRC 5-1983).
Murphy P, *Murphy on Evidence* (11th end, Oxford University Press 2009).
Parton N, *The Politics of Child Abuse* (Palgrave 1985).
Platt L, *Discovering Child Poverty: The Creation of a Policy Agenda from 1800 to the Present* (Policy Press 2005).
Radzinowicz L and Hood R, *A History of the English Criminal Law and its Administration since 1750, Volume V: The Emergence of Penal Policy in Victorian and Edwardian England* (Clarendon Press 1986).
Royal Commission on the Housing of the Working Classes, *Minutes of the Evidence of the First Report* (Cmnd 4402-1, 1885).
Smith C and Gallen J, 'Cáin Adomnáin and the Laws of War' (2014) 16 *Journal of the History of International Law* 63.
Stewart J, 'Children, Parents and the State: The Children Act 1908' (1995) 9(1) *Children and Society* 90.
Walker N, 'Morality and the Criminal Law' (1964) 11 *Howard Journal* 209.
Wasserstein B, *Herbert Samuel: A Political Life* (Oxford University Press 1992).
Wikeley N, *Child Support: Law and Policy* (Hart Publishing 2006).
Weeks J, *Sex, Politics and Society: The Regulation of Sexuality since 1800* (2nd ed, London, Longman, 1989).
Wolfram S, 'Eugenics and the Punishment of Incest Act 1908' [1983] *Criminal Law Review* 308.
Wolfram S, *In-laws and Outlaws: Kinship and Marriage in England* (Palgrave Macmillan 1987).

3 Children in the constitutional order of traditional modernity

Introduction

The idea that children occupy a particularly important position within Ireland's constitutional framework would, for a long time, have been a rather strange proposition. While it is true that children had been mentioned in Ireland's constitutional texts and cases, they most commonly appeared not as individual subjects or agents, but as a part of a wider network – the family. As a result, examining the position of children within the legal order of the Constitution itself can help us to understand how the relationship between state, families and children was thought about at a relatively abstract level. It can, therefore, allow us to bridge the gap between the legal and the sociological by seeing how the most basic and fundamental of legal texts bears the imprint of a particular form of modernity. This chapter will cover the constitutional position of children up to the publication of the report of the Kilkenny Incest Inquiry in 1993, with post-Kilkenny developments dealt with in Chapter 6. The Kilkenny Report can be seen as the event that most obviously marks the transition from simple to late modernity in Irish child protection law. It was the impetus for sustained discussion about the development of a constitutional amendment on children's rights, which was successfully passed in 2012. As will be seen, Irish constitutional law operated under conditions of simple modernity during the pre-Kilkenny era, with a more reflexive approach evident after the publication of that report.

The case law on children and children's rights will be dealt with after a more textual analysis of the relevant constitutional provisions, an analysis which will draw heavily on sources showing the drafting history of the text. This is because the case law and drafting of the texts took place in separate fora – judges decided on specific points of constitutional law and interpretation in the context of litigation, while parliamentarians and civil society representatives engaged in a more wide-ranging discussion of concerns affecting children, such as state intervention in family life, in the context of broader issues such as the nature of the state's underpinning principles.

Several images of children will emerge. The traditional approach to Irish constitutional law posits that children have been subsumed within a wider concept of the family. As this chapter will show, this is not quite the case. While it is true that the text adopted in the 1937 Constitution contains few references to children, and that the case law frequently did not emphasise their rights, this is not quite the same as invisibility.[1] The early decades of constitutional history show that the child was considered and was visible, but most frequently as an object of the law, passive, rather than being considered as an agent. In the wake of later child protection scandals, Irish constitutional law on the child came to an existential crossroads, opening up new possibilities for the child protection system and the possibility of the incorporation of children's rights into the legal order, marking children's full transition to the status of agents. During the time-frame examined in this chapter, however, it is evident that the recognition of children as agents in a meaningful sense had not yet developed.

The constitutional texts of traditional modernity

Before considering the relationship between children, their families, and the Constitution, it is worth considering briefly the role that the Constitution plays in Ireland. Constitutions do not only outline how a state is to be governed; they can contain examples of fundamental rights which must be protected, while also outlining broad principles which guide the drafting of other legislation, leading Kelly to describe constitutions as containing "manifesto statements".[2] Ireland's legal system is based on constitutional supremacy. This means that the Constitution serves as the fundamental law of the state. The parliament, known as the Oireachtas, is not permitted to pass any law which contravenes its provisions; the result of doing so would be to have the legislation declared void.[3] Second, constitutional lawmaking is regarded as somewhat different from ordinary law reform measures. Unlike ordinary legislation, which can be amended by a parliamentary vote, the Constitution can only be amended following a referendum.[4] Adjudication on constitutional issues relating to children and childhood in this context allows courts to engage with the construction of childhood.[5]

1 Aoife Nolan, 'The Battle(s) over Children's Rights in the Irish Constitution' (2007) 22(4) *Irish Political Studies* 495.
2 JM Kelly, '*Law and Manifesto*' in Frank Litton (ed), *The Constitution of Ireland: 1937–1987* (Institute of Public Administration 1988).
3 See generally, Gerard Hogan and Gerry Whyte, *JM Kelly: The Irish Constitution* (4th edn, Tottel Publishing 2003) 895–912.
4 See Articles 46 and 47 of the Constitution of Ireland.
5 On this, see generally, John Tobin, 'Courts and the Construction of Childhood: A new way of thinking' in Michael Freeman (ed) *Law and Childhood Studies* (Oxford University Press 2012).

The Irish constitutions before 1937

Ireland has a written constitution, *Bunreacht na hÉireann*, which dates from 1937. It replaced the 1922 Constitution which was closely tied to the Anglo-Irish Treaty of 1921, which created the Irish Free State; this, in turn, replaced an earlier constitutional document from 1919.[6] The earliest of these contained no specific reference to children, or indeed to any personal rights, as it was exclusively concerned with the relationship between the executive and the legislature. However, the statement of social and economic principles known as the Democratic Programme of the First Dáil was passed on the same day which, it has been argued, can be seen as a fundamental rights appendix.[7] This Democratic Programme did refer to children, stating that

> It shall be the first duty of the Government of the Republic to make provision for the physical, mental and spiritual well-being of the children, to secure that no child shall suffer hunger or cold from lack of food, clothing, or shelter, but that all shall be provided with the means and facilities requisite for their proper education and training as Citizens of a Free and Gaelic Ireland.[8]

As can be seen, these references to children contain references to a number of ideas which later became important – the recognition that the State has a duty to fulfil certain obligations towards children, the implicit recognition of their vulnerability, the recognition that children have social and economic needs. However, these are couched by the qualification that these needs shall be met so as to enable them to participate in a highly ideological and romanticised version of Ireland – the initial draft of the above clause made no mention of "Gaelic Ireland", referring instead to "free citizens of a free nation".[9] Additionally, this paragraph can be seen as more of a statement of intent that children should live "better" lives, rather than the creation of legal rights which could be enforced against the Executive.[10] In this way, it continues on the path set by the 1916 Proclamation of the Irish Republic, which promised to "cherish all children of the nation equally"; the legal quality of such statements can be doubted given both the lack of full legal authority to implement them and their legal vagueness, even if their rhetorical power cannot.

6 Constitution of Dáil Éireann, 1919.
7 Laura Cahillane, 'Ireland's Forgotten Constitutions' (2009) 27 *Irish Law Times* 243, 248. There is some dispute about this, however. See in particular, Brian Farrell, *The founding of Dáil Éireann: parliament and nation-building* (Gill and Macmillan 1971) and Emmet O'Connor, 'Neither Democratic nor a Programme: The Democratic Programme of 1919' (2016) 40(157) *Irish Historical Studies* 92.
8 Dáil Debates 21 January 1919, vol F 1, col 23, Seán Ó Ceallaigh TD.
9 See the differences between drafts of this provision highlighted by O'Connor (n 7) 107.
10 Farrell (n 7) and O'Connor (n 7) point out that the Programme may never have been designed for implementation.

The 1922 Constitution contained even fewer references to children, with the sole instance being a reference in Article 8 to "the right of any child to attend a school receiving public money without attending the religious instruction at the school". This should not be read, however, as a nascent right to freedom of conscience for children, as the reference to this right forms part of an article referring more generally to the separation of church and state, and is also a direct reference to the Treaty signed between Ireland and Great Britain, which guaranteed that

> Neither the Parliament of the Irish Free State nor the Parliament of Northern Ireland shall make any law so as either directly or indirectly to endow any religion or prohibit or restrict the free exercise thereof or give any preference or impose any disability on account of religious belief or religious status or affect prejudicially the right of any child to attend a school receiving public money without attending the religious instruction.

As such, the child's "right" to freedom from religious instruction can instead be seen as a guarantee to the minority community in each of the two jurisdictions that no proselytising would occur in schools operated by the public authorities. Far from being invisible, it can be surmised that children were clearly seen, although as objects, rather than subjects bearing distinct legal rights capable of enforcement.

The Constitution which emerged from the drafting process represented the views of the majority of the drafting committee, especially in respect of the type of clauses which should be contained in a constitution.[11] However, alternatives were mooted, which may have radically altered the constitutional position of children between 1922 and 1937. Two distinct alternatives emerged during the drafting process and during Dáil debates. First, a draft constitution was produced by Alfred O'Rahilly, who would also become involved in the drafting process of the 1937 text. This draft, known as Draft C, was apparently not seriously considered by the committee responsible for drawing up the final text, but it foreshadows some of the themes that were to re-emerge in the 1937 text.[12] Draft C was heavily inspired by Roman Catholic social teaching, and sought to include a new section entitled "Family, Education, Religion". In O'Rahilly's own words, it embodied the "Christian ideal of marriage, parental authority, protection of women and children, education, religion in a mixed State."[13] Brady highlights that the exclusion of these provisions from the final text does not mean that the other committee members opposed their content, but rather that they disagreed with O'Rahilly over the inclusion of statements of political principle

11 See Paul Brady, 'Social, Political, and Philosophical Foundations of the Irish Constitutional Order' in Denis J Galligan and Mila Versteeg, *Social and Political Foundations of Constitutions* (Cambridge University Press 2013).

12 For an account of the drafting process and the involvement of O'Rahilly in the drafting of the 1922 Constitution, see Bill Kissane, *New Beginnings: Constitutionalism and Democracy in Modern Ireland* (University College Dublin Press 2011) 34–40.

13 NAS 8 953, cited in Brady (n 11) 289.

in a constitution.[14] If O'Rahilly's proposal had been accepted, even in part or in modified form, the likelihood is that the constitutional position of children would likely have been similar to that which was seen in the 1937 text, given the emphasis on marriage and parental authority, and the linking of children to issues revolving around education and religion.

On the other hand, during the parliamentary debates leading to the adoption of the 1922 Constitution, the Labour Party proposed a new version of Article 10 which would have created some legally binding obligations towards children. The proposal in full read:

> The right of the children to food, clothing, shelter and education, sufficient for their proper physical welfare and training as citizens of Saorstat Eireann is guaranteed.
>
> It is the duty of all citizens to ensure that their children and wards receive adequate education. To this end provision shall be made by the State for the free education of the young up to an age to be prescribed by law. School attendance shall be compulsory. Provision shall be made by the State, so that secondary and higher educational institutions shall be readily accessible in the case of persons with small means.
>
> All schools and educational establishments, public and private, shall be controlled by the State, within limits to be determined by law.
>
> All schools and educational establishments shall aim at inculcating moral character, religious tolerance, and personal and vocational efficiency, and the teaching given therein shall be imbued with the spirit of Irish nationality and international goodwill. The duties of citizenship shall be a subject of instruction in all schools in order to fit the pupil for his responsibilities as a citizen.[15]

First, children are again thought of as possessing a right to education, an idea which was revived in the 1937 text. Second, children and education are linked, as in the 1919 Democratic Programme, with national identity. Third, the social and economic needs of children are recognised, much as in the 1919 Programme. Importantly, these are couched in the language of rights, a crucial difference when compared with later reluctance to recognise social and economic rights for children other than the right to education, but which more importantly seeks to recognise children as having rights capable of enforcement.[16] This proposal does not include many of the rights associated with children's agency today, but by

14 Brady, ibid.

15 Dáil Debates, 25 September 1922, vol 13, col 696, Thomas J O'Connell TD.

16 On the importance of rights and enforcement of rights for children generally, see Conor O'Mahony, 'Education, Remedies and the Separation of Powers' (2002) 24 *Dublin University Law Journal* 57, Conor O'Mahony, 'A New Slant on Educational Rights and Mandatory Injunctions?' (2005) 27 *Dublin University Law Journal* 363, and Aoife Nolan, 'A Role for the Courts in Ensuring the Enforcement of the Socio-Economic Rights of the Child: Overcoming the Counter-majoritarian Objection' in Andre Alen et al (eds), *The UN Children's Rights Convention: Theory meets Practice* (2nd edn, Intersentia 2007).

making claims to food, shelter and clothing enforceable as rights, children could, even indirectly, exercise influence on social structures.

The role of the State in this proposal seems to be enlarged somewhat, despite some tension over this being evident in the proposed text. While private educational establishments are recognised, they are to be "controlled by the State". Although schools were to be provided by the State, the primary responsibility for education rested with parents, as indicated by the statement that citizens shall ensure the education of "their" children. While the State was to guarantee the social and economic rights of children, the mechanism by which this may be done was not as clear as in the case of education, thereby marking out education rights as the primary social and economic right. The role envisaged for the State, therefore, does not seem to have been properly demarcated, especially outside of the educational context. Nonetheless, an interesting phrase appears in the second paragraph. Citizens were to be responsible for their "children and wards". This would have meant that not only the children of married couples would have to be provided for, but that those children in the care of adults not born within marriage would have to be given co-equal status, at least in respect of education. This is surprising in light of the later constitutional position, which accorded primacy to married family units. While this did not fully equalise the position of marital and non-marital children, it certainly did recognise that adults *in loco parentis* had duties towards children deriving from a child's dependent state, rather than the adult's marital status.

It similarly undermines any claim that the later constitutional position can be regarded as a non-ideological view of family life; rather it was clearly one that was constructed through the active expression of preference for one particular vision of the family. The early constitutional texts generally present a mixed view of children within political and legal discourse. Children were to have certain rights. These rights were both limited in scope, with education being given priority, and related to their dependent status, but the fact that they were seen as being capable of having rights raises the question of whether they could be regarded as agents. Support can also be found for the view that children were seen instead as objects, subject to the overriding imperative of national identity formation and subject to parental discipline. Yet they were also to be the passive recipients of welfare due to concern among some for child deprivation. No single paradigmatic view of children dominates these early documents.

The 1937 Constitution

Over the course of the 1920s and 1930s, the 1922 Constitution would be amended on many occasions, although none of these changes affected provisions relating to children, and it was regarded as being open to further revision, or even replacement.[17] Eventually, it was decided that the document should be

17 On this, see generally, Donal K Coffey, 'The Need for a New Constitution: Irish Constitutional Change 1932–1935' (2012) 47 *Irish Jurist* 275.

replaced by a new constitution, which was approved by a plebiscite in 1937. While Kelly has described the text as re-bottling of wine, most of which was then quite old and of familiar vintages,[18] the 1937 text did contain some radical changes. The new constitution introduced a "new symbolic system" for Irish law, policy and institutions,[19] due largely to the replacing of any references to Great Britain and its associated symbols with references to Irish nationality and Roman Catholicism.[20] While the new Constitution was not an entirely religious document, it did draw heavily on Catholic social teaching for certain aspects of its provisions relating to fundamental rights. This is reflected in the drafting process as much as in the final text.[21]

While the majority of the text was drafted by the Taoiseach, Éamon de Valera, and a small group of civil servants, recommendations relating to the drafting were also made by several clerical groups, in particular a group of Jesuits, the later Archbishop of Dublin John Charles McQuaid, and Alfred O'Rahilly, whose interventions are discussed further below.[22] Articles 40–45 do bear a strong Catholic imprint, so much so that the final text was described as "a fairly successful union of democracy and Catholic teaching."[23]

Several provisions of the 1937 Constitution are important for children. Those with the most obvious relevance are Articles 41 and 42, though as will be outlined later, Article 40.3 was also to become important. Articles 41 and 42 outline the State's view of the family, the rights of the family as against the state, and rights to education. The articles are so heavily intertwined that they will be considered together. Article 45 on non-justiciable directive principles of social policy also contains some references, particular to orphans, and will be considered briefly.

Article 41.1.1° "recognises the family as the natural and primary unit group of Society, and as a moral institution possessing inalienable and imprescriptible rights, antecedent and superior to all positive law". The following paragraph guarantees that the State will "protect the Family in its constitution and authority." Only one type of family is accorded constitutional recognition, given the terms of Article 41.3.2°, which pledges the State to "guard with special care the

18 JM Kelly, *The Irish Constitution* (Jurist Publishing 1980) xxviii.

19 Jeffrey Prager, *Building Democracy in Ireland – Political Order and Cultural Integration in A Newly Independent Nation* (Cambridge University Press 1986) 90–91.

20 For a brief overview of this process, see James Casey, *Constitutional Law in Ireland* (3rd edn, Round Hall 2000) 16–19.

21 See generally, JM Kelly, *Fundamental Rights in the Irish Constitution* (2nd edn, Allen Figgis & Co 1967) 57–58, Casey, ibid, 22, Patrick Hannon, 'In God's Name, What Next? Religion, The Constitution and the New Ireland' in Oran Doyle and Eoin Carolan (eds), *The Irish Constitution: Governance and Values* (Thomson Round Hall 2008) and Eoin Daly, *Religion, Law and the Irish State* (Clarus Press 2012) 28–33.

22 Though O'Rahilly was not at this time a priest, he was ordained following his retirement from academic life.

23 Enda McDonagh, 'Church and state in the Constitution of Ireland' (1961) 28(2) *Irish Theological Quarterly* 131.

institution of Marriage, on which the Family is founded".[24] Article 42.1 highlights that "the primary and natural educator of the child is the Family" and also protects the "inalienable right and duty of parents to provide" for the education of their children. While much of the remainder of the article deals largely with scholastic education,[25] the provisions of Article 42.5 have proven crucial in many of the debates concerning the constitutional rights of children.[26] This article stated that

> In exceptional cases, where the parents for physical or moral reasons fail in their duty towards their children, the State as guardian of the common good, by appropriate means shall endeavour to supply the place of the parents, but always with due regard for the natural and imprescriptible rights of the child.

This provision allows State intervention in family life where it is necessary to ensure the protection of the child and has had a controversial history. As will be outlined in Chapter 4, State intervention in marital families bordered on the routine during the early decades of independence, and even after the adoption of the 1937 Constitution, with children sent to reform and industrial schools for reasons such as parental poverty.[27] However, as this practice declined during the 1960s and 1970s, Article 42.5 came to be seen in a different light, permitting intervention only in the most egregious of cases, as the interpretation of the provision outlined below will demonstrate.

It has been argued that the provisions of Articles 41 and 42 are not so novel as is sometimes asserted. While some commentators claim that the provisions are virtually without precedent in modern constitutions,[28] Hogan has claimed that the terms of these articles are not so different from later constitutional documents or from the terms of later international human rights treaties, such as the International Covenant on Civil and Political Rights.[29] However, this claim

24 This view did shift somewhat with the gradual recognition that unmarried mothers enjoyed constitutional rights in respect of their family life with their children, although these rights were recognised as arising under Article 40.3, and so did not quite mirror the rights of married families under Article 41.

25 Although see the decision of *O'Donoghue v Minister for Health* [1993] IEHC 2, [1996] 2 IR 20 which extended the meaning of education beyond this narrow interpretation in the context of a child with severe disabilities.

26 Article 42.5 was repealed following a referendum in 2012, considered in Chapter 6. It will be referred to in the past tense, unless circumstances demand otherwise.

27 See also Moira Maguire, *Precarious Childhood in Post-Independence Ireland* (Manchester University Press 2012).

28 For an example, see Francis X Beytagh, *Constitutionalism in Contemporary Ireland: An American Perspective* (Round Hall 1997) 37.

29 Gerard Hogan, "Foreword" in Dermot Keogh and Andrew McCarthy, *The Making of the Irish Constitution 1937* (Cork University Press 2007) 22–25, citing the International Covenant on Civil and Political Rights (adopted 16 December 1966, entered into force 23 March 1976) 999 UNTS 171. Article 23 of the International Covenant provides:

underplays the sweeping nature of the provisions' language and scope; even where human rights treaties protect family life or even families based on marriage, none make use of natural law language to such an extent as to claim the family rights effectively supersede the law.[30]

This Catholic influence on Articles 41 and 42 is evidenced by the reliance placed on papal encyclicals during the drafting of the provisions. The preference for the collective entity of the family has its roots in the encyclical *Rerum Novarum*, which discusses the Catholic view of the proper balance of rights between the state and the family.[31] Although references to individual family members are largely absent from the constitutional provisions on the family, with priority given to the collective, the Constitution does highlight the role of parents.[32] In Article 42.1 they are described as the natural and primary educators of children, while Article 41.1.1° asserts the inalienability and imprescriptibility of parental rights. This draws specifically on the language of another encyclical, *Divini Illius Magistri*,[33] which describes the rights of families as "anterior to any right whatever of civil society and of the State, and therefore inviolable on the part of any power on earth".[34]

The secondary role afforded to the State in the constitutional text mirrors the theological understanding of the principle of subsidiarity, even if this has not been rigorously applied in practice. This principle holds that it is inappropriate for the state to control any activity or to take any action that can be accomplished at a

1. The family is the natural and fundamental group unit of society and is entitled to protection by society and the State.
2. The right of men and women of marriageable age to marry and to found a family shall be recognized.
3. No marriage shall be entered into without the free and full consent of the intending spouses.
4. States Parties to the present Covenant shall take appropriate steps to ensure equality of rights and responsibilities of spouses as to marriage, during marriage and at its dissolution. In the case of dissolution, provision shall be made for the necessary protection of any children.

30 See also, Article 10 of the *International Covenant on Economic, Social and Cultural Rights*, (adopted 16 December 1966, entered into force 3 January 1976) 993 UNTS and the various references to the family in the United Nations Convention on the Rights of the Child (adopted 20 November 1989, entered into force 2 September 1990) 1557 UNTS.

31 Pope Leo XIII, 'Encyclical Letter, *Rerum Novarum*: On Capital and Labour' (Papal Encyclical 1891) [12]: "we have the family, the 'society' of a man's house – a society very small, one must admit, but none the less a true society, and one older than any State. Consequently, it has rights and duties peculiar to itself which are quite independent of the State." www.vatican.va/holy_father/leo_xiii/encyclicals/documents/hf_l-xiii_enc_15051891_rerum-novarum_en.html, accessed 29 December 2019. See also, Keogh and McCarthy (n 29) 112–115.

32 See generally, Ursula Kilkelly, *Children's Rights in Ireland: Law Policy and Practice* (Tottel Publishing 2008) 60–61 and 104–110.

33 Pope Pius XI, 'Encyclical Letter, *Divini Illius Magistri*: On Christian Education' (Papal Encyclical 1929) www.vatican.va/holy_father/pius_xi/encyclicals/documents/hf_p-xi_enc_31121929_divini-illius-magistri_en.html, accessed 29 December 2019.

34 Ibid [32].

more local level, such as the education of children. Within Catholic social teaching, this can be effectively done at the parental level, and so the state should not concern itself with such matters. This view, originally found in *Rerum Novarum*, was repeated in *Quadragesimo Anno*,[35] which was published only a few years before the drafting of the new constitutional text began. This encyclical reasserted the centrality of the subsidiarity principle to Catholic thought, with the effect that the role of the state would be reduced, and restored to what was felt was its "rightful place, which is not to do anything itself, but to direct, watch, urge and restrain subsidiary organisations".[36] Further, *Divini Illius Magistri* promotes the idea of parental authority, stating that "it would be contrary to natural justice if the child, before the use of reason, were removed from the care of its parents, or if any disposition were made concerning him against the will of the parents."[37]

Limited provision is made for state intervention into the family by Article 42.5, which "in exceptional cases",[38] can be used to justify intervention in cases of failure to fulfil parental obligations to children. This also mirrors the language of *Rerum Novarum* which provides that for "the civil government [to] at its option intrude into and exercise intimate control over the family and the household is a great and pernicious error."[39] In cases of "exceeding distress ... it is right that extreme necessity be met by public aid"[40] so that the state can fulfil its obligations to families and the nation more generally. In language strikingly similar to that used in Article 42.5, *Divini Illius Magistri* provides that "[i]t also belongs to the State to protect the rights of the child itself when the parents are found wanting either physically or morally in this respect, whether by default, incapacity or misconduct."[41]

That the language used by the Constitution closely reflects that of papal encyclicals is clear.[42] However, it must be asked how consciously the language

35 Pope Pius XI, 'Encyclical Letter, *Quadrigesimo Anno*: On Reconstruction of the Social Order' (Papal Encyclical 1931) [79], "it is true that on account of changed conditions many things which were done by small associations in former times cannot be done now save by large associations. Still, that most weighty principle, which cannot be set aside or changed, remains fixed and unshaken in social philosophy: Just as it is gravely wrong to take from individuals what they can accomplish by their own initiative and industry and give it to the community, so also it is an injustice and at the same time a grave evil and disturbance of right order to assign to a greater and higher association what lesser and subordinate organizations can do." www.vatican.va/holy_father/pius_xi/encyclicals/documents/hf_p-xi_enc_19310515_quadragesimo-anno_en.html, accessed 29 December 2019.

36 JH Whyte, *Church and State in Modern Ireland 1923–1979* (2nd edn, Gill & McMillan 1980) 67.

37 Pope Pius XI (n 33) [33].

38 Article 42.5.

39 Pope Leo XIII (n 31) [14].

40 Ibid.

41 Pope Pius XI (n 33) [45].

42 See further Oran Doyle, 'Family Autonomy and Children's Best Interests: Ireland, Bentham and the Natural Law' (2010) 1 *International Journal of the Jurisprudence of the Family* 55.

paralleled Catholic doctrine, and what it tells us about the position of children in the constitutional and legal order. First, the archival work undertaken by Keogh, McCarthy, Hogan and Kissane highlights that clerical influence on what became the fundamental rights provisions was significant.[43] Alfred O'Rahilly's unused "Draft C" of the 1922 Constitution was reconsidered. De Valera was in contact with the Jesuit priest Fr Edward Cahill, who presented him with a copy of his own book *The Framework of a Christian State*. It is important, however, not to overplay the influence of Cahill, who was regarded by his own order as a marginal voice.[44] Cahill's main role seems to have been to act as an intermediary for a formally constituted Jesuit committee who lobbied for the adoption of a "Catholic Constitution".[45] The future Archbishop McQuaid, a personal friend of de Valera's, provided several draft articles relating to political authority, religion, education and social policy. De Valera also sent a delegate to Rome to attain the Pope's assent to the certain clauses of the Constitution.[46] This would seem to indicate that, contrary to Hogan's assertion that it does not really matter whether Thomas Aquinas or Thomas Paine was the main inspiration for constitutional provisions,[47] several parts of the Constitution was drafted with an explicitly Catholic approach in mind.

One further point relating to children in the Constitution must be made, even though it has attracted limited attention. Article 45 contains the "Directive Principles of Social Policy". The article states that these are for the "general guidance of the legislature", so that "justice and charity shall inform all the institutions of social life."[48] The idea of justice underpinning this vision appears rather communitarian in nature, allowing limitations to be placed on the exercise of autonomy in the interests of a common good;[49] as such the attention it has received has been mostly in the context of economic and social rights.[50] The article makes specific reference to ensuring that the state will safeguard with special care the "economic interests of weaker sections of the community" and makes particular reference to "orphans" in this respect.[51] Further, it pledges to endeavour to protect children from unsuitable employment, so that their "tender age ... shall

43 See Keogh and McCarthy (n 29), Kissane (n 12) and Gerard Hogan, *The Origins of the Irish Constitution: 1928–1941* (Royal Irish Academy 2012), especially chapters 6 and 11.
44 See generally Dermot Keogh, 'The Constitutional Revolution: An Analysis of the Making of the Constitution' in Litton (ed) (n 2).
45 Kissane (n 14) 66.
46 Keogh (n 44) 43–53.
47 Gerard Hogan, 'The Constitution, Property Rights and Proportionality' (1997) 32 *Irish Jurist* 373.
48 Article 45.1.
49 Hogan and Whyte (n 3) 2079. See further, Gerard Hogan, 'Directive Principles, Socio-Economic Rights and the Constitution' (2001) 36 *Irish Jurist* 175, and Gerry Whyte, *Social Inclusion and the Legal System: Public Interest Law in Ireland* (Institute of Public Administration 2002), 43–45.
50 These are discussed further in Chapter 6.
51 Article 45.4.1°.

not be abused".[52] Yet these provisions are expressly stated not be "cognisable by any Court",[53] rendering them effectively non-justiciable. This has meant that the article has not been used as a substantive ground of constitutional review, and has been limited to a background role as an interpretative aid.[54] This was seen in one case involving child labour, where Article 45 was seen as allowing the Oireachtas to deem that the prohibition of employment of children under ten in certain public entertainment contexts was necessitated by the common good.[55] Apart from this, there has been no meaningful engagement with the article in the context of children's rights or the construction of childhood.

Where did all of these provisions leave children? What does it matter whether the framers of the document were motivated by early modern reinterpretations of medieval natural law theory or classical liberalism? The answer lies in part in the Oireachtas debates on the final text of the Constitution and partly in the interpretation of the Constitution's text by the courts. This becomes especially important when the Constitution is later interpreted in a historicist or originalist manner by judges – the idea that one ought to interpret a constitutional provision in the way in which that constitution's drafters intended it would be interpreted.[56] This effectively requires that constitutional provisions be given the meaning they had when it was originally drafted. Although not the dominant method of constitutional interpretation, it has been utilised in some important cases.[57] If such an approach were adopted, it would effectively undermine any ability for courts to engage with children's rights in a meaningful way, because it would not be possible to extend the reach of constitutional provisions to account for modern needs or constructions of what it means to be a child, effectively restricting them to a more proprietary approach to litigation concerning children's issues.[58]

My primary research into the Dáil Debates demonstrated that a high level of emphasis was placed on parental authority. This can be seen from de Valera's assertion that Articles 40–44 "set down what are the rights which the individual and the family have as against the operation of the otherwise all-powerful Parliament".[59]

52 Article 45.4.2°.
53 Article 45.
54 See the discussion in Hogan and Whyte (n 3) 2079–2085.
55 *Landers v Attorney General* (1975) 109 ILTR 1.
56 On this idea, see generally, Michael J Perry, 'The Authority of Text, Tradition, and Reason: A Theory of Constitutional Interpretation' (1985) 58 *Southern California Law Review* 551, Antonin Scalia, 'Originalism: The Lesser Evil' (1988–89) 57 *University of Cincinnati Law Review* 849 and Keith Whittington, *Constitutional Interpretation: Textual Meaning, Original Intent, and Judicial Review* (University Press of Kansas) 1999.
57 See for example, aspects of the decisions in *Sinnott v Minister for Education* [2001] IESC 63, [2001] 2 IR 505 and *Zappone v Revenue Commissioners* [2006] IEHC 404, [2008] 2 IR 417.
58 On which see Tobin (n 4) and John Tobin, 'Judging the Judges: Are they adopting the rights approach in matters involving children? (2009) 33(2) *University of Melbourne Law Review* 579.
59 Dáil Debates 11 May 1937, vol 67, col 61, Éamon de Valera TD.

Clearly then, the articles outlining family rights were thought of as establishing a bulwark against the State, contemplating that legislation which sought to abrogate family rights would be unconstitutional. With respect to the interaction between family members, and specifically between children and parents, the debates are silent on the question when discussing Articles 41 and 42. However, some insight may be gleaned from the debate on Article 40.1, which provides for an Aristotelian version of equality – all are equal before the law, but differences in social capacity or function may justify differential treatment. In the context of this provision, de Valera specifically referred to the capacity of children.[60] He stated that

> [y]ou cannot deduce from that that our laws are not to take cognisance of absolute social or physical capacity. Is a child, for instance, to be held as responsible for certain actions, a child whose will and mind are not developed, as a matured person? Are our laws to insist that he should be held as responsible as a person who was mature? Clearly not. Therefore, if you want to make a statement with regard to the equality of persons before the law, you must modify such a statement by making clear in what sense they are equal before the law.[61]

This clearly positions children as immature, and in need of paternalist treatment, whether from the family or from the state. This view was not unique to Catholic teaching,[62] but the balance between the alternative sources of protective influence – state or parent – was strongly Catholic in outlook. The alternative inspiration of political liberalism, which drew heavily on Bentham's work, permitted greater intervention on utilitarian grounds.[63] While Maguire's argument that state intervention was commonplace in the early decades after the adoption of the Constitution is correct, the importance of the Catholic inspiration for the positioning of children in relation to their parents and the State emerges when the case law on this point is considered.

What the texts reveal about children

Before the case law under the 1937 Constitution is considered, it is worth pausing to consider what the texts of, and debates surrounding, Ireland's various constitutions tell us about how children were constructed as an ideological–discursive formation. The major documents discussed so far – the 1919 Democratic Programme, and the two constitutions of 1922 and 1937 – share significant similarities and were drafted over a period of fewer than two decades when Ireland underwent significant political, but not social or cultural, transformation. In these documents, children were clearly not regarded as agents in any

60 See Nolan (n 1).
61 Dáil Debates 11 May 1937, vol 67, cols 72–73, Éamon de Valera TD.
62 See Doyle (n 42).
63 Ibid.

meaningful way; rather they were seen as objects with needs rather than rights. This certainly reflected international thinking about children at the time – the League of Nations' Declaration of the Rights of the Child, adopted in 1924, also saw children as dependent, in need, and as objects of munificence rather than as rights-bearing agents.[64] The emphasis on education, and especially the ideological character of education designed to inculcate in children a sense of Gaelic Ireland, saw children as objects to be imbued with a sense of nationality. However, children were also seen as objects of concern – the Democratic Programme's emphasis on what would now be termed child poverty, along with the Labour Party proposal for the 1922 Constitution – demonstrate a clear concern with children's well-being.

The 1937 text brought these issues into sharper focus. While some concern with children's economic well-being is seen in Article 45, these references are vague, and, as indicated above, non-justiciable. The more substantive provisions of the text – those which create justiciable rights and responsibilities – mention that the child has natural and imprescriptible rights, but leaves these undefined, a point which will be dealt with when the case law is considered below. Further, they are mentioned only in the context of state intervention into family life. When read in the context of Articles 41 and 42 as a whole, it becomes clear that the state is to take a merely subsidiary role while respecting to an unusually high degree the principle of parental authority. Children were to be educated by parents but also more broadly subject primarily to parental governance, given both their own immaturity and the near unimpeachable position of marital parents. Further, children were embedded within a very traditional kind of social structure – the marital family – which is characteristic of the structure of simple modernity. The constitutional provisions and drafting process make clear that there was a heavy emphasis on the integrity of the structure of the family itself, and of the instrumental control of children within it. The fact that the law's approach to children was rooted in the outlook of the first modernity, yet survived into the era of reflexive modernity would be troublesome in its own right; the fact that it survived in a constitution which enjoys supremacy over other legal instruments and with which policy initiatives must comply would eventually create significant difficulties for children, especially those at risk, as will be shown in later chapters.

Children in constitutional case law

Early case law on children

Courts may approach children's issues in a variety of ways – by treating children as the bearers of rights, as property, or as the beneficiaries of a welfare-orientated

64 Geneva Declaration of the Rights of the Child of 1924, adopted September 26, 1924, League of Nations O.J. Spec. Supp. 21, 43 (1924). See Geraldine Van Bueren, *International Law on the Rights of the Child* (Martinus Nijhoff 1994) at 8–9 for an account of the issues giving rise to the Declaration.

fluoridation amounted to an attack on the authority of the family as it removed parental choice over whether children should receive extra fluoride, whereas the State argued that it was a necessary and proportionate response to dental hygiene concerns. The Supreme Court reasoned that

> The aspect of that authority which is in question is the authority of the family or the parents to provide for the health of its members in the way it thinks best. It is sought to establish, as a corollary, that parents are entitled to omit to provide for the health of their children if they so think fit. One of the duties of parents is certainly to ward off dangers to the health of their children, and in the Court's view there is nothing in the Constitution which recognises the right of a parent to refuse to allow the provision of measures designed to secure the health of his child when the method of avoiding injury is one which is not fraught with danger to the child and is within the procurement of the parent. The nature of the health problem here involved and the effectiveness of the means available for dealing with it have already been referred to. There is nothing in the Act which can be said to be a violation of the guarantee on the part of the State to protect the family in its constitution and authority.[78]

This statement is novel in the Supreme Court's early jurisprudence on the relationship between children and families. The view that there is no constitutional basis for a right allowing a parent to refuse the provision of measures which would secure the health of a child stands in stark contrast to later decisions.[79] It seems to indicate the non-absolute nature of parental rights; and by establishing that parental authority has a limit, it implicitly recognises that children have an interest which courts are entitled to vindicate in contravention of parental wishes. Similarly, it does not establish that children can be substantively regarded as rights-bearers, but the movement away from an invisibility approach to children is clear.

The courts also used the new constitutional provisions to move away from the common law rules relating to paternal authority. Under common law, a father had a virtually absolute hold over his children's upbringing, including in circumstances where parents had separated.[80] A practice developed in Ireland whereby couples of different religious beliefs would enter into antenuptial agreements relating to the custody and religious upbringing of children upon separation – usually, this meant that children were to be brought up as Catholics.[81] In several

78 Ibid 350.
79 See the discussion of the decision in *HW and CW v North Western Health Board* [2001] 3 IR 365 in Chapter 6.
80 *Re Agar-Ellis* (1883) LR 24 Ch D 317 (CA).
81 See generally Jesse Buck, 'The role of *ne temere* in the decline of an Irish custom regarding the religious affiliation of the children of mixed marriages' (2011) 11 *The Australian Journal of Irish Studies* 28.

decisions, these agreements were deemed to be of no effect, and the common law rule of paternal authority remained in place.[82] This principle was overturned in *Re Tilson, Infants*.[83] While much of the judgment concerns the questions of joint parental authority, as well as the extent to which common law forms part of the post-1937 Irish legal corpus, there are some interesting observations about children's interests. The antenuptial agreement was to be upheld because it was designed

> to safeguard the innate and imprescriptible right of the child to religious education, its most precious inheritance in the eyes of a Christian State. I apprehend that this Court is bound under the Constitution to cherish that inheritance of helpless citizens. Consequently, however wide the unfettered *patria potestas* may be, a judicial theory, which, under cover of public policy would freely allow a father to spoil his children's birthright by uprooting their creed at his pleasure in plain defiance of his gravest express obligations undertaken as husband and father, can find no place in a jurisprudence moulded to fit the Constitution of Ireland, whether the agreement be held to give them a moral claim before the Court or a legal right.[84]

As with *Ryan*, the movement in *Tilson* away from the invisibility of children's rights is obvious. This trend continued in *Re Article 26 and the Adoption (No 2) Bill, 1987*.[85] In assessing the constitutionality of legislation which sought to permit the involuntary adoption of children born to married parents, the Court had to consider Article 42.5 in detail. First, children were recognised as possessing all of the personal rights of citizens which were found in Articles 40–44. Secondly, legislation which permitted the permanent transfer of parental rights was regarded as not necessarily unconstitutional. Third, state intervention in family life can be seen as legitimate for compelling reasons, rather than for reasons of culpability.

Children's cases in the era of unenumerated rights

At this juncture, it can be argued that there was a trend toward greater recognition of children as having rights, but the case law would appear to fall short of the full substantive approach. The possibility of such an approach being adopted was opened up by one of the most important developments in Irish constitutional history in the *Ryan* case, where the High Court held that Article 40.3.1° of the Constitution, in which the State guarantees to respect, defend and vindicate the "personal rights" of the citizen, contained a previously unidentified corpus of unenumerated rights, rights which flow from the "Christian and democratic

82 *Re Frost, Infants* [1947] IR 3 (HC, SC); *Re Keenan, Infants* (1950) 84 ILTR 169 (HC).
83 [1951] IR 1 (HC, SC).
84 Ibid 18.
85 [1989] IR 656 (SC).

nature of the State".[86] This provision has permitted the extension of constitutional rights far beyond those listed in the text itself.[87]

The importance of this was seen in *G v An Bord Uchtála*,[88] where Finlay P, O'Higgins CJ and Walsh J recognised that children can be regarded as independent rights-bearers, that the rights concerned derive from Article 40.3 and that they do not need to rely on their membership of a constitutionally recognised family for these rights to be fulfilled.[89] The rights set out by the court were phrased in very broad language. In the High Court, Finlay P spoke about the child's right to bodily integrity, and the right to "an opportunity to be reared with due regard to her religious, moral, intellectual, physical and social welfare".[90] In the Supreme Court, O'Higgins CJ spoke in somewhat broader terms by outlining rights such as "the right to be fed and to live to be reared and educated, to have the opportunity of working and of realising his or her full personality and dignity as a human being."[91] Walsh J listed an even larger number of rights,[92] especially rights linked to life and welfare. With respect to parental power, he noted that parents did not have the power to exercise their duties to their children in such a way as to "intentionally or by neglect to endanger the health or life of the child."[93] He also indicated, in a statement that echoes the earlier statement in *Ryan*, that "[t]here is nothing in the Constitution to indicate that in cases of conflict the rights of the parent are always to be given primacy".[94]

This judgment could have indicated the beginning of a strong children's rights movement in Irish constitutional law and could have been the start of a more sustained movement towards the adoption of a substantive approach to children's rights. Yet the decision had a number of limitations. First, Finlay P's judgment spoke of a child having the "right to an opportunity to be reared with due regard to her religious, moral, intellectual, physical and social welfare".[95] It is implicit within this statement that the rights of children, limited as they are to opportunities to develop or achieve some other aim, require that parents play the lead role

86 *Ryan* (n 77) 314.

87 For a thorough analysis of the provision, see Gerard Hogan, 'Unenumerated Personal Rights: *Ryan's* Case Re-evaluated' (1990–1992) 25–27 *Irish Jurist* 95. See further, Oran Doyle, "Legal Validity: Reflections on the Irish Constitution" (2003) 25 *Dublin University Law Journal* 56, Desmond M Clarke, 'The Constitution and Natural Law: A Reply to Mr. Justice O'Hanlon' (1993) 11 *Irish Law Times* 177, Desmond M Clarke, 'Unenumerated Rights in Constitutional Law' (2011) 34 *Dublin University Law Journal* 101, Gerard Casey, 'Are There Unenumerated Rights In The Irish Constitution?' (2005) 23 *Irish Law Times* 123, Richard Humphreys, 'Interpreting Natural Rights' (1993–1995) 28–30 *Irish Jurist* 221.

88 [1980] IR 32 (SC).

89 Ibid 44 (Finlay P), 56 (O'Higgins CJ), and 73, 75 (Walsh J).

90 Ibid 44.

91 Ibid 56.

92 Ibid 69.

93 Ibid.

94 Ibid 78.

95 Ibid 44.

in realising that opportunity. The judgment of O'Higgins CJ also addressed the issue of opportunity,[96] but this was the more sophisticated concept of the opportunity to develop and achieve self-fulfilment. This obviously also relies on parents but O'Higgins CJ's comments were phrased in a way which reflected a greater awareness of the realities of children's evolving capacities for fulfilling rights by themselves. It is a more satisfactory judgment from a children's rights perspective because it realises that this "right to opportunity" must be vindicated alongside other, more substantive rights such as rights to life, education and protection. The role of the state is explicitly recognised as being instrumental for some children in terms of their attaining self-fulfilment. Fulfilment and development are also key themes in the judgment of Walsh J – he explicitly recognises issues such as recreation as being essential for children – as is the way in which parents discharge their duties.[97]

The concept of parental duty is perhaps one of the enduring legacies of the *G* decision. Each of the three judgments discussed relies heavily on the idea that parents have duties towards their children which must be properly discharged. If parents fail in these duties, then Article 42.5 allows the state to intervene. The case gives no guidance on how this is to be achieved. The judgment of Henchy J contains perhaps the clearest statement on this point. While speaking in the context of the difference between children of married and unmarried parents, he noted that although the children of married parents have rights with correlative duties placed on parents, parents who are not married have no such correlative duties.[98] This is because their children's rights derive from Article 40.3 which makes no reference to, and according to Henchy J allows no interpretation imposing, duties to respect or vindicate rights. While it would appear difficult for Henchy J to maintain a position that rights can exist without duties, it nevertheless remains important to realise that the courts are slow to recognise unenumerated duties alongside unenumerated rights.[99] By emphasising the role of parental duties as opposed to children's rights, the Supreme Court indicated that its gaze would in future be fixed on whether the family has discharged its duties to the child and not on whether the rights of the child have been vindicated.

On this more pessimistic view, the *G v An Bord Uchtála* decision does nothing more than merely allow for the possibility that children's rights may trump

96 Ibid 56.

97 Following this theme, Denham J in *DG v Eastern Health Board* [1998] 1 ILRM 622, 722 (SC) highlighted that children have the right to be reared with due regard to their welfare and to be fed, accommodated and educated. She also argued that children had certain developmental rights including the opportunity to work and realise their personality and dignity as a human being. The final aspect of children's rights included in this judgment was protective rights – the right to suitable care and treatment.

98 *G* (n 88) 85–88.

99 See *Crowley v Ireland* [1980] IR 102 (SC) which seems to indicate that the provisions of Article 40.3 cannot be invoked by one person against another in a private legal dispute.

those of parents, should parental behaviour be extreme enough to warrant such an outcome and be seen as a failure of duty, a possibility which goes no further than that contemplated by a minimalist reading of Article 42.5. Although the case implicitly recognises the existence of a separate body of rights for children within Article 40.3, it does not demarcate their extent nor indicate their level of importance vis-à-vis the explicitly established rights of the parents. This may be unduly pessimistic. While there are certain limitations built into the decision, it includes the first clear recognition that children had unenumerated constitutional rights, and allows for the possibility, also unheard of at the time, that the rights of children could take priority over those of parents. In this way it presaged the decision in *PW v AW*.

In *PW v AW*,[100] Ellis J highlighted that the concept of parental duty, and its observance or breach, was helpful in deciding whether the child's rights had been breached. In particular, it was recognised that in the event of a conflict between the constitutional rights of a legitimate child and its mother's right to custody, the rights of the child should prevail; there was no need to demonstrate a failure of parental duty. Thus, the rights accorded to the family under Article 41 attach not only to the familial unit but also to each member of the family, including children. Additionally, the child has an unenumerated right under Article 40.3 to have its welfare regarded as the first and paramount consideration in any dispute relating to its custody.[101] This is an extremely strong statement in favour of children's rights, at least in the context of clashes with parental rights, especially when compared with earlier decisions. The *PW* case, however, has had its value as a precedent undermined by later decisions on family autonomy and the presumption that child welfare is best secured by deferring to parents.[102]

This first major case which undermined *PW* was the Supreme Court decision of *Re JH, an infant*.[103] In this case, the importance of family autonomy was heavily emphasised, and it was to shape children's rights case law for decades to come, especially as it related to the relationship between parents and children. The Supreme Court regarded children's rights as being dependent upon the existence of a family whose rights could not be reduced or interfered with by law – the child was described as having the right

> to belong to a unit group possessing inalienable and imprescriptible rights antecedent and superior to all positive law … to protection by the State of the family to which it belongs … to be educated by the family and to be provided by its parents with religious, moral, intellectual, physical and social education.[104]

100 High Court, 21 April 1980.
101 Ibid 73–74.
102 Geoffrey Shannon, *Child Law* (2nd edn, Round Hall 2011) 20.
103 [1985] IR 375 (SC).
104 Ibid 394.

As can be seen, none of these rights exists independently of the family; children's rights, indeed appear to be merely incidental to family rights. In effect, the Supreme Court ruled that where a dispute existed between the parents of a legitimate child and third parties, it was presumed that the welfare of the child would be best protected by the parents. This radically reinforced the concept of parental authority and undermined the position of children as rights-bearing subjects, highlighting that Irish constitutional law at this point in time was deeply rooted in simple modernity.

Adoption as a potential gateway to children's rights

Many of the cases just outlined dealt with adoption. Although a comprehensive review of adoption law is beyond the scope of this work, there are some interesting insights to be gleaned from the case law and political commentary on this issue. First, the decision which led to the most expansive reading of Art 40.3 for children – *G v An Bord Uchtála* – was an adoption case. This alone would be noteworthy as it represents the point at which the child is regarded as having rights of its own, separate from those of family members. Secondly, the adoption case of *Re JH* saw the restriction of children's independent rights, and the recognition of the inability of children's rights to break free completely from the rights of the family outlined in Article 41, because it emphasised that questions relating to children were to be viewed primarily through the prism of their parent's marital status.

Adoption in this period of Irish history most commonly occurred when a child was born to a single woman outside of marriage, with children frequently being placed for adoption in the first few months of life.[105] In order for a valid adoption order to be made, the mother had to give consent twice during the process – once when placing the child for adoption, and once at the making of the final adoption order. Significant controversy was generated over several cases concerning the validity of the consent obtained and over the ability of the courts to dispense with the mother's consent in certain circumstances.[106] Adoption was, generally, an adult-centred process with little emphasis on the child's individual needs and rights.

However, following controversy caused by the decision in *M v An Bord Uchtála*, which saw a six-year-old boy returned to his biological parents having been placed for adoption shortly after his birth,[107] calls were first made for the

105 See generally, Kerry O'Halloran, *Adoption Law and Practice* (2nd edn, Round Hall 2010), Geoffrey Shannon, *Children and Family Relationships Law in Ireland: Practice and Procedure* (Clarus Press 2016) chapter 7 and Diarmaid Ferriter, *Occasions of Sin: Sex and Sexuality in Modern Ireland* (Profile Books 2009).

106 For an extensive treatment of these, see O'Halloran ibid.

107 [1977] IR 287 (SC). On the aftermath to this decision see generally, Diarmaid Ferriter, *Ambiguous Republic: Ireland in the 1970s* (Profile Books 2012) 381–383.

amendment of the Constitution to provide for the rights of children.[108] Despite campaign groups having already highlighted problems with adoption legislation, it was noted at the time that

> It's funny but that decision seemed to generate more interest in the problem of children and the law than all the campaigning of groups such as CARE, Children First, the ISPCC and all the others over the last 10 years.[109]

A protest march attracted 2,000 people who heard the reading of a "Proclamation of Children's Rights".[110] Ultimately, a constitutional amendment was mooted which would have provided for the personal rights of children.[111] In particular, this would have provided that, in any adoption situation, the child's interests would prevail, although some initial scepticism was expressed over this proposal.[112] While the question of an amendment was mentioned in the Oireachtas on several occasions,[113] it appeared that the proposed amendment would be limited to adoption and not a more wide-ranging proposal for the inclusion of children's rights more generally.[114] This more general proposal received only limited support in the Oireachtas at the time.[115]

Eventually, constitutional reform did occur in 1979, but of a very limited nature. The Sixth Amendment to the Constitution essentially provided that no adoption order would be declared invalid merely by virtue of the fact that the person who made it was not a judge. There was continued criticism of the narrow scope of constitutional reform,[116] especially as it failed to deal with the fundamental problem of the conflict between parents' and children's rights. To address this, Senator Robinson highlighted a Labour Party proposal to reform Article 42.5 which would have removed the reference to the inalienable and imprescriptible rights of the child, and replaced it with the following provision:

1. That children shall enjoy special protection by law and other means to enable them to develop physically, mentally, morally and spiritually to their fullest potential and in conditions of freedom and dignity and in the enactment of laws relating to children the welfare of the child shall be the first and paramount consideration.

108 Paul Murray, 'Child care groups mount adoption decision attack' *The Irish Times* (Dublin, 5 June 1976). The question of constitutional reform is discussed further in Chapter 6.
109 Anonymous, quoted in Christina Murphy, 'Children have no independent rights under Constitution' *Irish Times* (Dublin, 9 June 1976).
110 '2,000 protest at child-care laws' *The Irish Times* (Dublin 14 June 1976).
111 Dick Walsh, 'Referendum on adoption in autumn' *The Irish Times* (Dublin, 17 June 1976).
112 'Support from all sides for Adoption Bill' *The Irish Times* (Dublin, 18 June 1976).
113 See Dáil Debates 17 June 1976, vol 291, col 1225, Gerard Collins TD.
114 'Concerned on adoption referendum' *The Irish Times* (Dublin, 24 June 1976).
115 Seanad Debates 6 July 1976, vol 84, cols 1073–1075, Senator Mary Robinson.
116 See in particular, Dáil Debates 14 February 1979, vol 311, cols 1092–1105, Jim O'Keeffe TD and Eileen Desmond TD.

2. Equality of rights under the law shall not be denied to any child on the basis of status at birth or parentage.
3. The State acknowledges the family as the social unit best fitted to provide the continuity of care essential to the upbringing of a child. Where, however, the welfare of the child requires it, whether by reason of the death of the parents or by reason of their unwillingness, neglect or inability to discharge their parental duties, the State shall supply the place of the parents by appropriate means which may include the enactment of laws providing for the transfer of parental rights to substitute parents.[117]

This far-reaching, and at the time radical, proposal was never put to a referendum. Significant strides had been made in the advancement of children's rights – not only had decisions such as *G*, *PW* and the *Adoption Bill* reference advanced the cause in the Irish courts, the issue also began to gain traction at a political level. Even if these decisions and political discourse had not yet moved towards a more substantive approach to children's rights, there was a clear sense of travel in that direction, as the transition away from simple modernity at a societal level was beginning.[118] However, the decision in *Re JH* was to prove highly influential in later cases concerning children's welfare. The combination of the compelling reasons test, the emphasis on the right to belong to a family whose autonomy was protected and the presumption that welfare coincided with protecting familial autonomy found in that case served only to halt the developments seen elsewhere. It must be conceded that children were not consistently recognised as agents, but there was a growing recognition of the ability of children to develop agency as well as the realization that children were individuals whose identity and needs were not necessarily coterminous with those of the family. Yet *Re JH* effectively ensured that any attempt to construct children as subjects must usually yield to parental wishes. This ambivalence was shaken by the impact of the Kilkenny Inquiry, and by later high-profile incidents concerning child protection and children's rights.

Conclusion

In the Irish context, it is necessary to understand the constitutional relationship between the family and the state in order to understand how children have been thought about. Historically, in conditions of simple modernity, children were largely subsumed within the wider marital family, and there was little evidence that the thinking behind the early draft constitutional texts which sought to grant rights to children had any impact on later judicial approaches to children's rights. What limited political or civil enthusiasm there was for the separateness of children's interests from those of their parents seemed to disappear with the

117 Seanad Debates 7 March 1979, vol 91, col 428, Senator Mary Robinson TD.
118 For more on this, see Chapter 6.

preference for strict adherence to Catholic social teaching in designing the text of the 1937 Constitution.

This chapter has argued for a version of constitutional history in which children were visible and present, but largely passive. This chimes with the idea that Ireland operated during this period under the conditions of simple, traditional modernity with all of the solidity of social relationships that implies. Children were provided for in terms of education and as part of a family whose autonomy would be protected by the state. That the state could intervene in the family was not disputed, but the threshold for intervention was set at a high level which was difficult to reach. The final text of the Constitution, and much of the case law relating to it, demonstrated the solidity of social relationships and traditional hierarchies of simple modernity. That the preservation of family integrity was an end to which the Constitution aimed is indicative of this. Yet when the legislative and social work history of this period is told in the coming chapters, this vision of the family as a sacred space becomes significantly more complicated. Children were recognised as having interests, but they were also taken from their families for problematic reasons. Their treatment once removed and placed in the care of the state also undermined the idea that children were recognised in their own right. While the courts, in constitutional litigation, were beginning to recognise children as being capable of being rights-bearers, legislative policy seemed to cleave even more stubbornly to the model of traditional modernity. It is to this aspect of the law affecting children that we must now turn.

References

Anonymous, '2,000 Protest at child-care laws' *Irish Times* (Dublin, 14 June 1976).

Anonymous, 'Concerned on adoption referendum' *Irish Times* (Dublin, 24 June 1976).

Anonymous, 'Support from all sides for Adoption Bill' *Irish Times* (Dublin, 18 June 1976).

Beytagh FX, *Constitutionalism in Contemporary Ireland: An American Perspective* (Round Hall 1997).

Brady P, 'Social, Political, and Philosophical Foundations of the Irish Constitutional Order' in Denis J Galligan and Mila Versteeg (eds), *Social and Political Foundations of Constitutions* (Cambridge University Press 2013).

Buck J, 'The Role of *ne temere* in the Decline of an Irish Custom Regarding the Religious Affiliation of the Children of Mixed Marriages' (2011) 11 *The Australian Journal of Irish Studies* 28.

Cahillane L, 'Ireland's Forgotten Constitutions' (2009) 27 *Irish Law Times* 243.

Casey G, 'Are There Unenumerated Rights In The Irish Constitution?' (2005) 23 *Irish Law Times* 123.

Casey J, *Constitutional Law in Ireland* (3rd edn, Round Hall 2000).

Clarke DM, 'The Constitution and Natural Law: A Reply to Mr. Justice O'Hanlon' (1993) 11 *Irish Law Times* 177.

Clarke DM, 'Unenumerated Rights in Constitutional Law' (2011) 34 *Dublin University Law Journal* 101.

Coffey DK, 'The Need for a New Constitution: Irish Constitutional Change 1932–1935' (2012) 47 *Irish Jurist* 275.
Daly E, *Religion, Law and the Irish State* (Clarus Press 2012).
Doyle O, 'Legal Validity: Reflections on the Irish Constitution' (2003) 25 *Dublin University Law Journal* 56.
Doyle O, 'Family Autonomy and Children's Best Interests: Ireland, Bentham and the Natural Law' (2010) 1 *International Journal of the Jurisprudence of the Family* 55.
Farrell B, *The Founding of Dáil Éireann: Parliament and Nation-Building* (Gill and Macmillan 1971).
Ferriter D, *Occasions of Sin: Sex and Sexuality in Modern Ireland* (Profile Books 2009).
Ferriter D, *Ambiguous Republic: Ireland in the 1970s* (Profile Books 2012).
Hannon P, 'In God's Name, What Next? Religion, The Constitution and the New Ireland' in Oran Doyle and Eoin Carolan (eds), *The Irish Constitution: Governance and Values* (Thomson Round Hall 2008)
Hogan G, 'Unenumerated Personal Rights: *Ryan's* Case Re-evaluated' (1990–1992) 25–27 *Irish Jurist* 95.
Hogan G, 'The Constitution, Property Rights and Proportionality' (1997) 32 *Irish Jurist* 373.
Hogan G, 'Directive Principles, Socio-Economic Rights and the Constitution' (2001) 36 *Irish Jurist* 175.
Hogan G, 'Foreword' in Dermot Keogh and Andrew McCarthy (eds), *The Making of the Irish Constitution 1937* (Cork University Press 2007)
Hogan G, *The Origins of the Irish Constitution: 1928–1941* (Royal Irish Academy 2012).
Hogan G and Whyte G, *JM Kelly: The Irish Constitution* (3rd edn, Butterworths 1994).
Hogan G and Whyte G, *JM Kelly: The Irish Constitution* (4th edn, Tottel Publishing 2003).
Humphreys R, 'Interpreting Natural Rights' (1993–1995) 28–30 *Irish Jurist* 221.
Kelly JM, *Fundamental Rights in the Irish Constitution* (2nd edn, Allen Figgis & Co 1967).
Kelly JM, *The Irish Constitution* (Jurist Publishing 1980).
Kelly JM, 'Law and Manifesto' in Frank Litton (ed), *The Constitution of Ireland: 1937–1987* (Institute of Public Administration 1988).
Keogh D, 'The Constitutional Revolution: An Analysis of the Making of the Constitution' in Frank Litton (ed), *The Constitution of Ireland 1937-1987* (Institute of Public Administration 1988).
Keogh D and McCarthy A, *The Making of the Irish Constitution 1937* (Cork University Press 2007).
Kilkelly U, *Children's Rights in Ireland: Law Policy and Practice* (Tottel Publishing 2008).
Kissane B, *New Beginnings: Constitutionalism and Democracy in Modern Ireland* (University College Dublin Press 2011).
Maguire M, *Precarious Childhood in Post-Independence Ireland* (Manchester University Press 2012).
McDonagh E, 'Church and State in the Constitution of Ireland' (1961) 28(2) *Irish Theological Quarterly* 131.

Murphy C, 'Children have no independent rights under Constitution' *Irish Times* (Dublin, 9 June 1976).
Murray P, 'Child care groups mount adoption decision attack' *Irish Times* (Dublin, 5 June 1976).
Nolan A, 'A Role for the Courts in Ensuring the Enforcement of the Socio-Economic Rights of the Child: Overcoming the 'Counter-majoritarian Objection' in Andre Alen et al (eds), *The UN Children's Rights Convention: Theory Meets Practice* (2nd edn, Intersentia 2007).
Nolan A, 'The Battle(s) over Children's Rights in the Irish Constitution' (2007) 22(4) *Irish Political Studies* 495.
O'Connor E, 'Neither Democratic nor a Programme: The Democratic Programme of 1919' (2016) 40(157) *Irish Historical Studies* 92.
O'Halloran K, *Adoption Law and Practice* (2nd edn, Round Hall 2010).
O'Mahony C, 'Education, Remedies and the Separation of Powers' (2002) 24 *Dublin University Law Journal* 57.
O'Mahony C, 'A New Slant on Educational Rights and Mandatory Injunctions?' (2005) 27 *Dublin University Law Journal* 363.
Perry MJ, 'The Authority of Text, Tradition, and Reason: A Theory of Constitutional Interpretation' (1985) 58 *Southern California Law Review* 551.
Pope Leo XIII, 'Encyclical Letter, *Rerum Novarum*: On Capital and Labour' (Papal Encyclical 1891).
Pope Pius XI, 'Encyclical Letter, *Divini Illius Magistri*: On Christian Education' (Papal Encyclical 1929).
Pope Pius XI, 'Encyclical Letter, *Quadrigesimo Anno*: On Reconstruction of the Social Order' (Papal Encyclical 1931).
Prager J, *Building Democracy in Ireland – Political Order and Cultural Integration in A Newly Independent Nation* (Cambridge University Press 1986).
Scalia A, 'Originalism: The Lesser Evil' (1988–89) 57 *University of Cincinnati Law Review* 849.
Shannon G, *Child Law* (2nd edn, Round Hall 2011).
Shannon G, *Children and Family Relationships Law in Ireland: Practice and Procedure* (Clarus Press 2016).
Tobin J, 'Judging the Judges: Are They Adopting the Rights Approach in Matters Involving Children? (2009) 33(2) *University of Melbourne Law Review* 579.
Tobin J, 'Courts and the Construction of Childhood: A New Way of Thinking' in Michael Freeman (ed), *Law and Childhood Studies* (Oxford University Press 2012).
Van Bueren G, *International Law on the Rights of the Child* (Martinus Nijhoff 1994).
Walsh D, 'Referendum on adoption in autumn' *Irish Times* (Dublin, 17 June 1976).
Whittington K, *Constitutional Interpretation: Textual Meaning, Original Intent, and Judicial Review* (University Press of Kansas 1999).
Whyte G, *Social Inclusion and the Legal System: Public Interest Law in Ireland* (Institute of Public Administration 2002).
Whyte JH, *Church and State in Modern Ireland 1923–1979* (2nd edn, Gill & McMillan 1980).

4 Children and risk in independent Ireland, 1921–1970

Introduction

Law and social attitudes to children developed radically during Ireland's first seven decades of self-governance in a way that neatly illustrates the transition from traditional modernity to a society on the cusp of reflexive modernity. Within the period between independence and the Kilkenny Incest Report, there are two distinct stages in the evolution of both law and social attitudes that require separate examination. First, the period 1921–1970 was a period where Roman Catholic social teaching dominated public discourse and shaped virtually all aspects of social life. It is this period which will be the focus of the present chapter, with the period between 1970 and 1991 examined in Chapter 5. Each of these chapters deals with the law as it developed in conditions of simple modernity, with an emphasis on traditional social structures, a lack of individualization and an attitude to risk which held that risks could be eliminated, or at least sequestered and hidden from public sight.

The period under examination in the present chapter represents in some ways a continuation of, or even a partial regression from, the processes begun by the Westminster parliament in the 1880s, in that there was a mixed view of children, both as threats and as victims. As Ireland began to design its own regulatory systems governing childhood, especially in the constitutional texts outlined in Chapter 3, the idea of children as agents was seldom seen in these years, reflecting the conditions of simple modernity. The formative years of independent Ireland were "a time when there was overwhelming agreement that traditional Catholic values should be maintained, if necessary by legislation".[1] Maguire highlights how the interests of children were of secondary importance to the pressing political desires of upholding a nationalist identity, pacification of the Catholic hierarchy and the perpetuation of male sexual privilege, suggesting that these policy aims constituted a greater good for which children's interests were sacrificed.[2]

1 JH Whyte, *Church and state in modern Ireland, 1923–1979* (2nd edn, Gill and Macmillan 1980) 60.

2 Moira Maguire, *Precarious Childhood in Post-Independence Ireland* (Manchester University Press 2009) 113–114.

This idea will be tested first through an assessment of the criminal law reforms – primarily around the age of consent – undertaken after independence, and second through the way in which children were "protected" by their confinement on "welfare" grounds in religiously run institutions. As a combination of historical scholarship and official reporting over the last two decades has made clear, there was at least some official knowledge of sexual offending against children. While the work of the Carrigan Committee has been extensively analysed,[3] I will also utilise material drawn from Oireachtas debates on a range of child protection measures to examine how children and risk were thought about within a legal system rooted in traditionalism.

Child protection and criminal law

Early attempts at criminal law reform

Personal, and especially sexual, morality, was a significant concern for legislators in newly independent Ireland. During the first decade of the state's existence, several statutes, including criminal law statutes, were passed in an attempt to restrain perceived sexual immorality through censorship of literature and broadcasting.[4] Official reports also recommended reform of the criminal law related to personal sexuality, so that issues like prostitution, single motherhood and regulation of behaviour in dance halls and motor cars could be addressed from a moral purity perspective.[5] Legislative change relating to child sex offences was sought as early as 1925, with the Minister for Justice indicating that legislation was being prepared to amend the Criminal Law Amendment Act 1885 as well as to deal with other issues relating to illegitimate children.[6] There was an understanding that new technologies and forms of entertainment could both undermine traditional family life and pose new risks to children. A further link between sexual misconduct and public entertainment was made when a Dáil question was asked

3 See in general, Mark Finnane, 'The Carrigan Committee of 1930–31 and the moral condition of the Saorstát' (2001) 32(128) *Irish Historical Studies* 519, James Smith 'The Politics of Sexual Knowledge: The Origins of Ireland's Containment Culture and the Carrigan Report (1931)' (2004) 13(2) *Journal of the History of Sexuality* 208, Moira Maguire, 'The Carrigan Committee and Child Sexual Abuse in Twentieth-century Ireland' (2007) 11(2) *New Hibernia Review* 79, Finola Kennedy, 'The Suppression of the Carrigan Report: A Historical Perspective on Child Abuse' (2000) 89 *Studies: An Irish Quarterly Review* 354 and Diarmaid Ferriter, *The Transformation of Ireland 1900–2000* (Profile Books 2005).

4 See, for example, Censorship of Films Acts 1923–1930, and the Censorship of Publications Act 1929.

5 See generally, Inter-Departmental Committee of Inquiry Regarding Venereal Disease, *Report of the Inter-Departmental Committee of Inquiry Regarding Venereal Disease* (Stationery Office 1925), the Committee on Evil Literature, *Report of the Committee on Evil Literature* (Stationery Office 1927) and the Commission on Relief of the Sick and Destitute Poor, *Report of the Commission on the Relief of the Sick and Destitute Poor Including the Insane Poor* (Stationery Office 1927).

6 Dáil Debates 28 April 1925, vol 11, col 369, Minister Kevin O'Higgins TD.

about the possibility of children being subjected to sexual assaults in cinemas at night-time.[7]

A more substantive discussion of sexual offences reform took place when a private member's bill was tabled in 1929 to amend the 1885 Act.[8] The Bill was heavily inspired by the UK Criminal Law Amendment Act 1922, which did not apply to Ireland.[9] The Bill would have raised the age of consent to 18, removed the possibility of consent being raised as a defence where a victim was under 18 and provided for a defence of reasonable mistake for men under the age of 23. However, the Bill was withdrawn so that a committee could be established to investigate these matters further.[10] Nonetheless, an examination of the records of this brief debate on the legislation provides some insight into how young people and sexual offending were thought about. First, there was a general consensus among the participants that the age of consent should be raised. While the Bill aimed to make 18 the new age of consent, some TDs proposed the age of 17,[11] while others again felt that public opinion may favour an even higher age.[12] It was also recognised that the level of sexual offending against young people was increasing, although no data was provided to support this statement.[13]

These views could be taken as indicating growing recognition of the need to continually strengthen the protection afforded to children's interests, but there are some other statements which undermine that view and which were to re-emerge in later discussions on the matter. First, there was a reversion to the language of blackmail which characterised the debates leading to the 1885 Act. In supporting a revised age of consent of 17 rather than 18, the Minister for Justice stated that "if a girl of eighteen is a loose woman she may become a most terrible blackmailer. She may look to be very much older, and she may become a most desperate blackmailer."[14] Questions were raised as to why a girl who had sex under the age consent should not also be criminalised along with the man, regardless of the circumstances,[15] as "[e]verybody in this House knows, that girls of 16, 17 and 18 years of age are really more responsible for this offence which it is desired to punish under this Bill, than are the persons whom this Bill would punish."[16] Finally, a link was made between the age of consent and juvenile prostitution, although the exact nature and extent of that link was not

7 Dáil Debates 27 November 1929, cols 1439–1440, Eamonn Cooney TD and Minister James FitzGerald-Kenney TD.
8 Criminal Law Amendment Bill 1929.
9 The Act applied to the UK as a whole; however, section 4 makes certain allowances for Scots law.
10 Dáil Debates 27 March 1930, vol 34, col 270.
11 Dáil Debates 27 March 1930, vol 34, col 260, Minister James FitzGerald-Kenney TD.
12 Ibid, col 270, Dr Myles Keogh TD.
13 Ibid, col 266, Thomas J O'Connell TD.
14 Ibid, col 260, Minister James FitzGerald-Kenney TD. See also the statement of by Deputy O'Connell, ibid, col 264, that men were also in need of protection.
15 Ibid, col 263, Gearóid O'Sullivan TD.
16 Ibid, col 264, Gearóid O'Sullivan TD.

made explicit, save to say that dealing with one without the other would not adequately address either issue.[17] The Minister's comments show that age of consent reform and elimination of juvenile prostitution were part of the same overarching morality-based policy agenda. This is made explicit when the blaming of young victims, and female victims especially, would impact on the future development of criminal law reform, beginning with the conduct of the Carrigan Committee and the subsequent passage of the Criminal Law (Amendment) Act 1935 (the 1935 Act).

The work of the Carrigan Committee

Following the withdrawal of the 1929 Bill, the *Committee on the Criminal Law Amendment Acts (1880–85) and Juvenile Prostitution* was established to review the legislative position.[18] The committee was designed to be non-political, staffed by a leading criminal law barrister, William Carrigan, after whom the Committee came to be named, one clergyman of each of the main Christian denominations present in Ireland, two doctors and a social welfare official. The Committee and its influence on later legislation have been subjected to sustained analysis by Irish historians.[19] This literature requires some prior attention before the workings of the Committee are examined. Several common themes emerge from it: the Committee's emphasis on a specifically Catholic view on morality, the emphasis on institutionalization as a means of dealing with those tainted by sexual immorality, the lack of emphasis on social conditions contributing to sexual immorality, and the side-lining of the interests of victims, but perhaps most crucially, the importance of the disputes that emerged in political circles following the completion of the Report. Finnane and Smith, in particular, have claimed that the Committee sought to impose a hegemonic morality on child victims. The evidence contained in the Committee's Report, but especially its Minute Book, does not necessarily bear these themes out. There is an undeniable overlap between many of the Committee's views and Christian, if not specifically Catholic, moral teaching on sexuality and femininity. Witnesses often spoke the language of moral decline or of unmarried mothers being "first time offenders".[20] Despite this language, the underlying approach to children, and child sexual offences victims, can be characterised as more protective in nature.

With respect to the concern that the Committee did not seem to recognise any significant connection between social conditions and social problems,[21] the

17 Ibid, col 260, Minister James FitzGerald-Kenney TD.
18 See Committee on the Criminal Law Amendment Acts, *Report of the Committee on the Criminal Law Amendment Acts (1880–1885) and Juvenile Prostitution (1931)*, National Archives of Ireland (NAI), Department of Justice (D/Jus) file S5998 (Carrigan Report).
19 See the works cited at n 3 above.
20 See, for example, the testimony of District Judge Gleeson, Committee on the Criminal Law Amendment Acts, *Minute Book*, (NAI, D/Jus S5998) 70.
21 Smith (n 3).

evidence adduced to the Committee demonstrated that housing conditions were a significant factor influencing the level of sexual offending in urban areas.[22] Only one witness could be regarded as taking a very extreme view on sexual morality even by the standards of the time by positing that all extra-marital sexual activity should be treated as a crime.[23] This view was neither taken up by the Committee nor referred to in its Report. Signs of technological and social change were a major concern for witnesses; in particular, the rise of popular new modes of entertainment like the dance hall and motor car, and the loosening of parental authority were seen as significant causes of a generally lowered moral tone.[24] Such markers of modernity were seen as risks to the existing social fabric, risks that could be controlled.[25] It has been argued that more attention was paid to the visible aspects of sex and sexuality, such as illegitimate children, than to the harm of serious sexual offending.[26] In reality, both were addressed, although not equally, with the more visible aspects of sexuality certainly receiving greater attention. When focus is drawn away from the overarching morality discourse and towards the specific recommendations of the Committee and its witnesses, and the ways in which they viewed sexual offences against children and young people, a quite different picture emerges. Its work demonstrates an uneasy mixture of desire to control risks by controlling potential victims' behaviour through curbing their access to supposed sources of moral danger, and the recognition that those who transgressed against young people had offended against their victims' legitimate interests in being protected.

This more complex picture of the Committee's work is illustrated clearly when the age of consent issue is considered. The vast majority of witnesses suggested raising the age of consent from 16 to 18 so as to afford greater protection to young girls, a view which became one of the Committee's recommendations.[27] It did so "for the better protection of young girls against sexual offences."[28] Some witnesses indicated that many members of their organizations would prefer to see an age of consent of 19 or 21.[29] A significant number of witnesses also called for a higher age of consent to be imposed in situations when sexual activity occurred between a woman and her employer or another person in a position of authority,[30] although this proposal was not recommended by the Committee. Virtually all witnesses stated their opposition to the reasonable belief defence, even in circumstances where the offender was a young man.[31] The potential for

22 Committee on the Criminal Law Amendment Acts (n 20), testimony of Eoin O'Duffy, 25.
23 Ibid, testimony of Kathleen Kirwan, 62.
24 Ibid, testimony of Very Rev John Canon Lee, 41.
25 Ibid, testimony of Reverend RJ Devane SJ, 10.
26 See generally, Finnane (n 3).
27 Committee on the Criminal Law Amendment Acts (n 18) 16–18.
28 Ibid 40.
29 For example, Committee on the Criminal Law Amendment Acts (n 20), testimony of Miss Ita Dodd representing the Irish Women Citizen's and Local Government Association, 13.
30 See, for example, ibid, testimony of Mrs Margaret Gavan Duffy and Mrs Ita Brady, 59.
31 Ibid.

by young men.[49] Another witness proposed the best remedies for this ignorance would not only be to raise the age of consent but for sex education to be provided by doctors attending girls' schools.[50]

The Committee also recommended certain reforms in criminal procedure. Evidence from a District Court judge to the Committee suggested that the rules of evidence governing sexual offence trials were in need of revision. He suggested in that cases where the child was deemed not fit to give sworn testimony, the rules governing the admission of "extraneous evidence" should be relaxed.[51] The warning which had to be given by a judge to a jury about the dangers of convicting on the basis of the uncorroborated evidence of a young person was seen to have a negative effect on conviction rates – "in many cases of this kind, the jury acquitted the prisoner even though his guilt was apparent."[52] A witness from the NSPCC supported this view, as in her experience prosecutions of offences against girls under ten often failed due to lack of evidence. In her view, if a child made an immediate complaint, the statement of the person to whom it was made should be treated as corroboration.[53] The Committee was clearly swayed by this evidence, recommending that the rules of practice which had grown up among judges of giving a warning of convicting a person based on the uncorroborated evidence of a single witness in sexual offence cases should be abrogated.[54] They made a similar recommendation in respect of the rules of evidence regarding accomplices.[55] There was a feeling among the Committee that in cases where the accused raised the consent of the victim as a defence, she might be treated as an accomplice, and so a warning about dangers of uncorroborated evidence of accomplices would have to be given. The Committee, therefore, recommended doing away with such a warning in cases where the victim was under the age of consent.[56] They also recommended the use of joint trials where one person was accused of multiple assaults within a 12 month period, so as to increase the likelihood of obtaining a conviction.[57]

The proposed reforms of the evidentiary and other rules demonstrate clearly that a sense of concern over sexual offending was held by the Committee and its witnesses. There was not an attempt to suppress knowledge about or prosecutions of sexual offences, but an attempt to make convictions easier. This was underpinned by a belief that the men committing such acts were in need of punishment, that other men needed to be warned of the consequences and so deterred, while the interests of children in being protected from such dangers

49 Committee on the Criminal Law Amendment Acts (n 20), testimony of Miss Edith Tancred, 49.
50 Ibid, testimony of Mrs Gavan Duffy, 59.
51 Ibid, testimony of District Judge Dermot Gleeson, 55.
52 Ibid, 55.
53 Ibid, testimony of Mrs Hannah Clarke, 71.
54 Report of the Committee on the Criminal Law Amendment Acts (n 18) 26–27.
55 Ibid.
56 Ibid 27–28.
57 Ibid 28–29.

justified these significant legal changes. There are some problems with the approach of the Committee, however; there was relatively little express attempt to disentangle the experiences of boys and girls who had been victimised, and what this meant for the various sources of risk that they faced. There was also no meaningful attempt to think about the family itself as a site of abuse, which is particularly important in light of the near-contemporary drafting of a series of constitutional provisions which would make intervention in family life difficult.[58] Nonetheless, the examination of the minutes of the Committee does reveal some new insights into the construction of children within child protection discourse.

Political and legal responses to the Carrigan Report

It is the responses to the Committee's findings that demonstrate a definite lack of concern about children's interests. Having been delivered to the Government, the Report was not published, and its contents were the subject of several years of private correspondence among politicians, senior civil servants and a handful of outside parties.[59] The Department of Justice prepared a memorandum for Government which was critical of the Report, calling into question its impartiality, suggesting that it was driven by a desire to increase prosecutions for sexual immorality and that its witnesses presented a very narrowly defined version of the facts they presented. It labelled the desire to raise the age of consent to 18 as punitive and vindictive.[60] Following a general election and the election of a new government in 1932, a further committee of Dáil deputies was established to consider the Report,[61] and two senior clerics were invited by the new Minister for Justice to make submissions. They deemed it to be too "drastic, lacking in judgment, and unworkable".[62] That further comment was sought from clerics is not entirely surprising; however, the decision to bypass normal parliamentary procedures is striking.

The Dáil Committee produced heads of a Bill that would form the basis of the Criminal Law (Amendment) Act 1935. The unpublished deliberations of that informal Committee effectively replaced the usual parliamentary procedure of what are known as "second stage debates", where the principles of the legislation would be debated, effectively shutting down the possibility of significant parliamentary dissent, which in turn hampers our ability to assess how children

58 See above the discussion of the drafting of Articles 41 and 42 in Chapter 3.

59 Kennedy (n 3).

60 A copy entitled "Department of Justice Memorandum" is attached to "For Agenda of Meeting of Executive Council" dated 27 October 1932, NAI D/Jus 90/3, cited in Maguire (n 3).

61 "Department of the President Memorandum, to Each Member of the Executive Council" dated 10 November 1933, attached to the "For Agenda of Meeting of Executive Council" dated 15 November 1933, NAI D/Jus 90/4, cited in Kennedy (n 3).

62 NAI D/Jus H247/41 B, cited in Kennedy (n 3).

and the risks they faced were understood by lawmakers.[63] The Dáil committee recommended several significant changes from the Carrigan Report. Primarily, it suggested that the age of consent should be set at 17 rather than 18, that there be no extension of the use of whipping and that there be no publication or blacklisting of convicted offenders.[64] Furthermore, the proposed changes to corroboration rules and judicial practice were criticised by the Department of Justice on the basis that children's evidence should not be readily believed:

> It is understood that many competent authorities have grave doubts as to the value of children's evidence. A child with a vivid imagination may actually live in his mind the situation as he invented it and will be quite unshaken by severe cross-examination.[65]

The Minister responsible for piloting the Bill through the Oireachtas commented that in the context of sexual offence trials, "the sympathies of the court may be more in favour of the accused than the accuser".[66]

The Act which resulted from this torturous process largely remained in place until the late modern child protection era. Indeed, its core provisions were to stand until constitutional problems surfaced in 2006 – for non-familial sexual offending, or sexual offending falling short of incest, the 1935 Act was to remain the main statute governing sexual offending into the twenty-first century.[67] The main effects of the 1935 Act were to raise the age of consent to 17,[68] the defilement of a girl under 15 now being treated as a felony,[69] and the penalties for various offences against young people being increased. A maximum life sentence could now be imposed.[70] Further, section 14 stated that if a person was charged with indecent assault against a person under 15, it would be no defence to prove that the victim consented to the acts alleged. This clearly sought to impose a more disciplinary approach not on children themselves, but on those who posed risks to children. The increase in penalties was designed to be of deterrent effect, while the increase in age of consent was designed to afford greater protection to young people. Other aspects of the legislation were clearly designed to further a

63 There was a second stage debate – Dáil Debates 28 June 1934, vol 53, col 1246, but the proceedings of that debate were not of the normal variety. No substantive discussion was entered into and the Bill was referred to a further committee. At the second stage in the Seanad debates, another Committee was formed – see *Report of the Special Committee on the Criminal Law Amendment Bill, 1934* (Stationery Office 1935).

64 See Department of Justice Memorandum entitled "To each Member of the Executive Council" dated 10 November 1933, and "Heads for a Bill to amend the Criminal Law (Amendment) Acts" NAI D/Jus H247/41 E, cited in Smith (n 3) 218.

65 NAI D/Jus 90/4, Department of Justice memorandum, 10, cited in Smith (n 3).

66 NAI, Department of Justice memo, D/J/ 90/4/3, cited in Maguire (n 3).

67 See the discussion of the constitutional controversy it generated in Chapter 6.

68 Section 2. See also *CC v Ireland* [2006] 4 IR 1 (SC), discussed in Chapter 6.

69 Section 1.

70 On penalties generally see sections 1, 2 and 6.

highly moralistic agenda,[71] but as regards sexual offending against children, the 1935 Act went some way to addressing the concerns outlined in the Carrigan Report. There was no attempt, however, to reform the law of evidence, which is unsurprising in light of the political and civil service attitudes mentioned in the previous paragraph.

Clearly, a variety of motivations helped to determine the final shape of the legislation – on the one hand, control of sexuality and a moralising agenda were prominent features within the legislation, yet on the other, there was a limited recognition of children's interests in being protected. Care must be taken not to push this latter point too far; the recognition and acceptance of the importance of children's interests were limited to the provision of a regime of criminal liability designed to deter and punish a wider range of behaviour. It did not extend to the recognition of the interests of child victims who sought to bring such behaviour to police attention. Children were, therefore, not really regarded as agents in any meaningful way, with evidential reform permitting greater participation in the trial process ignored. The approach of criminal law in the early decades of independence maps very closely onto the social landscape of simple modernity. Traditional social structures, reliance on certainty and trust in authority, and an approach to risk underpinned by the belief that risks could be eliminated are all present in and informed the legal processes relating to children.

Children, families and institutionalization

The legal framework of child protection and institutionalization

The early decades of post-independence Irish history are not synonymous with child protection. Revelations about the operation of childcare institutions and the ways in which members of religious orders were able to engage in systematic child abuse without fear of consequences have demonstrated that little regard was had for children, and vulnerable children in particular.[72] However, what emerges from the legal history of this period is, in fact, the presence of two quite distinct attitudes towards children – official attitudes which perpetuated the concern for children's interests, and the attitudes of those tasked with the care that children actually experienced, an attitude which saw children as "moral dirt"[73] and social dangers. When discussing criminal law in the previous section of this chapter, I drew the conclusion that the 1935 Act did not really take children's interests seriously, given its emphasis on sexual morality more generally. However,

71 In particular, section 17 which criminalised the sale and importation of contraception.

72 See generally, Commission to Inquire into Child Abuse (CICA), *Report of the Commission to Inquire into Child Abuse* (Stationery Office 2009), Mary Rafferty and Eoin O'Sullivan, *Suffer the Little Children: The Inside Story of Ireland's Industrial Schools* (New Island Books 2000), Bruce Arnold, *The Irish Gulag: How the Irish State Betrayed its Innocent Children* (Gill and Macmillan 2009).

73 Harry Ferguson, 'Abused and looked after children as moral dirt: Child abuse and institutional care in historical perspective' (2007) 36(1) *Journal of Social Policy* 123.

there was much more official concern with those interests when engaging with the reform of the civil law as it applied to children. The need to have stronger child protection mechanisms because protecting children was seen as something valuable was a greater influence on this aspect of law reform than it was in the criminal sphere. Child victims of abuse were therefore accorded differing levels of priority, and constructed in different ways, depending on which area of the law they encountered. Subsequent revelations have made clear, however, that this was not reflected in practice.

In order to describe the development of these two distinct attitudes, it is important to highlight that the main means by which children were "protected" outside of the criminal law relating to sexual offences was through institutionalization. Legislation permitted children who themselves were guilty of criminal offences, or who were seen as being at risk of committing such offences in the future due to a problematic family environment, to be removed from their homes and placed in institutions designed to provide training for young people to enter employment and to ensure moral reform of their characters.[74] This institutional accommodation and training was provided in two distinct kinds of institutions – reformatory schools or industrial schools.[75] The former was designed to deal with children convicted of criminal offences, while the latter dealt with non-criminal children deemed to be at risk of engaging in crime. These were originally designed by Quaker groups to train children for future reintegration into society.[76] The schools provided technical and industrial training for boys, while girls were mostly trained to enter domestic service.[77] In time, however, industrial schools came to undertake a greater role in accommodating children who experienced what would now be termed child abuse, including children who experienced neglect, a role that persisted until quite late in the twentieth century.

Reformatory and industrial schools were operated by religious institutions – of the 61 industrial schools in the territory of the Free State, 56 were under the auspices of the Roman Catholic Church, with five under the control of Protestant denominations.[78] The reasons for the high level of church involvement in these schools stems in part from the desire to instil a socially ordained moral rectitude in the children resident there. In addition, political, cultural and

74 See generally, Jane Barnes, *Irish Industrial Schools, 1868–1908: Origins and Development* (Irish Academic Press 1989).

75 The passing of the Reformatory Schools (Ireland) Act 1858 and the Industrial Schools (Ireland) Act 1868 gave these institutions a statutory basis.

76 Michael Freeman, *The Rights and Wrongs of Children* (Continuum 1983) 66. See also CICA, *CICA Investigation Committee Report Volume I* (n 72) 35–36, where it is noted that the schools were based on models used in Germany, Switzerland and Scandinavia. See also Linda Mahood and Barbara Littlewood, 'The "vicious girl" and the "street-corner boy": sexuality and the gendered delinquent in the Scottish child-saving movement 1850–1940' (1994) 4(4) *Journal of the History of Sexuality* 549.

77 See Barnes (n 74) 85–86, and CICA (n 72) 40.

78 CICA Volume I (n 72), ibid 36–37.

interdenominational rivalry inhibited the coordination of services at a governmental level,[79] giving greater autonomy to the religious orders involved. Catholic organizations were particularly concerned at the prospect of proselytization by Protestant groups.[80] However, it must be remembered that what would nowadays be regarded as state duties to protect vulnerable individuals were, during the nineteenth and early twentieth centuries, regarded as aspects of a largely philanthropic enterprise. The development of these schools and the delegation of responsibility to private groups must be understood in the context of the history of philanthropy itself.[81] The voluntary and philanthropic history of child protection work shows that it did not always have a professional, scientific basis, but that morality played a crucial role in how people viewed vulnerable children. Child protection work was often, therefore, not child-centred, but focused on the failings of adults. Thus, according to Buckley, "the term 'protection' hardly referred to protecting children from 'cruel' treatment by parents; rather, it referred to 'protecting' children from the criminal and moral consequences of parental 'neglect'".[82]

As Ireland became independent, the main legislation governing how children could be removed from parental care and placed in an institution was the Children Act 1908, which was discussed in Chapter 2. Section 58 of the 1908 Act provided a series of reasons permitting the removal of children. These included begging, homelessness, destitution, parental drunkenness, living with or associating with a known thief or prostitute, or being the daughter of a man convicted under the Criminal Law Amendment Act 1885. These grounds sometimes relied on the criminalization of the children themselves. Before a child could be "protected" because they were found begging, for instance, a court had to first convict the child of the offence in question before sending them to a certified school.[83] Provision was also made in the 1908 Act for the making of fit person order, whereby the child would not be institutionalised but instead placed in the care of a designated individual.[84] Cretney maintains that very few of these orders were ever made in the United Kingdom,[85] meaning that institutionalization was the only means

79 Fred Powell, Martin Geoghegan, Margaret Scanlon and Katherina Swirak, 'Child Outcasts: The Ryan Report into Industrial and Reformatory Schools' in Kenneth Burns and Deborah Lynch (eds), *Children's Rights and Child Protection: Critical Times, Critical Issues in Ireland* (Manchester University Press 2012) 16.

80 CICA Volume I (n 72) 38.

81 Caroline Skehill, 'Child Protection and Welfare Social Work in the Republic of Ireland: Continuities and Discontinuities between the Past and the Present' in Noreen Kearney and Caroline Skehill (eds), *Social Work in Ireland: Historical Perspectives* (Institute of Public Administration 2005) 134–135.

82 Sarah-Anne Buckley, *The Cruelty Man: Child welfare, the NSPCC and the State in Ireland, 1889–1956* (Manchester University Press 2013) 114–115.

83 Section 58(1)

84 Section 58(7). See also sections 21 and 59.

85 Stephen Cretney, *Family Law in the Twentieth Century: A History* (Oxford University Press 2005) 648.

by which children were accommodated having been taken from parental care. Reviewing the operation of this provision, the Kennedy Report of 1970 came to the same conclusion as Cretney – the fit person order was under-utilised, leading to an over-reliance on institutional approaches to child protection.[86]

Current understandings of the institutions rightly see them as places where systematic abuse took place. Children who experienced abuse in their families were placed in near prison-like conditions, where physical and sexual abuse by staff were commonplace.[87] However, the image of the schools, and of the children resident in them, held by political figures helps to demonstrate that they were seen as safe, protective spaces. A Dáil committee debate in 1925 on the financing of schools showed this particularly well. The Labour leader Thomas Johnson TD spoke of his gradual conversion to the cause of industrial and reform schools. Outlining his initial understanding of these institutions, he said:

> I always visualised the reformatory school as something very like a gaol. The idea of boys and youths being sent to a reformatory was somewhat repulsive because of the knowledge that a boy of 12, 13 or 14 years of age, if he were to go into the surroundings and the atmosphere of a gaol, or anything like a gaol, would not come away with an improved character.[88]

Having visited a school, he changed his mind and praised not only the training the boys received but also the atmosphere in the school.[89] He retained concerns, however, over the manner in which staff were selected,[90] an issue which would have drastic consequences in light of later knowledge of child protection scandals. Despite this concern, the overwhelming majority of speakers supported the schools. The manual labour regime employed in them was seen as a necessary part of "working out the beast" of criminal tendencies.[91] The archetypal circumstances leading to committal to a school were outlined by Deputy Sears:

> It would be better to have them there for the reason that they would be taken away from their present surroundings, where they have little but bad example before them. Their parents, perhaps, may be people who are sent to jail occasionally, or it may be that their parents are drunkards, as unfortunately too often is the case.[92]

While some minor opposition was raised against the practice of institutionalization on the grounds that it contaminated young children with a "brand" while

86 Eileen Kennedy, *Reform and Industrial Schools System Report* (Stationery Office 1970) 71.
87 CICA, *Volume IV: Conclusions* (n 72).
88 Dáil Debates 18 June 1925, vol 12, col 1263, Thomas Johnson TD.
89 Ibid, col 1264.
90 Ibid.
91 Ibid, col 1272, Professor William Magennis TD.
92 Ibid, col 1278, William Sears TD.

separating them from their families for inordinate periods of time,[93] the general mood was that opponents of institutionalization were harming the public interest. This view was best exemplified by WT Cosgrave's statement that "this city [Dublin] has not benefited much by the extraordinarily lopsided soft-heartedness" of those critics.[94] Such views were also seen as harmful to the boys in question, as they would be left at the mercy of neglectful parents, with no instruction of how to tell right from wrong, and deprived of training that they could gainfully use in later life.[95]

This attitude represents a recognition that some parents failed to provide for those interests, especially when alcohol abuse was a major part of family life, and the state was entitled to step in through the legalised separation of parent and child in a way that was believed to facilitate the furthering of both the child's and the community's interests. Buckley writes that "the first decades of Irish independence were typified by an erosion of the rights of parents as carers and educators", citing legislation on a range of matters ranging from compulsory education to welfare and illegitimacy.[96] She characterises the legislation as "repressive" and focused on working-class families.[97] This view is understandable if one sees the gaining of political independence as a radical break with the past child protection system. However, when set alongside the gradual discursive changes that occurred over the preceding decades, it is doubtful that the political and legal attitudes of the 1920s and 1930s really represent a major modification of what went before. There was less emphasis on Protestant-influenced ideas of self-reliance in the early years of the Free State. There was less emphasis on the suffering of children, and more on the reform and reintegration of children back into civilised society. Nonetheless, the official attitude was broadly similar to that which led to the 1908 Act, which is usually seen as a "late flowering of Victorian reformism" pushed through by a Liberal government.[98] Buckley's view is perhaps more representative of the "real" experiences of children who suffered callous familial separations followed by systematic abuse in institutions, rather than "official" attitudes towards the need to have effective protection mechanisms.

Approaches to children and families in political discourse

Further evidence of the presence of complicated official attitudes to questions of child protection can be seen from the legislative reforms undertaken in the early decades of independence. Children's interests were advanced and prioritised over those of parents by legislation such as the School Attendance Act 1926, one of

93 See the speech of Deputy Byrne, ibid, cols 1278–1279.
94 Ibid, col 1280, President WT Cosgrave TD.
95 Ibid.
96 Buckley (n 82) 28.
97 Ibid.
98 CICA, *Volume 1: History of Industrial Schools and Reformatories* (n 72) 37.

the Acts sometimes characterised as repressive.[99] While not a child protection statute in the classic sense, it is helpful in understanding how the state thought about the extent of legitimate intervention in family life, and thus serves as a template for how later child protection law reform initiatives were undertaken. Dáil debates on the legislation show that there was not much principled objection to the legislation, but instead, much like the child protection statutes passed in the later years of British governance, discussion focused on where to draw the legislative limits of compulsory attendance.[100]

Measures were introduced that were designed to ensure compliance with the legislation. School attendance inspectors and Gardaí were empowered to visit the homes of truant children, issue formal warnings to their parents, summon the parents to court where they could be issued with fines and ultimately, request the removal of the child to an industrial school.[101] These were certainly coercive measures but there is a major difference between coercion and repression. Fahey makes the point that the enforcement of school attendance was seen as a law enforcement issue,[102] but this is again consistent with emerging views of how the state ought to relate to families – part of its function was that it would act as a guarantor, through coercive means if necessary, of the interests of children whose needs were not being met. Law enforcement was undoubtedly a blunt tool by which to meet these interests, and the use of it to ensure the separation of families through institutionalization had disastrous consequences for many of those children. The point is, though, that the state did not at the time recognise the existence of those consequences, and so official pronouncements on the practice of institutionalization continued to present it as a force for good. Fahey points to a great irony in this position in his consideration of the role of children's rights in the school attendance debates.[103] He characterises the "right" to education for children classified as habitual truants as a duty enforced by punishment in a quasi-carceral institution.[104] References to children's rights as a justification for compulsion should be, he posits, best regarded as an "ideological device with ambiguous significance for parents and children".[105]

The desire to make the institutionalization of children on child protection grounds easier was evident in the passage of the Children Act 1929, which greatly facilitated the admission of children to industrial schools. As indicated earlier, under the 1908 Act, a child could not be admitted to an industrial school simply due to lack of, or inadequate, parental care, or poverty. There was a need to prove some additional factor, such as the child begging, homelessness or lack of

99 Buckley (n 82).
100 Dáil Debates 3 December 1925, vol 13, cols 1206, William Hewat TD.
101 Section 16, School Attendance Act 1926.
102 Tony Fahey, 'State, Family, and Compulsory Schooling in Ireland' (1992) 23(4) *The Economic and Social Review* 369, 380.
103 Ibid, 390.
104 Ibid, 391.
105 Ibid, 392.

parental capacity due to alcoholism.[106] Until the passage of the 1929 Act, the practice of the courts when dealing with a situation like this was to "inspire the police sergeant on various pretexts to arrest the children for begging".[107] This was the easiest way to ensure the child's admittance to an industrial school but nonetheless involved bringing a criminal prosecution against a child for what essentially amounted to living in poverty. The words of one District Judge were quoted in the Senate as the source of inspiration for the legislation:

> It would be a red-letter day for the poor, destitute, hungry children of our city and country if our legislators could be induced to pass a short Act allowing a Justice, in his discretion, to send a destitute child not an orphan to an industrial school without any formal charge being brought against the poor little urchin.[108]

There was little opposition to the legislation in either House. Some comments were made about the legislation being unnecessary outside of Dublin due to similar legal powers being available under other legislation,[109] but this gained no traction. In any event, it was not an objection to the principle of the Bill. Only one statement of that kind was made in the debates, and even then it was qualified. Deputy O'Kelly stated that he believed that in principle it was simply wrong for a child to be torn from the side of their parent when the only crime the parent has committed was to be destitute.[110] However, an amendment allowing for parental consent and for a clause governing the withdrawal of the child from the school would be sufficient to assuage his concerns.[111] As a result, the Act eventually provided that if a child was found destitute and their parents were unable to support them, they could be committed to an industrial school,[112] provided that the parents consented to the order and that if an application was made to the Minister for Education by the parents for the discharge of the child, the Minister was obliged, if satisfied that they were able to support the child, to order the child to be released.[113]

The first significant inquiry into the operation of the industrial and reform school sector was completed in 1936 by District Judge George Cussen. It painted a broadly positive picture of the schools, recommending that the system be maintained, subject to some modifications, and that the religious orders remain in control of the schools.[114] The standard of care provided was stated to be generally

106 Section 58(1).
107 Seanad Debates 13 June 1928, vol 10, col 647, Senator Jane Wyse Power.
108 Ibid, col 644, Senator Patrick J Brady.
109 Dáil Debates 28 February 1929, vol 28, col 731, Minister General Richard Mulcahy TD.
110 Ibid, col 729, Robert Briscoe TD.
111 Ibid, col 727, Seán T O'Kelly TD.
112 Section 1(1), inserting section 58(1)(h) into the 1908 Act.
113 Section 1(2) amending section 58(1) of the 1908 Act.
114 George Cussen, *Commission of Inquiry into the Reformatory and Industrial School System 1934–1936* (Stationery Office 1936) 49.

good.[115] In light of more recent revelations, it might appear that findings of the Cussen Inquiry are largely worthless.[116] Nonetheless, the report did express concern for the children living in the schools and did present some criticism of the regime then in place. Early in the report, it stated that there was a concern that children institutionalised in industrial schools because of familial destitution were associated in the public mind with criminal wrongdoing, and that these prejudices very seriously affected the prospects of the children in later life.[117] Given the problem of poverty underlying familial conditions for children sent to reform schools, the Report highlighted "that such young persons cannot in any sense fairly be looked upon as criminals."[118] Conditions in schools were not uncritically supported – silence at meals was seen a "harsh and unnecessary disciplinary measure",[119] while the practice of substitution of "monotonous marching around a school yard" in a "drill-like exercise" in place of recreation was seen as having a "deleterious" impact on the children.[120]

These indicate a more concern-based attitude to the children, a view borne out by an examination of the Report's attitude to the role of the state in supporting the children in these schools. It was seen as "essential to give each child the impression that he is an individual in whose troubles, ambitions, and welfare a lively interest is being taken".[121] To this end, the educational aspect of the schools was seen as in need of reform;[122] in language that would echo that used a year later in Article 42.5 of the Constitution, the Report stated that

> [t]he State being in effect in the position of guardian to the children sent to these schools has in our view an obligation to ensure that they are afforded a primary education at least as good as that provided for other children.[123]

Local authorities were castigated for failure to live up to their own responsibilities.[124] Crucially, the Children Act 1929 was seen as necessary, but insufficient to meet children's needs. The Report criticised the Act for not permitting the

115 Ibid 20.

116 See the comment by Buckley and Riordan that the Report had little impact – Sarah-Anne Buckley and Susannah Riordan, 'Childhood since 1740' in Eugenio F Biagini and Mary E Daly (eds), *The Cambridge Social History of Modern Ireland* (Cambridge University Press 2017) 340.

117 Ibid 10.

118 Ibid 11.

119 Ibid 22.

120 Ibid 23.

121 Ibid 21.

122 See the extensive recommendations at ibid 51–53.

123 Ibid 27. For comparison, this is the wording of Article 42.5: "In exceptional cases, where the parents for physical or moral reasons fail in their duty towards their children, the State as guardian of the common good, by appropriate means shall endeavour to supply the place of the parents, but always with due regard for the natural and imprescriptible rights of the child."

124 Ibid 11.

Minister for Education when discharging a child from an industrial school to "provide for any safeguard in the matter of the fitness of the parents or parent on moral or other grounds to resume control of the child".[125] The attitude towards children and the risks they faced was a clear break with the past. The desire for children's welfare to be taken more seriously at all levels of government and in the operation of the schools themselves marks the Cussen Report as a milestone in the legal construction of children during this period.

Child law, 1941–1964 and the influence of the Constitution

The debates around the Children Act 1941 presented the first opportunity for the Dáil to show how it thought about children, and the risks they faced, since the enactment of the 1937 Constitution. It was, in essence, an Act amending the Children Act 1908, mostly concerned with making administrative changes to the management of schools, and with clarifying certain points relating to the admission of children to schools. Yet the debates touched upon the social construction of children and the interplay between different constitutional rights in a way that had not been seen before.

In a reflection of the often-confused thinking about childhood, children were sometimes seen as victims, as threats, and as having interests in need of safeguarding. The Minister for Education stated when presenting the Bill to the Seanad that the legislation would deal with those children "for whom the advantages of family life are unfortunately not available [and] … a small number of children who require greater discipline and control than is normally afforded by family life."[126] This binary view presents children as either victims of circumstances or as threats to the social and moral order in need of correction. Yet in the same debate, another speaker stated that "the central motive in all legislation in regard to children … should be inspired with a desire to promote the child's interests."[127] While the speech continued in a child rescue vein,[128] the rhetoric of rescue was here predicated on the idea that children had interests separate from those of their parents, and separate from the interests of the state. The debates were largely conducted with "every feeling of consideration and sympathy for that weak and helpless section of the community."[129] The recognition of children as holding interests, even limited ones springing from their position as victims of circumstance, is presented in a very forthright way throughout the parliamentary debates. As will be seen below, when the constitutional questions relevant to the legislation were addressed, it became clear that though children were beginning to be thought of as having interests, this was not a consensus view.

125 Ibid 16.
126 Seanad Debates 5 March 1941, vol 25, col 495, Minister Thomas Derrig TD.
127 Ibid, col 520, Senator Professor William Magennis.
128 See for example, ibid, col 523, Senator Professor William Magennis: "every Christian will hold that it is the duty of civilised society to come to their rescue."
129 Ibid, col 537, Senator Seán Patrick Campbell.

One significant legislative amendment brought in by the 1941 Act was to change the way in which the consent rules introduced by the 1929 Act operated. This was eventually embodied in section 10 of the 1941 Act.[130] This provided that a child who was found destitute could not be committed to an industrial school unless parental consent was first obtained, or had been dispensed with owing to mental incapacity, desertion, or the imprisonment of one or both parents.[131] The purpose behind these changes was to increase the discretion enjoyed by judges.[132] It was suggested that such a change would be in children's best interests, especially in cases where consent was being maliciously withheld. By not having to obtain the consent of both parents, it was reasoned, the court would now have the discretion to commit the child to an industrial school in these "very exceptional or ... borderline" cases.[133] Parental consent was, however, described as a "fundamental principle",[134] which could only be disregarded in exceptional cases where destitution was the main reason for committal.

The parental consent question highlights perhaps the most significant legal point raised by the introduction of the 1941 Act – it was the first time in Dáil debates since the passage of the 1937 Constitution that the interplay between parental rights under Article 41 and children's rights under Article 42 was considered. The Bill was described as tightening up the law with respect to exceptional cases, but in doing so clashed with a fundamental principle of constitutional law and state policy.[135] While it was admitted that the Bill was designed to deal with exceptional cases, the following quotation captures very well the influence of the new constitutional arrangements:

> it is not wise further to restrict the fundamental rights of the parent, which I was under the impression was one of the things that still remained guaranteed by the Constitution ... what you are doing is taking discretion away from the parents and putting it in the power of a district justice—I do not care whether he is a district justice or the Chief Justice—for a reason that he thinks fit—not that this House thinks fit, but that he thinks fit—to deprive the natural guardians of the child of their rights and their duties.
>
> Now, I question very much the wisdom of the adoption of a policy of that kind in order to meet a few exceptional cases. I think that, in a matter of this kind, the first consideration ought to be—and I thought that we had, if not guaranteed it, at least expressed a pious opinion to that effect in the Constitution—apart from any provision of the Constitution, that there is no undue interference with the rights of the family, and that if it is found necessary to interfere with them, then it will be done on stated grounds, and not

130 This amended section 58(1) of the 1908 Act.
131 Section 10(e) of the 1941 Act.
132 Dáil Debates 11 December 1940, vol 81, cols 1102–1103, Minister Thomas Derrig TD.
133 Ibid, col 1102.
134 Ibid, col 1107.
135 Ibid, col 1111, Professor John Marcus O'Sullivan TD.

> have the *carte blanche* that is given here to a judge to determine it according as suits his fancy.[136]

In framing opposition to the new section 10 in this way, the fundamental tension within Irish child protection law as it stood until the recent constitutional change is encapsulated by the idea that while reform may legitimately be seen as being in the best interests of children, the constitutional arrangements place a high premium on parental discretion. This premium would in effect prevent further reform in children's interests.

The provision was later ruled unconstitutional by the Supreme Court. In the 1955 decision of *Re Doyle*,[137] a father had consented for his daughter to be sent to an industrial school, having been deserted by his wife. The wife's consent was dispensed with by the District Court, but when the father applied to have his daughter released, this was refused on the grounds that the consent of both parents was statutorily required for the release. The Supreme Court ruled that the statute was unconstitutional as it effectively removed from the father the right to care for his daughter if he was willing and able to do so. Further, it was held that the rights guaranteed to parents by virtue of Article 42.1 could not be removed or invalidated, even by reference to Article 42.5. The Court held that this provision

> does not enable the Legislature to take away the right of a parent who is in a position to do so to control the education of his child, where there is nothing culpable on the part of either parent or child.[138]

In situations where such "culpability" may exist, such as through parental desertion, the court reasoned that, at least in the circumstances of the present case, the authority of the family as a constitutional entity is unaffected, and that the desertion of one parent does not diminish the constitutional rights of the other.[139]

During the Dáil debates on the 1941 Bill, children's interests began to play a role in the shaping of legislation.[140] The Minister responsible for the Bill (which became the 1941 Act) quoted the terms of Article 42.5 in support of the proposals to widen the circumstances in which children could be admitted to schools for destitution without parental consent before stating

> [m]y only interest in this matter is to see that the interests of the child are safeguarded, and, while I am Minister for Education, feeling that I have a special responsibility towards those children, to recommend to the Dáil

136 Ibid, cols 1110–1111.
137 *In Re Doyle, an Infant* (SC) 21 December 1955, [1989] ILRM 277.
138 Ibid 5, 282.
139 Ibid.
140 Dáil Debates 11 December 1940, vol 81, cols 1142–1143, Minister Thomas Derrig TD.

> whatever steps I consider necessary to amend the law so as to make better provision in their regard.[141]

This is the first time that Article 42.5 was used in the Dáil to support greater intervention in family life. In the Seanad, the Article was referred to indirectly by a speaker who commented that in the debates so far "[w]e heard a great deal about the rights of parents, but we heard very little about the rights of children."[142] Here, the idea that children had interests and rights was seen clearly. In later Seanad debates, opposition to the Bill was expressed due to it not going far enough to protect children's rights. It was argued that the provision allowing a child to be released from a school following a parental application to this effect was not in compliance with Article 42.5 if it did not permit a court to consider whether the welfare of the child would be provided for on release. The language of rights was specifically used; it was argued that

> It is because the child has rights, the exercise of which is denied to it by the failure of the parent that the State as guardian of the common good must interfere, and it is the duty of the State … to see to it that the child gets a proper bringing up.[143]

Further, it was stated that

> the idea that it is the parent's right to do what he likes with the child is a wrong conception of the parent's right and duty here. Parental right is based on parental duty … [t]he State, in this case, must become the custodian and must intervene on behalf of the rights of the child, notwithstanding what may be put forward on behalf of the rights of the parent.[144]

The recognition of children as agents in the sense advocated by David Oswell, evident in the passages just considered, was also a live issue in two of the major child and family law reforms undertaken in this period – the introduction of a legal mechanism for adoption in 1952 and the revision of guardianship, custody and access rules in 1964. Neither of these were child protection measures in a strict sense, and so they will not be considered in detail. Yet they share some noteworthy features, especially in how they understand the relationship between children and their families, the idea of children having their own interests, and ways in which the concept of rights was used to promote or oppose reform. The Adoption Act 1952 established an adoption board, *An Bord Uchtála*,[145] which was empowered to make adoption orders transferring legal responsibility for a

141 Ibid, col 1142.
142 Seanad Debates 5 March 1941, vol 25, col 525, Senator Helena Concannon TD.
143 Seanad Debates 2 April 1941, vol 25, col 914, Senator Professor William Magennis.
144 Ibid, col 916–917.
145 See section 8.

child to another family in certain circumstances.[146] One of the main restrictions on the board's ability to make orders was that children could only be adopted if they were illegitimate or an orphan[147]; it was therefore impossible to adopt a child born to married parents in any circumstances except if the child were an orphan.

During the legislative debates on the 1952 Act, it was stated by the responsible Minister that there was "a danger that the Bill would be held to be unconstitutional if it provided for the adoption of legitimate children whose parents are alive."[148] It was also posited that the main need for the legislation arose in respect of orphans or illegitimate children,[149] and that in matters such as this, reform ought to be incremental,[150] suggesting that, even if there were a need for the adoption of children of married families, legislation would not be immediately forthcoming. There was some discussion in the debate about the nature of the constitutional rights of the various parties involved. One participant spoke of how it was impossible for the Dáil to legislate in contravention of natural law, which itself was thought of as governing the limits of positive constitutional rights: "In relation to children, natural rights can only cease in circumstances of full and free consent on the part of the natural parent. No legislation of ours can change that."[151] This was an exceptionally strong endorsement of parental rights, yet there was also some indication that children's interests were to be regarded as central to the process. While the legislation as passed contained no reference to the interests or welfare of a child as a primary consideration in adoption in proceedings, one TD specifically referred to the rights of the child – "[e]ven though there is only an infant in question, his rights under the Constitution should be guaranteed."[152] It was also recognised by another TD that birth parents could not always be regarded in a positive light – first, he posited that it would be unfair for a child placed with adoptive parents to be removed from their care should the parents change their minds, especially when they had neglected the child's interests,[153] and thought that parents could be thought of as lacking legitimate authority because of their behaviour towards their children.[154]

The tone of the debate at the passing of the Guardianship of Infants Act 1964 was quite different. The debate on this critically important statute, which is still largely in place today, was in fact quite limited, with second stage debate being dealt within a single day. As such, there are a limited number of statements from which to draw information or conclusions about how children were thought about. Indeed, it may be argued, the fact that there was so little debate

146 See generally, Part II of the Act.
147 Section 10(c).
148 Dáil Debates 11 June 1952, vol 132, col 1106, Minister Gerald Boland TD.
149 Ibid.
150 Ibid, col 1107, Minister Gerald Boland TD.
151 Ibid, col 1176, TF O'Higgins TD.
152 Ibid, col 1108, Major-General Seán MacEoin TD.
153 Ibid, col 1117, Patrick McGrath TD.
154 Ibid, col 1118.

shows a level of consensus among the legislature over the principles of the Act. Introducing the Bill, the Minister for Justice outlined that one of the two legal principles to be given effect by the legislation was the principle that "in any proceedings affecting a child, the child's welfare must be the first and paramount consideration."[155] He further explained that "The aim is always the ultimate welfare of the infant."[156] Certain limited rights were afforded to the natural fathers of illegitimate children, specifically the ability to apply for directions from a court in respect of the child. The purpose of this provision was stated to be as a means of affording greater protection to the child, such as in cases when the father may wish to apply for custody where the child was being neglected by the mother.[157] There was very limited opposition to the Bill. The only significant point of contention for present purposes was the concern that providing that the welfare of an individual child would always be the paramount consideration would create constitutional difficulties. While it was stated that there was no objection to this in principle, it was noted that "there are very definite provisions in the Constitution which seem to … to provide that the family unit as a whole, not the individual component parts of that unit, must be regarded as of first and paramount importance."[158]

This limited recognition not only of children's interests but of the priority they were to be accorded marks an important staging post in the development of the Irish legal framework relating to children. The idea that children's interests could supersede those of parents was expressly enshrined in legislation, with no meaningful opposition. Children's agency was not expressed through, for example, participation mechanisms, but it was clearly recognised that the law needed to place their welfare at the centre of any court decision, thereby creating the conditions of possibility for their interests to shape the lives of others. It was a limited, but important, recognition that helped to move children away from being seen as mere objects.

Conclusion

In the early decades of Ireland's self-governance, children were at times seen as risks to the social order that had to be controlled, but there was a clear trend towards seeing children as victims, victims whose interests required recognition and concern on the part of the state. In Chapters 7 and 8, I will consider the abusive practices within institutions and in families towards children, including practices undertaken in the period examined in this chapter. Therefore, any statement that the law began to take a more concern-orientated approach needs to be tempered by later revelations. Even on a legal level, there was some ambivalence over

155 Dáil Debates 29 January 1964, vol 207, col 141, Minister Charles Haughey TD.
156 Ibid, col 143.
157 Ibid, col 142.
158 Ibid, col 144, Michael Joseph O'Higgins TD.

children and families – the Constitution was acknowledged to protect the private domain of married family life, yet interventions in family life were increasingly permitted where children lived in destitution. Criminal law reform was predicated on widening the scope of the law as well as increasing punishments for the guilty. However, these were incomplete reforms. Families were separated when support may have brought about better outcomes; reforms of the law of evidence making it easier to prosecute sexual abuse cases were ignored in favour of reform of the substantive law.

Despite this ambivalence, there does appear to have been a shift in the discursive construction of children in legal sources, particularly in legislative debates from late in the period covered in this chapter. While the conditions of simple or traditional modernity clearly prevailed in this era, agency, at least in a highly circumscribed form, was beginning to emerge as a property possessed by some children. On occasion, children were described in the Dáil as having rights, separate and distinct from the marital family. These references were not particularly common or forceful, but their existence cannot be denied. Towards the end of the period examined in this chapter, children's interests and needs started to take on a greater role in policy formulation. The passage of the Adoption Act 1952 and the Guardianship of Infants Act 1964 are testimony to this. Of particular interest is the lack of real dispute over one of the central reforms of the 1964 Act – that the child's welfare would be the paramount consideration. While it took time for this approach to reach other areas of the law affecting children, its recognition set the scene for the period of reform of children's services that began in the early 1970s.

References

Arnold B, *The Irish Gulag: How the Irish State Betrayed its Innocent Children* (Gill and Macmillan 2009).

Barnes J, *Irish Industrial Schools, 1868–1908: Origins and Development* (Irish Academic Press 1989).

Buckley SA, *The Cruelty Man: Child Welfare, the NSPCC and the State in Ireland, 1889–1956* (Manchester University Press 2013).

Buckley SA and Riordan S, 'Childhood Since 1740' in Eugenio F Biagini and Mary E Daly (eds), *The Cambridge Social History of Modern Ireland* (Cambridge University Press 2017).

Commission on Relief of the Sick and Destitute Poor, *Report of the Commission on the Relief of the Sick and Destitute Poor Including the Insane Poor* (Stationery Office 1927).

Commission to Inquire into Child Abuse (CICA), *Report of the Commission to Inquire into Child Abuse* (Stationery Office 2009).

Committee on Evil Literature, *Report of the Committee on Evil Literature* (Stationery Office 1927).

Committee on the Criminal Law Amendment Acts, *Report of the Committee on the Criminal Law Amendment Acts (1880–1885) and Juvenile Prostitution (1931)*, National Archives of Ireland (NAI), Department of Justice (D/Jus) file S5998.

Cussen G, *Commission of Inquiry into the Reformatory and Industrial School System 1934–1936* (Stationery Office 1936).

Ferguson H, 'Abused and Looked After Children as Moral Dirt: Child Abuse and Institutional Care in Historical Perspective' (2007) 36(1) *Journal of Social Policy* 123.

Ferriter D, *The Transformation of Ireland 1900–2000* (Profile Books 2005).

Finnane M, 'The Carrigan Committee of 1930–31 and the Moral Condition of the Saorstát' (2001) 32(128) *Irish Historical Studies* 519.

Freeman M, *The Rights and Wrongs of Children* (Continuum 1983) 66.

Inter-Departmental Committee of Inquiry Regarding Venereal Disease, *Report of the Inter-Departmental Committee of Inquiry Regarding Venereal Disease* (Stationery Office 1925).

Kennedy E, *Reform and Industrial Schools System Report* (Stationery Office 1970).

Kennedy F, 'The Suppression of the Carrigan Report: A Historical Perspective on Child Abuse' (2000) 89 *Studies: An Irish Quarterly Review* 354.

Maguire M, 'The Carrigan Committee and Child Sexual Abuse in Twentieth-century Ireland' (2007) 11(2) *New Hibernia Review* 79.

Maguire M, *Precarious Childhood in Post-Independence Ireland* (Manchester University Press 2009).

Mahood L and Littlewood B, 'The "Vicious Girl" and the "Street-Corner Boy": Sexuality and the Gendered Delinquent in the Scottish Child-Saving Movement 1850–1940' (1994) 4(4) *Journal of the History of Sexuality* 549.

Milner A, 'Sodomy as a Ground for Divorce' (1960) 23 *Modern Law Review* 50.

Powell F, Geoghegan M, Scanlon M and Swirak K, 'Child Outcasts: The Ryan Report into Industrial and Reformatory Schools' in Kenneth Burns and Deborah Lynch (eds), *Children's Rights and Child Protection: Critical Times, Critical Issues in Ireland* (Manchester University Press 2012).

Rafferty M and O'Sullivan E, *Suffer the Little Children: The Inside Story of Ireland's Industrial Schools* (New Island Books 2000).

Skehill, C 'Child Protection and Welfare Social Work in the Republic of Ireland: Continuities and Discontinuities between the Past and the Present' in Noreen Kearney and Caroline Skehill (eds), *Social Work in Ireland: Historical Perspectives* (Institute of Public Administration 2005).

Smith J, 'The Politics of Sexual Knowledge: The Origins of Ireland's Containment Culture and the Carrigan Report (1931)' (2004) 13(2) *Journal of the History of Sexuality* 208.

Stone L, *Road to Divorce: England 1530–1987* (Oxford University Press 1990).

Whyte JH, *Church and State in Modern Ireland, 1923–1979* (2nd edn, Gill and Macmillan 1980).

5 Child protection law and policy, 1970–1993

Introduction

The period between 1970 and 1991 marked a period of increasing concern about the state of child protection law and policy. In 1970, two significant breaks with the previous decades occurred – the publication of the Kennedy Report which hastened the closure of reformatory and industrial schools, and child protection social work became the responsibility of the newly established Health Boards. The passing of the Child Care Act 1991 coincided with a new public interest in child protection leading to a period of significant legal reform, a change that resulted in a new consciousness about risk that has shaped the discourse surrounding child protection. As a result, this chapter will be bookended by these developments. The period in between saw the early indications of the emergence of a reflexive society that was to be more clearly seen in the 1990s – following the publication of the Kilkenny Incest Report in 1993, traditional child protection structures were reformed, and the interests of the marginalised increasingly recognised as relevant, if not always fully empathised with. Risks were also being recognised as something that could not be suppressed, but that needed to be managed. The shift in thinking about risk was one of the most important developments in this period and is clear evidence of the first stirrings of late modernity.

This chapter will examine the shift in the discursive practice that took place in respect of child protection work between 1970 and the passing of the Child Care Act 1991. It will first focus on the way in which children were presented in reports into the child care and protection system. Second, the development of new social work guidelines for child protection will be outlined, followed by an analysis of how the law began to deal with the problems of child abuse prior to the passage of the 1991 Act. Finally, the main aspects of this Act will be analysed in detail, with particular attention paid to how the Act sought to manage risk and the interests of children. This will leave an examination of the ways in which the Kilkenny case and other child abuse scandals impacted on child protection law reform to the next chapter.

Children in child care reports

The period discussed in this chapter saw the development of an attitude to child protection in official circles that could best be characterised as increasingly willing to undertake fundamental reform, but able to carry out only incremental, but significant change. As such, it represents an early stage of institutional reflexivity, a process described by Giddens as involving the "regularized use of knowledge about circumstances of social life as a constitutive element in its organization and transformation".[1] While there was a gradual movement towards child protection as a more expert and state-led enterprise from the 1930s in the United Kingdom, Ireland was slower to develop this kind of approach. A state-led approach to social work can be traced to the early 1960s,[2] with this becoming entrenched in the child protection context from the 1970s onwards.[3] A number of reasons for the importance of this time period can be offered – internationally, child abuse had been "rediscovered" by Henry Kempe and his colleagues.[4] Specific guidelines were developed in Ireland for the first time to deal with this problem, which will be discussed below. Government reports began to recognise the need for fundamental reform of the child care system.[5]

The Kennedy Report

The first major driver of reform that needs to be addressed is the role of government and civil society reports and inquiries into the operation of the child care system. A report published in 1966 by Tuairim, an NGO concerned with child welfare, called for legislative reform, a movement away from institutional care and the reorganization of children's services under the auspices of the Department of Health.[6] Civil society groups such as CARE,[7] Children First and the Irish

1 Anthony Giddens, *Modernity and Self-Identity: Self and Society in the Late Modern Age* (Polity Press 1991) 20.

2 Charlie Delap and Terry Kelleher, 'Local Authority Social Work in Ireland: Origins, Issues and Developments' in Noreen Kearney and Caroline Skehill, *Social Work in Ireland: Historical Perspectives* (Institute of Public Administration 2005). See generally Helen Buckley, Caroline Skehill and Eoin O'Sullivan, *Child Protection Practices in Ireland: A Case Study* (Oak Tree Press 1997) 11 and Robbie Gilligan, 'Policy in the Republic of Ireland: Historical and Current Issues in Child Care' in Pam Carter, Tony Jeffs, and Mark Smith (eds) *Social Work and Social Welfare Yearbook 1* (Open University Press 1989) 61.

3 Caroline Skehill, *History of the Present of Child Protection and Welfare Social Work in Ireland* (Edwin Mellin 2004) ch 3.

4 Henry Kempe et al, 'The Battered Child Syndrome' (1962) 181 *Journal of the American Medical Association* 17. See also Harry Ferguson, 'Protecting Irish Children in Time: Child Abuse as a Social Problem and the Development of the Child Protection System in the Republic of Ireland' (1996) 44(2) *Administration* 5, 7.

5 See in particular the Report of the Task Force on Child Care Services, discussed below.

6 Tuairim, *Some of Our Children – A Report on the Residential Care of the Deprived Child in Ireland* (Pamphlet No 13, Tuairim 1966).

7 CARE, *Children Deprived: CARE Memorandum* (CARE 1972).

Association of Social Workers also developed proposals for reform.[8] Underpinning all of these reports was a recognition that children's interests needed to be given greater priority than was presently occurring.

However, the most important report for present purposes was the Report of the Kennedy Commission, published in 1970. This grew out of concerns over the conditions in reform schools raised with government ministers in the mid-1960s.[9] The Report itself states that the late Minister for Education, Donogh O'Malley realised that the Children Act 1908 was "not suitable to an era of changing conditions. He felt that the Community was not doing all it should to help underprivileged children, particularly those who had to be placed in these schools".[10] This attitude of concern permeated the Committee's Report. One of the major recommendations was that the "whole aim of the Child Care system should be geared towards the prevention of family-breakdown", with admission to care a matter of last resort when there was no satisfactory alternative available.[11] The Report was clear in recommending that the existing institutional system should be abolished, that several institutions be closed immediately, that aftercare become a fundamental part of the system and that adequate training be compulsory for everyone involved in child care work.[12]

Overall, the feeling was that the system then in place had placed too much emphasis on providing "accommodation for children and on safeguarding them from moral and physical dangers" to the detriment of the child's developmental needs.[13] The system was "haphazard and amateurish".[14] A functioning, modern child care system would require a much more collaborative approach, involving "doctors, psychologists, social workers, counsellors, remedial and special teachers who will work as a team".[15] This emphasis on interagency working was a radical departure from the institutional system which relied on clerics, members of religious orders and a handful of lay personnel to provide care. It also highlighted the emphasis on prevention of admissions to care, to which the Committee devoted an entire chapter of its Report, where the need for adequate housing, financial support and family support services was made clear.[16]

On the basis of this summary, the Kennedy Report would appear to be a trailblazer, a pivotal moment in the development of a modern, robust, child care system. Concern for children clearly permeated the Report. Keating demonstrates

8 See generally Ann Lavan, 'Social Work in Ireland' in Steven Shardlow and Malcolm Payne (eds), *Contemporary Issues in Social Work – Western Europe* (Arena 1998).
9 For a comprehensive account of the origins, and inner workings, of the Committee, see Anthony Keating, 'A contested legacy: the Kennedy Committee revisited' (2014) 22(3) *Irish Studies Review* 304.
10 Eileen Kennedy, *Reform and Industrial Schools System Report* (Stationery Office 1970) 4.
11 Ibid 6.
12 Ibid.
13 Ibid 12.
14 Ibid 13.
15 Ibid 18.
16 Ibid 61–66.

how this led to its warm reception by the media.[17] In particular, he points to media and civil society reaction to the Report which described it as "courageous" and "long overdue".[18] However, criticism was also made of the Report, including in the decades after its publication, for failure to report on the real lives of children in the institutions, thereby allowing the perpetuation of a deception as to what was really happening in institutions.[19] It has been claimed that the Committee

> omitted to print its most damaging evidence of the awful conditions children were warehoused in, their meagre rations, substandard clothing, and the abuse and neglect they experienced in some of the institutions, choosing instead to address these issues behind closed doors.[20]

The Report also suffered from significant implementation problems. While the institutional care system did decline, the radical overhaul of many aspects of child care called for in the Report did not materialise, at least in the short term. The difficulties experienced in implementing many of its recommendations have been characterised as stemming not from

> a lack of effort by any party, but reflected that despite a broad consensus on what should be done in the area of child welfare, interested parties held opposing views on the precise mechanisms, principles and pace of change required.[21]

What is clear even from a reading of the Report itself is the notable absence of emphasis on children's rights, or any indication that children could be considered to have attained the status of agent. Children's rights are referred to on three separate occasions; it is stated that children ought to enjoy the right to personal property while in care,[22] that the voluntary detention system may impact particularly on young girls who are not aware of their rights[23] and that a juvenile over the age of 15 charged with murder or manslaughter had a right to elect a trial by jury rather than by a judge sitting alone.[24] By any reading, this is not a document based on the idea that children have clearly articulable or legally enforceable rights. This ought not to be surprising given the constitutional position of children at the time – even international law did not fully recognise children as

17 Keating (n 9) 314.
18 Ibid.
19 Bruce Arnold, 'Still Missing Full Story Behind Children "Shovelled Into Schools" *Irish Independent* (Dublin, 21 May 2009).
20 Keating (n 9) 314–315.
21 Denis O'Sullivan, 'Social Definition in Child Care in the Irish Republic: Model of the Child and Child-care Intervention' (1979) 10(3) *Economic and Social Review* 309.
22 Kennedy (n 10) 19.
23 Ibid 39.
24 Ibid 68.

rights-holders until almost two decades later. When the rights of girls accommodated under a voluntary scheme are mentioned, these are not spelt out, their content either assumed to be known by all readers, or, more likely, existing as unquantifiable ephemera.

The Task Force on Child Care Services

Following the Kennedy Report, a Task Force on Child Care Services was established. In its 1980 Report, some progress towards the recognition of children as rights-holders can be seen. The Report sought to foreground children's needs as the overriding concern in child care work, but rights rather than mere needs were used as justifications for reform; indeed children were recognised as a "significant minority" whose constitutional rights required special protection by the State.[25] It recognised that children's rights were human rights,[26] and cited the 1959 UN Declaration on the Rights of the Child.[27] This was a critical staging post on the path to the recognition that children were to be thought of as agents, at least in professional child care circles; among the rights it recommended that children within the care system be extended was the right to separate legal representation in child care hearings.[28] This aspect of participation in legal proceedings could only have been conceived of if children were first credited with the ability to contribute to the proceedings in some way, and by recognising that their voices were sufficiently important to hear.

Having recognised children as agents, the Task Force was moved towards advocating for the entrenchment of children's constitutional rights; in particular, it attempted to guide the drafting of the 1976 constitutional amendment on adoption.[29] When the need for a new constitutional provision to safeguard the rights of children in the adoption process became clear, the Task Force's Final Report indicates that it attempted to intervene by suggesting that the

> proposed amendment be drafted in such a way that it secured the constitutionality of this principle for the wider range of children whose best interests might require their being placed in the care of persons other than their natural parents. We suggested that the principle of paramountcy should be enshrined clearly in the Constitution in a way which would cover all cases (other than cases involving an offence on the child's part) in which decisions are taken about the placement and custody of children, and not just in adoption cases.[30]

25 Task Force on Child Care Services, *Final Report* (Stationery Office 1980) 38.
26 Ibid 45.
27 UN General Assembly, *Declaration of the Rights of the Child*, 20 November 1959, A/RES/1386(XIV).
28 Task Force (n 25) 273.
29 See Chapter 3.
30 Task Force on Child Care Service (n 25) 215.

The authors of a supplemental report continued to argue that there was a need to take constitutional rights for children more seriously. They argued that "children have *constitutional rights* which must take precedence over the constitutional rights of their parents when this is necessary to ensure a child's current or future welfare."[31] They called for a clearer enunciation of what the natural and imprescriptible rights of the child were, and posited that this must include "the right of a child to receive adequate care, if necessary through the compulsory intervention of the state."[32]

These reports demonstrate a significant shift in how children were thought about. In the decade that separated the Kennedy Report from the Task Force Report, children's agency was clearly recognised and children's rights went from being seen an issue of marginal concern to one which required constitutional clarification in order to safeguard both children and the child protection system itself. Children were now beginning to be recognised as subjects by those tasked with reviewing child care at a systematic level. It was clear that a consensus had been reached that, whatever about the precise nature of children's constitutional or legal rights, children at the very least had an interest in the operation of an effective child protection system. The changing understanding of how to implement that protection system, and of the risks that children needed to be protected from, is evidenced by the reforms undertaken within child protection social work itself.

Child abuse in law and policy, 1970–1991

The development of child protection social work guidelines and the evolution of risks

At around the same time that the Kennedy Report was recommending the dismantling of the institutional system, social work principles came to dominate child care work. The 'social risk' model of children and childhood was replaced with an approach much more rooted in developmental psychology; such an approach saw the lack of attention to child development as itself constituting a form of deprivation.[33] As outlined above, Ireland had begun to develop a more welfare-orientated approach to social work in the early 1970s. For Ferriter, "it was not until the 1970s that social workers were accepted as the most appropriate professionals to take on child welfare responsibilities."[34] This approach has been linked with the rediscovery of child abuse more generally, as the period from 1970 onwards showed the development of a more sophisticated child protection

31 Ibid 299, emphasis in original.

32 Ibid 300.

33 O'Sullivan (n 21). Much of this owes an intellectual debt to the work on attachment theory done by John Bowlby. See Victoria A Fitton, 'Attachment Theory: History, Research, and Practice' (2012) 19(1–2) *Psychoanalytic Social Work* 121.

34 Diarmuid Ferriter, *The Transformation of Ireland 1900-2000* (Profile Books 2005) 450.

system reflecting the first impact of the conceptualization of the "battered baby syndrome" as requiring a multi-disciplinary approach.[35]

With the establishment of the Irish Society for the Prevention of Cruelty to Children in 1956 and the Health Boards in 1970,[36] a more developed child protection system began to emerge. The idea behind the Health Boards was to ensure that health and social decisions were taken at a more local level and that the services provided would be more focussed on the person receiving these services. Part of the Boards' function was the provision of personal social services for children and families.[37] This necessitated movement away from the delegation of responsibility to voluntary and religious groups and towards the direct provision of care to children whose welfare and development was at risk. The result was that the priest or member of a religious order was replaced by the public health nurse or social worker as the point of contact for a child in need of protection. A key aspect of this state-based service is the variety of professionals who may be involved in a child's care – teachers, doctors, nurses, social workers, psychologists and police – necessitating a high degree of multi-disciplinary interaction and interagency cooperation.

As part of the professionalization of social work practice, it became necessary to develop new ways of thinking about and working with the risks children faced. One particularly important aspect of this will have been evident from the material covered in the previous chapter. While the criminal law was concerned with sexual offending against children, the debates about child care and protection tended to focus on parental capacity and deprivation. Sexual abuse had disappeared from official discourse by the mid-twentieth century. Ferguson has argued that due to the Irish state having an established "a traditional order, characterised by cultural denial, patriarchal social relations and repression, sexual abuse was not classified and worked with in practice."[38] This is part of a broader international trend, as it was in the 1970s that adult–child sexual contact again came to be conceptualised as abuse.[39]

This view of the slow emergence of the understanding the sexual offending was a risk faced by children which was within the remit of child protective services is partially verified when the development of child protection guidelines is considered. O'Sullivan traces the beginnings of this process to 1975 when a meeting

35 Ferguson (n 4) 13–14.

36 Health Act 1970.

37 Catherine McGuinness, *Report of the Kilkenny Incest Investigation* (Stationary Office 1993) ch 4. See also Department of Health, *Guidelines for the Development of Social Work Services (In Community Care Programmes)* (Department of Health 1973) cited in Skehill (n 3) 69.

38 Harry Ferguson, 'Child Abuse as a Social Problem in Post Traditional Ireland' in CN McElwee (ed), *Irish Society: A Reader in Applied Social Studies* (StreetSmart Press 1997) 31.

39 See generally, Carol Smart, 'A History of Ambivalence and Conflict in the Discursive Construction of the 'Child Victim' of Sexual Abuse' (1999) 8(3) *Social and Legal Studies* 391.

was held at the Department of Health to discuss the problem of "non-accidental injury to children" that had been identified in hospitals.[40] The following year, a committee reported on the matter,[41] which focused on clinical matters relating to "battered children." It provided largely clinical guidance on detecting physical abuse, with "proportionately marginal emphasis" on other aspects of what would now be called child abuse.[42] The Report provided an "index of suspicion" to assist the identification of child abuse, which was almost entirely based on physical symptoms of injury, with a limited focus on "nutritional deprivation, neglect and emotional deprivation and trauma".[43] This, and the expected lead role of hospital staff in any further investigations, was criticised by social workers.[44] Nonetheless, the emphasis on physical injury formed the basis of subsequent guidelines on the reporting and management of concerns, first issued in 1977.[45] These were replaced in 1980 with another set of guidelines which again did not use the term "child abuse", and retained the focus on "non-accidental injury".[46]

Child sexual abuse came to be recognised as a distinct phenomenon in Ireland during the 1980s. A new set of Guidelines issued in 1983 contained the first official mention of child sexual abuse in a policy document.[47] Civil society groups began to take notice of a wider understanding of child abuse. The Irish Association of Social Workers hosted a workshop on child sexual abuse in 1983, which led to the development of an Incest Crisis Service, while the Rape Crisis Service also began identifying survivors of childhood sexual abuse as a significant group requiring support.[48] *Magill* magazine referred to an unpublished Department of Health report highlighting that one in four Irish girls may be sexually abused before the age of 18.[49] Revised child protection guidelines from 1987 marked the first time that child sexual abuse was considered as necessitating

40 Commission to Inquire into Child Abuse (CICA), *Report of the Commission to Inquire into Child Abuse, Volume IV: Residential child welfare in Ireland, 1965–2008: an outline of policy, legislation and practice: a paper prepared for the Commission to Inquire into Child Abuse* (Stationery Office 2009) 256.

41 Department of Health, *Report of the Committee on Non-Accidental Injury to Children* (Stationery Office 1976).

42 CICA (n 40) 256.

43 Department of Health (n 41) 10.

44 CICA (n 40) 257.

45 Department of Health, *Memorandum on Non-Accidental Injury to Children* (Stationery Office 1977). See generally Denis Greene, 'Legal Aspects of Non-accidental Injury to Children' (1979) 27(4) *Administration* 460.

46 Department of Health, *Guidelines on the Identification and Management of Non-Accidental Injury to Children* (Stationery Office 1980).

47 Department of Health, *Guidelines on Procedures for Identification and Investigation on Non-Accidental Injury to Children* (Stationery Office 1983).

48 CICA (n 40) 258. See also Irish Council of Civil Liberties, *Report of the Child Sexual Abuse Working Party* (Irish Council for Civil Liberties 1988) 12 and Kevin McKeown and Robbie Gilligan, 'Child Sexual Abuse in the Eastern Health Board Region of Ireland in 1988: An Analysis of 512 Confirmed Cases' (1991) 22(2) *The Economic and Social Review* 101.

49 Fintan O'Toole, 'The Betrayal Of The Innocents', *Magill* (Dublin, July 1986).

a state response.[50] The language of "non-accidental injury" was replaced with the language of "child abuse". The 1987 Guidelines are also notable for making clear that all reports of child abuse should be investigated and that all suspicions of child sexual abuse should be reported to the Gardaí. The Ombudsman for Children later noted that the relationship between the Gardaí and other branches of the child protection network was somewhat neglected as there was "[n]o real guidance" given on how the relationship between Gardaí and other agencies was to work.[51] Nonetheless, the 1987 Guidelines envisaged a wider range of professionals as having a role in child protection work in contrast to the narrow emphasis on medical personnel seen in earlier iterations, while at the same time mirroring what was occurring in wider society – the recognition of child abuse, and child sexual abuse in particular, as a not uncommon risk in children's lives.

Child abuse and the development of the Child Care Act 1991

During this period, the need for significant legal change also became clear. The Children Act 1908 had been amended in earlier decades, but the various reports mentioned above highlighted the need for ever more far-reaching reform. The period between 1980 and 1991 has been characterised as a "period in waiting" where the law struggled to catch up with developments elsewhere in the child protection field, as the services sank into a state of apathy while waiting for reform.[52] Legal reform in child protection tends to occur slowly in the absence of crisis.[53] Nonetheless, there was a clear recognition that legal reform was essential.

Concerns over the constitutional propriety of the Health Boards' use of the "fit person" procedure under the 1908 Act were raised in the Dáil in 1978.[54] The Law Reform Commission issued recommendations in 1989 and 1990 that radical reform of the law was required, including the creation of a new offence of child sexual abuse, significant changes to the law of evidence, and the introduction of mandatory reporting of child abuse concerns.[55] The need for urgent action was demonstrated by the Supreme Court decision in *State (D and D) v Groarke*,[56] which clarified that the Health Boards had no power to act as a fit person under the 1908 Act. Emergency legislation granting the Health Boards proper legal

50 Department of Health, *Guidelines on Procedures for the Identification, Investigation and Management of Child Abuse* (Stationery Office 1987).

51 Ombudsman for Children, *A report based on an investigation into the implementation of Children First: National Guidelines for the Protection and Welfare of Children* (Stationery Office 2010) 88.

52 Skehill (n 3) 83.

53 For an example of an expeditious legal response to a child protection issue, see the comments in Chapter 8 about the Criminal Law (Sexual Offences) Act 2006.

54 Dáil Debates 28 June 1978, vol 307, col 2144, Jim O'Keeffe TD and Minister Charles Haughey TD.

55 Law Reform Commission, *Consultation Paper on Child Sexual Abuse* (LRC CP-2 1989), Law Reform Commission, *Report on Child Sexual Abuse* (LRC-32 1990).

56 [1990] 1 IR 305 (SC).

authority was introduced as the Children Act 1989. These developments came against the background of the broader reform initiatives contained in the Child Care and Protection Bill 1985 and its successor, the Child Care Bill 1988, both of which aimed to replace the 1908 Act.

Perhaps the most important shift to occur in this period was the recognition in political discourse that children could be, and for some organizations were, right-holders and agents. The shift in legal attitudes is illustrated in a 1979 paper on proposed changes to sexual offences legislation: commenting on the potential for removing the right of a parent to seek damages where an offence had been committed against the child, the Law Reform Commission stated that "the notion of a person recovering damages on the basis of a proprietary interest in another is now outdated."[57] The Commission expressly recommended in 1990 that children be given a right to be heard in care proceedings unless it would be inappropriate to do so.[58] Limited understanding of change in social attitudes can be drawn from the reports of a technical, specialist agency, or from the Task Force on Child Care's views; greater evidence of a wider attitudinal shift can be seen in an analysis of the Dáil debates on the 1985 Bill. In the opening statement, it was asserted that there was "greater acceptance that they have rights of their own."[59] Opposition TDs went further, arguing that while children did indeed have rights, it was

> urgent that we provide for a constitutional referendum to clearly set out the rights of children so as to ensure that where there is a conflict between the right of the child to have its welfare protected and the right of parents to have custody of their child, the right of the child to welfare and full development during childhood will take precedence over any parental right vested in parents under our Constitution.[60]

This approach was repeated in later years during subsequent debates.[61] While, as will be outlined in Chapter 6, constitutional change was not to occur until 2012, the above quotation represents a significant cultural shift in the perception of children. The realization that children did, and should, have constitutional rights, and that these rights needed to be strengthened in both constitutional law and statutory provisions relating to child protection was a radical break in legal discourse with the construction of children as mere objects of concern. However, the legislation emanating from these debates, the Child Care Act 1991, was required to take account of the contemporary constitutional provisions relating

57 Law Reform Commission, *The Law Relating to Seduction and the Enticement and Harbouring of a Child* (Working Paper No. 6 – 1979) 59.
58 Law Reform Commission, *Report* (n 55) 28.
59 Dáil Debates 30 May 1985, vol 359, col 65, Minister Barry Desmond TD.
60 Dáil Debates 5 June 1985, vol 359, col 472, Alan Shatter TD.
61 For example, Special Committee on Children (Child Care and Protection Bill 1985) 24 September 1986 and Dáil Debates 14 June 1988, vol 382, col 153, Mary Flaherty TD.

to the primacy of parental rights. It also took a series of major public scandals beginning with the Kilkenny Incest Inquiry for many of the recommendations of the Law Reform Commission and other agencies to be implemented beginning in the mid-2000s. It is important to first examine the 1991 Act to see, despite its limitations, quite how far it went in reconstructing children, the risks they faced and child protection work more generally.

The Child Care Act 1991

The Child Care Act 1991 introduced a range of "new and extensive responsibilities" on the state,[62] which were better suited to the needs of modern child care. Systematic changes to the legal powers available to those engaged in child protection work were introduced by the Act, such as new powers for taking children into care.[63] It was also supposed to mark a significant philosophical departure from the reactive model of child saving to one with a greater emphasis on child welfare. Both sections 3 and 24 of the Act outline that the welfare of the child is to be the "overriding concern" of Health Boards and courts.[64] This was said to imply "a shift from a reactive deployment of resources to a more proactive approach which aims to involve parents, children and carers and a desire to facilitate inter-agency collaboration".[65] The spirit of the legislation was summed up by Gilligan who contends that

> The Act is not some draconian charter that compels health boards to act coercively against families to which such children belong. Rather the human spirit of the legislation requires, for the first time, the state, through the agency of the health boards, to be alert and active in promoting the welfare of vulnerable children in society.[66]

The 1991 Act made some significant improvements to its predecessor. First, it covers all children up to 18 years of age.[67] This increases the protection afforded to older teenagers, as section 131 of the 1908 Act made a distinction between children and young people. The latter category covered teenagers between the ages of 15 and 17 and different care and protection regimes were utilised for these two groups. Now all children could avail of a universal system of protection.

62 Alan Shatter, *Family Law in Ireland* (4th edn, Butterworths 1997) 623.
63 See generally Part IV of the 1991 Act.
64 Geoffrey Shannon, *Child Law* (Round Hall 2005) 111.
65 Buckley, Skehill, O'Sullivan (n 5) 17. See also Harry Ferguson, 'Child Welfare, Child Protection and the Child Care Act 1991: Key Issues for Policy and Practice' in Harry Ferguson and Pat Kenny (eds), *On Behalf of the Child: Child Welfare, Child Protection and the Child Care Act 1991* (A & A Farmar 1995) 17–18.
66 Robbie Gilligan, 'The Child Care Act 1991: An examination of its scope and resource implications' (1992–1993) 40(4) *Administration* 347, 352.
67 Child Care Act 1991, s 2.

Second, the 1991 Act envisages a much greater role for the state in child protection. Whereas the 1908 Act created significant space within which the voluntary sector could, and indeed was expected to, function, the 1991 Act designated the state as the main providers of child protection services through the Health Boards, and later the Health Service Executive (HSE) and currently through the Child and Family Agency (CFA).[68] Finally, the 1991 Act envisages a greater role for cooperation and engagement with families. The 1991 Act itself envisages that alongside more traditional methods of intervention, the state may utilise family support in order to help prevent children coming into the care system. This supportive model was to be thought of as "an invaluable synthesizing term that challenges traditional welfare policies and accommodates the changing nature of families and their needs."[69]

The nature of the state's child protection duties

Welfare lies at the heart of the new obligations. Section 3 of the 1991 Act states that it is the function of the Health Boards to promote the welfare of children not receiving adequate care and protection. This includes taking steps to identify children not receiving adequate care and to coordinate information from all relevant sources relating to such children. This marks a significant philosophical divergence from the 1908 Act, in that it imposes clear obligations on the state rather than on the private or voluntary sectors. This function has been described as "broad-based" and "challenging".[70] These are apt descriptors because adequate care and protection is not defined in the legislation, and so it is clear that the extent of the Health Boards' task may be subjected to differing interpretations, by Health Boards, courts, parents, or children, as to what constitutes adequacy in the care and protection of vulnerable children. More fundamentally, when the 1991 Act was introduced, there were significant statutory and constitutional constraints imposed on child protection work.[71] The Health Boards must regard the welfare of the child as the first and paramount consideration,[72] but they must do so having regard to the rights and duties of parents and the principle that it is in the best interests of a child to be brought up in their own family.[73] These tensions are repeated later in the 1991 Act, in section 24, which refers to the need to have

68 The 1991 Act referred to Health Boards, which were abolished and replaced by the Health Services Executive (HSE) under the Health Act 2004, with the Child and Family Agency Act 2013 establishing a new body, the Child and Family Agency (CFA) with responsibility for child protection functions. Generally, this chapter will refer to the term in use at the time the legislation was initially passed, or when an incident occurred, unless otherwise necessary.

69 Helen Buckley, *Child Protection and Welfare: Innovations and Interventions* (Institute of Public Administration 2002) 8.

70 Ursula Kilkelly, *Children's Rights in Ireland: Law Policy and Practice* (Tottel Publishing 2008) 277–278.

71 Ibid 278.

72 Section 3(2)(b)(i).

73 Section 3(2)(b) and (c).

regard to the constitutional rights and duties of parents. Prior to the insertion in 2015 of the new Article 42A on children's rights into the Constitution,[74] there was a clear priority afforded to the interests of parents over those of children,[75] which created a very high threshold for intervention in family life, and led to the prioritization of child protection work over child welfare work.[76] While case law since the enactment of these constitutional changes has clarified that children's interests do indeed take priority,[77] the making of orders is still described as an "exceptional" measure made when "truly necessary" and is limited by the requirements of proportionality.[78]

In order to do this, the state was given the function of ensuring the welfare of vulnerable children. In practical legal terms, section 2 of the 1991 Act is significant. As mentioned above, section 3 states that it is the Health Boards' function to promote the welfare of children. Although the word "function" is used instead of duty in section 3, section 2 of the 1991 Act defines "function" as including "powers and duties", and so this carries with it the public law implications, meaning that failure to fulfil the statutory function could be enforced by way of judicial review.[79] This means that the state, through the Boards, is "not merely entitled but obliged to provide … protection" to children who lack adequate care.[80] The extent of the duty imposed on the state is quite wide-ranging; with the exception of the injunction with regard to parental rights, there is little guidance given in the legislation on how the duty is to be discharged, save for stating that in order to carry out this function, it shall "take such steps as it considers requisite to identify children who are not receiving adequate care and protection and co-ordinate information from all relevant sources relating to children in its area",[81] as well as providing "child care and family support services".[82] This was the first time that such actions were seen as being legitimate state functions. It seemed to allow for active participation by the state in child welfare and family support.

Courts have pronounced on the nature of the duty in a limited number of cases. In *Eastern Health Board v E (No 1)*[83] Laffoy J briefly considered the role of the applicant in preventing a private adoption. Since the passing of section 7 of the

74 The new Article 42A became part of the Constitution after the signing of the Thirty-First Amendment to the Constitution Act by the President on 28 April 2015, following a referendum in 2012.
75 For greater detail on this issue, see Chapter 6.
76 Ferguson (n 65).
77 See, for example, *Child and Family Agency v SMcG and JC* [2017] IESC 9.
78 *Child and Family Agency v LH* [2017] IEDC 17.
79 Kilkelly (n 70) 278 citing *Paul Stephens v Eastern Health Board*, 24 July 1994 (HC). See further, Paul Ward, *The Child Care Acts: Annotated and Consolidated* (3rd edn, Round Hall 2014) 18–19.
80 Shannon (n 64) 230.
81 Section 3(2)(a), Child Care Act 1991.
82 Section 3(3), Child Care Act 1991.
83 [2000] 1 IR 430 (HC).

Adoption Act 1998, it had been illegal to place a child for adoption without utilising official state procedures. Laffoy J considered that if such an event occurred, the welfare of the child concerned could be compromised and it therefore fell to the child protection services in discharging their duties under section 3 of the 1991 Act to seek to negative such a placement.[84] *Comerford v Minister for Education* saw McGuinness J address issues relating to the education of a child with behavioural difficulties.[85] It was noted, however, that many of these difficulties stemmed directly from neglect he suffered at home. McGuinness J noted that when discharging section 3 duties, the child protection services may have staged intervention earlier in order to prevent these difficulties arising but that the "extremely strong rights given to parents and the family in the Constitution and the comparative lack of express constitutional rights for the child as against the parents" at the time compromised their ability to fulfil these duties.[86]

The orders available under the Act

The Child Care Act allows for a wide variety of orders to be made by courts in order to safeguard the welfare of children. It is the role of the Health Boards to apply for these orders if the making of an order would ensure the welfare of the child. Section 16 states that

> Where it appears to a health board with respect to a child who resides or is found in its area that he requires care or protection which he is unlikely to receive unless a court makes a care order or a supervision order in respect of him, it shall be the duty of the health board to make application for a care order or a supervision order, as it thinks fit.

First, it is a duty for the particular Health Board to apply for an order in the specified circumstances. It "shall" apply for an order, emphasising the mandatory nature of such an obligation. The only discretion vested in the Health Board lies in determining which order it seeks. However, as mentioned within the discussion of section 3 and the decision in *Comerford v Minister for Education*,[87] it is incumbent on the Health Board to bear parental rights in mind when making such a decision. Given the strong constitutional presumption in favour of parental rights which existed until 2015, the decision to seek an order under the 1991 Act, and a care order in particular, requires careful justification. Shannon points out that "the [Board] should look at all other options which maintain the family relationship while still protecting the rights of the child."[88]

84 Ibid 449.
85 [1997] 2 ILRM 134 (HC).
86 Ibid 145.
87 Ibid.
88 Shannon (n 64) 245.

The extent of the duty imposed by section 16 was not considered until the 2010 judgment in *CLT v Health Service Executive*.[89] The applicant was the grandmother of the child at the centre of the proceedings and sought to compel the Health Board's successor, the HSE, to begin care proceedings under the 1991 Act. She claimed that the child's mother was unstable and was being influenced by the child's natural father, who was known to have drug problems and a series of criminal convictions which resulted in custodial sentences and who had recently recommenced his relationship with the child's mother. The HSE sought to resist the application on the basis that it had conducted an investigation and saw no reason to begin any formal care proceedings, due to the fact that the applicant was caring for the child and there was no serious cause for concern.

The court reasoned that the wording of section 16 of the 1991 Act made clear that it was the duty of the HSE to apply for either a care order or supervision order if it appeared that the child was unlikely to receive adequate care and protection in the absence of such an order.[90] Given that the grandmother had no legal rights in relation to the child, she would be powerless to prevent the mother from seeking to regain care and custody rights if she wished.[91] More importantly, the court reasoned that the HSE had paid inadequate attention to the risk that the child's natural father becoming involved posed to her welfare. In the event that the child's natural parents did seek the return of the child to their custody, the court saw the potential for "high risk of serious damage to the child."[92] Whilst cognisant of the difficulties that commencing care proceedings may present, McMahon J was adamant that for the HSE "not to act is to risk too much".[93]

This judgment is novel in its understanding of future risk, as previous court judgments had simply not considered risk as thoroughly. The Court reasoned that in order to fulfil its duties under section 3, it was necessary for the HSE to utilise a more risk-orientated approach in their deliberations over whether to institute care proceedings than had previously been the case. It would also appear to be an attempt to manage the risks faced by a particular child, and also the organizational risks of potentially ineffective child protection work. In this sense, it seems to be a consciously reflexive judgment, designed to assist the future direction of an individual child's life chances and the manner in which services respond to risky situations. The approach of *CTL* was reinforced in the decision of *Child and Family Agency v OA* which spoke of section 16 imposing a duty to institute proceedings where it is apparent that a child requires care and protection on the basis that the Act "imposes a precautionary principle of protection."[94]

89 [2011] 3 IR 29, [2010] IEHC 467.
90 Ibid [7].
91 Ibid [9].
92 Ibid [11].
93 Ibid.
94 *Child and Family Agency v OA* [2015] IESC 52, [6].

The 1991 Act radically reformed the options available to those engaged in child protection social work. Voluntary care was placed on a statutory basis by section 4 of the Act, ensuring that parents can voluntarily place a child in the care of the state without the need for a full care order being made, and placing an obligation on the state to take the child into its care where it is unlikely to receive care and protection unless admitted to voluntary care. There is also a duty on the Health Board to maintain the child in its care for as long as required and to have regard to the wishes of any parent having custody of the child or any other person acting in loco parentis.[95] The Act also caters for emergency situations. Section 12 allows the Gardaí to remove, without warrant, a child where there are reasonable grounds for believing that there is an immediate and serious risk to the health or welfare of a child, and where seeking an emergency care order would be insufficient to protect the child's welfare given the immediacy of the risks they face. This is a power that is to be exercised in only the most extreme cases, with Nestor going so far as to state that "it must really be a matter of life and death."[96] Section 13 provides for emergency care orders. If the health or welfare of a child faces immediate and serious risk, the Health Board may apply for an emergency care order. These may last for a maximum of up to eight days. If a child is removed from their home under section 12, then they must either be released back into the custody of their parents or an emergency care order must be sought. As releasing a child back to their parents would raise the question of why they were removed in the first place,[97] it follows that while all section 12 actions should be followed by an emergency care order application, it is not a necessary prerequisite to such an application that the Gardaí have intervened under section 12.[98]

Part IV allows the HSE to apply for a variety of orders – care orders under section 18, interim care orders under section 17 and supervision orders under section 19. Shannon has argued that it is "notable in that it not only empowers but rather obliges" an application for a care order or a supervision order if a child is in need of care and protection,[99] a view confirmed in *CTL v HSE*.[100] Section 18 allows a care order to be made in respect of a child in circumstances where:

(a) the child has been or is being assaulted, ill-treated, neglected or sexually abused, or
(b) the child's health, development or welfare has been or is being avoidably impaired or neglected, or

95 Section 4(3).
96 Jim Nestor, *Law of Child Care* (2nd edn, Blackhall Publishing 2009) 156.
97 Kilkelly (n 70) 292.
98 Shannon (n 64) 237–245 outlines some of the procedural requirements in emergency situations, including differences between the procedures under sections 12 and 13.
99 Ibid 247. See also *Bedford County Council v M; A v Child and Family Agency* [2017] IEHC 583, [116]–[123].
100 *CTL* (n 89).

(c) the child's health, development or welfare is likely to be avoidably impaired or neglected.

In addition to these criteria, the court must also be satisfied that the child is unlikely to receive adequate care and protection if the order is not made. In addition to being satisfied that a threshold requirement has been met, the court must be satisfied that any harm suffered by a child is attributable to care given by the child's parents.[101] The 1991 Act leaves it open to the court to make a finding that state intervention is required to protect the welfare of the child on the basis of historic evidence of past harm, the presence of ongoing abuse, or the risk that some harm is likely to occur in the future.[102] Section 17 permits the court to make an interim care order. This order can be made where the requirements for a care order are met but it can only be used as a "short-term and temporary measure".[103] This is made clear by section 17(2)(a) which stipulates that the order may last for a maximum of 28 days, although this period may be extended by court order or consent of the parties. This is because the court must be satisfied that an application for a care order has been or is about to be made in respect of the child. While this would indicate that an interim care order can be used in situations where the Health Board does not have time to apply for a full care order, the relationship between interim care orders, care orders and the emergency provisions of sections 12 and 13 needs to be outlined. If an interim order is to be made, the court must have "reasonable cause" that the evidence warrants such an order.

However, for a full care order, the court must "be satisfied" of the necessity of the order. This indicates that the evidential threshold that the Health Board needs to meet is significantly lower for interim care orders than it is for a full care order.[104] However, if there is an immediate danger to a child, then the appropriate course of action would likely be to apply for an emergency care order under section 13. While the court needs to be satisfied to the higher standard of "reasonable cause" for this order, it must be remembered that it is specifically designed for emergency situations.[105]

In certain cases, a child's welfare may not be best served by removing them from the home without alternatives being explored by the Health Board and indeed by their parents. It is in these circumstances that the supervision order, provided for in section 19 of the Act, may be most useful. This order allows the Health Board to visit the child's home as it appears necessary to do so in order to monitor the level of care and protection being provided for the child by their carers. In essence, the supervision order creates visitation and monitoring rights for

101 Nestor (n 96) 166–167.
102 Kilkelly (n 70) 295.
103 Ibid 302.
104 Ibid.
105 See for example, the discussion of the procedural requirements for section 13 applications in Ward (n 79) 43–49.

the Health Board and empowers them to work with families to achieve increased welfare for their children. Shannon is of the view that the knowledge that the state is keeping an eye on them will perhaps prompt certain families to engage positively with the Health Board, or that the Health Board will find their initial fears to be unfounded.[106]

However, such positive outcomes are entirely contingent upon the family concerned cooperating with the Health Board and seeing their involvement as beneficial. If the family object to involvement, seeing it instead as interference, any attempt to impose the Health Board's views will be futile. This led one commentator to the conclusion that the supervision order is an "unusual way of providing assistance to such families",[107] given that breaching the terms of a supervision order carries the threat of criminal sanction, thereby making reluctant families even more reluctant to engage. It had been thought that a court could impose certain obligations on parents, such as a duty to undergo assessments, under the authority of a supervision order. However, it has been held that the supervision order does not allow the imposition of obligations such as these, as the section can only be used to mandate the examination of the child.[108] The same is true of the court's jurisdiction under section 47 which, despite being widely drafted so as to enable the court to give directions relating to the welfare of the child, cannot be used to impose personal obligations on third parties.[109]

The duty to share information

One specific aspect of the Act has radically impacted on the development of cooperation structures and information-sharing processes. While section 3(1) outlines the general function to promote the welfare of children, the following subsection contains the cooperation clause, which details that the Health Board "shall take such steps as it considers requisite to identify children who are not receiving adequate care and protection and co-ordinate information from all relevant sources relating to children in its area."[110] This was the first time that a legal basis had been given for information sharing, which previously had existed only as an administrative practice. Further, the Act was clear in stipulating that it "shall" be a function to co-ordinate information relating to child protection issues. This means that it is mandatory to identify children at risk, and ensure that information relevant to those children is collated from all relevant professionals and other sources and that it is shared among the appropriate bodies.

106 Shannon (n 64) 258–259.
107 Kilkelly (n 70) 301.
108 *JG v Judge Staunton* [2013] IEHC 533, [2014] 1 IR 390 (HC).
109 Ibid, and see also the decision in *NK v SK* [2017] IECA 1 which clarifies that section 11 of the Guardianship of Infants Act 1964 also cannot be read in so expansive a fashion.
110 Child Care Act 1991, s 3(2) (a).

While child protection agencies enjoy discretion in how they discharge this function and are only required to take such steps as they consider necessary, section 3(2) would seem to imply that the Health Board should play a lead role in coordinating information gathered from a variety of agencies which would allow a proper assessment of a child's needs to be made. This point was only briefly referred to in Dáil debates on the Act. The provision was not included in the original Bill but was proposed as an amendment by the Opposition. The attitude towards the cooperation clause is best illustrated by the speech of Deputy Yates introducing the amendment when he stated that

> We have already referred to the different roles of the Departments of Justice and Education and I feel as a minimum there should be an obligation on the health board to have up to date information of the children's needs within an area, be they recreational, related to housing or crime, or whatever. There is a need to co-ordinate all the relevant information.[111]

Although this specifically mentions the coordination of information gathered by different government departments, a wider interpretation of the extent of the Health Board's coordinating responsibilities is given in a later speech by the same deputy when he spoke of "the lack of co-ordination between school attendance officers, juvenile liaison officers and voluntary organizations such as the ISPCC who run the Childline service."[112] He then went on to mention members of the general public as holders of information about children at risk which should be considered by the Health Board. Curiously, this coordinating function was described in the same speech as "not a major issue", indicating that the coordination clause was regarded merely as a housekeeping matter introduced to encourage best practice rather than something to be taken very seriously.[113] The proposal was met with limited opposition. Deputy Coughlan drew on her own experience as a social worker to point out that social workers themselves always took on the job of gathering relevant information from a variety of sources.[114]

The significance of the cooperation clause was keenly felt by child care practitioners. Gilligan posited that section 3(2)(a)

> seems to require health boards to establish structures for bilateral and multilateral consultation and communication with other relevant sources … the Act would seem to imply a requirement on each health board to establish formal channels of communication with each of the following: schools, An Garda Síochána, the Department of Justice Probation and Welfare Service, youth services, housing authorities.[115]

111 Dáil Debates 1 November 1989, vol 392, col 1248, Ivan Yates TD.
112 Dáil Debates 11 December 1990, vol 403, col 1761, Ivan Yates TD.
113 Ibid.
114 Ibid, col 1761–1762.
115 Gilligan (n 66) 353.

Although the Act does not speak in such specific terms and despite the limited attention paid to the matter in the Oireachtas,[116] it would appear that Gilligan's analysis is correct. In order for the Health Board to properly coordinate information from the variety of agencies involved, proper protocols would have to be in place as it is impossible to ensure that all relevant information is gathered and disseminated in a systematic fashion without such a protocol in place. Information-sharing had now been given a clear statutory basis and was to become one of the main characteristics of child protection work. The following chapter will examine the development of the case law examining the extent of the section 3 duty as well as the legislative responses to the increasing importance of information in working with risk in child protection.

Conclusion

This chapter has traced the evolution of political and legal attitudes during a significant period of reform that showed the early signs of late modernity. The early decades of Ireland's self-governance, examined in the previous chapter, saw children regarded at times as threats to be controlled and disciplined, but also as victims whose interests required recognition and concern from the state. The material analysed in this chapter demonstrates the early stages of change within the political and social order, and especially the role of individualization, as children were being recognised as agents. This period also saw the beginning of new approaches to risk being used in an institutionally reflexive manner. Reforms in social work practice, as well as the legal framework, were increasingly predicated on the belief that children had rights. With respect to the risks children faced, moralistic and religious concerns for children disappeared from the discourse, to be replaced by a more scientific approach, and new concern with sexual abuse in particular. These risks were no longer sees as being eliminated through punishment or institutionalization, but reduced through information management and coordination. The next chapter will see the culmination of this process. Knowledge of child abuse scandals became part of the social fabric, and helped to drive the process whereby children finally became subjects, and risk management came to dominate the legal and social work approaches to child abuse.

References

Arnold B, 'Still missing full story behind children "shovelled into schools" *Irish Independent* (Dublin, 21 May 2009).

116 It should be noted that although the matter received only one mention in the Seanad, where it was described as a "fine platitude which nobody would oppose" by Senator O'Reilly, who then spoke about the difficulty of adequately funding such coordination when the health boards were already under-resourced: Seanad Debates 21 February 1991, vol 127, cols 1581–1582, Senator Joe O'Reilly.

Buckley H, Skehill C and O'Sullivan E, *Child Protection Practices in Ireland: A Case Study* (Oak Tree Press 1997).

Buckley H, Skehill C and O'Sullivan E, *Child Protection and Welfare: Innovations and Interventions* (Institute of Public Administration 2002).

CARE, *Children Deprived: CARE Memorandum* (CARE 1972).

Commission to Inquire into Child Abuse (CICA), *Report of the Commission to Inquire into Child Abuse, Volume IV: Residential Child Welfare in Ireland, 1965–2008: An Outline of Policy, Legislation and Practice: A Paper Prepared for the Commission to Inquire Into Child Abuse* (Stationery Office 2009).

Delap C and Kelleher T, 'Local Authority Social Work in Ireland: Origins, Issues and Developments' in Noreen Kearney and Caroline Skehill (eds), *Social Work in Ireland: Historical Perspectives* (Institute of Public Administration 2005).

Department of Health, *Report of the Committee on Non-Accidental Injury to Children* (Stationery Office 1976).

Department of Health, *Memorandum on Non-Accidental Injury to Children* (Stationery Office 1977).

Department of Health, *Guidelines on the Identification and Management of Non-Accidental Injury to Children* (Stationery Office 1980).

Department of Health, *Guidelines on Procedures for Identification and Investigation on Non-Accidental Injury to Children* (Stationery Office 1983).

Department of Health, *Guidelines on Procedures for the Identification, Investigation and Management of Child Abuse* (Stationery Office 1987).

Ferguson H, 'Child Welfare, Child Protection and the Child Care Act 1991: Key Issues for Policy and Practice' in Harry Ferguson and Pat Kenny (eds), *On Behalf of the Child: Child Welfare, Child Protection and the Child Care Act 1991* (A & A Farmer 1995).

Ferguson H, 'Protecting Irish Children in Time: Child Abuse as a Social Problem and the Development of the Child Protection System in the Republic of Ireland' (1996) 44(2) *Administration* 5.

Ferguson H, 'Child Abuse as a Social Problem in Post Traditional Ireland' in CN McElwee (ed), *Irish Society: A Reader in Applied Social Studies* (StreetSmart Press 1997).

Ferriter D, *The Transformation of Ireland 1900–2000* (Profile Books 2005).

Fitton VA, 'Attachment Theory: History, Research, and Practice' (2012) 19(1–2) *Psychoanalytic Social Work* 121.

Giddens A, *Modernity and Self-Identity: Self and Society in the Late Modern Age* (Polity Press 1991).

Gilligan R, 'Policy in the Republic of Ireland: Historical and Current Issues in Child Care' in Pam Carter, Tony Jeffs and Mark Smith (eds), *Social Work and Social Welfare Yearbook 1* (Open University Press 1989).

Gilligan R, 'The Child Care Act 1991: An Examination of Its Scope and Resource Implications' (1992–1993) 40(4) *Administration* 347.

Greene D, 'Legal Aspects of Non-accidental Injury to Children' (1979) 27(4) *Administration* 460.

Irish Council of Civil Liberties, *Report of the Child Sexual Abuse Working Party* (Irish Council for Civil Liberties 1988).

Keating A, 'A Contested Legacy: The Kennedy Committee Revisited' (2014) 22(3) *Irish Studies Review* 304.

Kempe H et al, 'The Battered Child Syndrome' (1962) 181 *Journal of the American Medical Association* 17.
Kennedy E, *Reform and Industrial Schools System Report* (Stationery Office 1970).
Kilkelly U, *Children's Rights in Ireland: Law Policy and Practice* (Tottel Publishing 2008).
Lavan A, 'Social Work in Ireland' in Steven Shardlow and Malcolm Payne (eds), *Contemporary Issues in Social Work – Western Europe* (Arena 1998).
Law Reform Commission, *The Law Relating to Seduction and the Enticement and Harbouring of a Child* (Working Paper No. 6 – 1979).
Law Reform Commission, *Consultation Paper on Child Sexual Abuse* (LRC CP-2 1989).
Law Reform Commission, *Report on Child Sexual Abuse* (LRC-32 1990).
McGuinness C, *Report of the Kilkenny Incest Investigation* (Stationary Office 1993).
McKeown K and Gilligan R, 'Child Sexual Abuse in the Eastern Health Board Region of Ireland in 1988: An Analysis of 512 Confirmed Cases' (1991) 22(2) *The Economic and Social Review* 101.
Nestor J, *Law of Child Care* (2nd edn, Blackhall Publishing 2009).
O'Sullivan D, 'Social Definition in Child Care in the Irish Republic: Model of the Child and Child-care Intervention' (1979) 10(3) *Economic and Social Review* 309.
O'Toole F, 'The betrayal of the innocents', *Magill* (July 1986).
Ombudsman for Children, *A Report Based on an Investigation Into the Implementation of Children First: National Guidelines for the Protection and Welfare of Children* (Stationery Office 2010).
Shannon G, *Child Law* (Round Hall 2005).
Shatter A, *Family Law in Ireland* (4th edn, Butterworth 1997).
Skehill C, *History of the Present of Child Protection and Welfare Social Work in Ireland* (Edwin Mellin 2004).
Smart C, 'A History of Ambivalence and Conflict in the Discursive Construction of the 'Child Victim' of Sexual Abuse' (1999) 8(3) *Social and Legal Studies* 391.
Task Force on Child Care Services, *Final Report* (Stationery Office 1980).
Tuairim, *Some of Our Children – A Report on the Residential Care of the Deprived Child in Ireland* (Pamphlet No 13, Tuairim 1966).
Ward P, *The Child Care Acts: Annotated and Consolidated* (3rd edn, Round Hall 2014).

6 Children's rights and constitutional change

Introduction

Irish constitutional law was revolutionised during the 1990s. The courts had to balance competing interests in cases dealing with the beginning and ending of life, referenda were held on divisive social issues like divorce and abortion, and issues involving constitutional questions were extensively litigated by citizens dealing with an increasingly complex regulatory system. As the post-independence landscape against which the Constitution was drafted receded from living memory to written history and the interpretative upheavals of the 1960s and 1970s on fundamental rights questions produced established doctrine, the courts were faced with the problem of applying a foundational document rooted in simple modernity, but onto which new principles had been grafted, in an increasingly reflexive era.

This chapter explores the ways in which the relationship between children, their families and the state was thought about during this more reflexive period of constitutional law. Taking the publication of the Kilkenny Report as its departure point, it first examines how the courts handled children's issues. It does so by examining the extension of children's rights to include new concepts such as participation, the problem space that arises between the rights of children and parents when questions of parental misconduct arise, and finally the rights of particularly vulnerable children. In doing so, the limitations of the existing constitutional framework will become clear. The political reactions to the question of constitutional reform will then be examined. Several committees examined the question, beginning in 1996, before a referendum was eventually passed in 2012 which inserted the new Article 42A into the Constitution. The new provision has generated some case law, which will be briefly examined before the chapter concludes.

The Constitution, children and the courts, 1993–2006

The Report of the Kilkenny Inquiry, published in 1993, led to the first sustained examination of the place of children within the constitutional order since the brief consideration of this issue in the late 1970s.[1] This Inquiry, chaired by Judge Catherine McGuinness, was established following revelations of physical and sexual abuse of a woman by her father over the course of 13 years. The abuse had come to the attention of the child protection professionals, but knowledge of the abuse was not acted upon. The reaction to this report was critical in helping Irish legal and social policy towards children to transition from simple to late modernity. The Report itself recognised that children were largely absent from the constitutional text, that the case law interpreting the relevant constitutional provisions seemed to place a premium on parental interests, and it was, therefore, important to incorporate children's rights into the Constitution. In the course of the report, McGuinness argued that "the very high emphasis on the rights of the family in the Constitution may consciously or unconsciously be interpreted as giving a higher value to the right of parents than to the rights of children" and went on to recommend the amendment of the Constitution to include "a specific and overt declaration of the rights of born children".[2] The existing constitutional basis for state intervention in family life, outlined in Article 42.5, was coming to be seen as a "very narrowly drawn provision"[3] which established that even in cases warranting state intervention, parental rights were often seen having as a higher priority due to the need to protect the authority and autonomy of the family. As such, the Kilkenny Inquiry Report shows how Ireland, and its legal system, were deeply rooted in simple modernity. Tradition and hierarchy grounded the constitutional provisions relating to children and families, and crucially, how they were worked with. There was no realistic possibility for children to be recognised as agents in a meaningful way, let alone that they could be thought of as holding meaningful rights.

In the post-Kilkenny era, marked by the emergence of reflexive modernity, the rights of children have taken on a more prominent role in both legal and political discourse. However, the developments within that period should not be thought of as the unchecked progress of children's rights-based thinking to the pinnacle of the constitutional value system. There remains a somewhat ambivalent construction of children within constitutional law. While a 'children's rights' amendment has been passed by referendum, a pervasive uncertainty remains over how constitutional law thinks about children. This ambiguity about the potential for dissolving traditional notions of familial autonomy in favour of a concept of the family, and child protection, more grounded in ideas like agency and rights is representative of the shift to reflexive modernity. Troubling knowledge about abuse within the family now had to be worked with. The embedding of individuals within a traditional social role

1 Catherine McGuinness, *The Kilkenny Incest Investigation: Report Presented to Mr Brendan Howlin TD, Minister for Health by South Eastern Health Board* (Stationery Office 1993). The report and the ensuing controversies will be deal with in detail in Chapter 7.

2 Ibid 96.

3 Ursula Kilkelly, *Children's Rights in Ireland: Law, Policy and Practice* (Tottel Publishing 2008) 61.

based on received ideas of family life would no longer be tenable. The uncertainty and anxiety that flow through late modernity were now becoming part of the constitutional framework.

Establishing new children's rights

In 1980, the decision in *G v An Bord Uchtála* established that children have a range of rights including the right "to be fed and to live, to be reared and educated, to have the opportunity of working and of realising his or her full personality and dignity as a human being".[4] In that case, Walsh J made clear that there is nothing in the Constitution to indicate that the rights of parents were always to be given supremacy over children's rights.[5] Several decisions from the post-Kilkenny era took up the idea that children's rights could not only be found in the Constitution, but that they could rank equal to those of parents. In the 1996 decision of *Southern Health Board v CH*,[6] O'Flaherty J was of the view that

> It is easy to comprehend that the child's welfare must always be of far greater concern to the court [than the procedural rights of the father in a dispute about the admissibility of hearsay evidence]. We must, as judges, always harken to the constitutional command which mandates, as the prime consideration, the interests of the child in any legal proceedings.7

Such a statement would have been unlikely without the earlier statement of Walsh J in *G v An Bord Uchtála* that nothing demands that parental rights are to be placed above those of children. Yet this view of children's rights as trumping the rights of parents would appear to have been at odds with the constitutional text. Even comparing the language of Articles 40, 41 and 42 reveals a disparity weighted in favour of parents. As outlined in Chapter 3, parents are given rights by Articles 41 and 42 which are described as being inalienable and imprescriptible, and as occupying a space which is antecedent and superior to all positive law. On the other hand, children's rights are described as inalienable according to Article 42.5 and the state is obliged to respect and defend them only as far as practicable by Article 40.3.[8] O'Flaherty J was engaging in an expansive reading of Article 40.3, as it appears that he has found a version of the paramountcy principle within the Article, which principle states that that in all decision affecting a child, their welfare or best interests should be the paramount consideration in the mind of the decision-maker.

4 *G v An Bord Uchtála* [1980] IR 32 (SC) 56, per O'Higgins CJ.
5 Ibid 78.
6 [1996] 1 IR 231 (SC).
7 Ibid 238.
8 See the literature on unenumerated rights generally cited in Chapter 3.

This expansive reading of the Constitution was followed by Finlay Geoghegan J in the 2004 decision of *FN v CO*.[9] A dispute had arisen between the father of two teenage girls and their maternal grandparents. The grandparents sought guardianship, and so the question arose as to whether this would be in the girls' best interests. Finlay Geoghegan J held that she was statutorily bound by section 3 of the Guardianship of Infants Act 1964 to consider the child's welfare as the first and paramount consideration. She also considered section 25 of the 1964 Act which requires that a child's wishes be taken into account if the court thinks this appropriate considering the age and understanding of the child. The decision saw the entrenchment of the idea that a child's welfare must be considered paramount as a child's constitutional right. The court stated that

> The right of a child to have decisions in relation to guardianship, custody or upbringing, taken in the interests of his/her welfare is a personal right of the child within the meaning of Article 40.3 and therefore one which the State pledges to vindicate as far as practicable.[10]

It was further held that Article 40.3 contains the right to have a decision made in accordance with the principles of constitutional justice, including the right to have one's wishes taken into account.[11] Participation rights were given a wide interpretation in *Z v Y*.[12] The case concerned the parentage of a girl who was nearly 16 years old, and the putative father was seeking to have her birth re-registered so as to reflect the fact of his paternity. The question arose as to whether the girl concerned was entitled to be informed of the proceedings to re-register her birth. Laffoy J ruled that, in line with the decision in *FN v CO*,[13] the child had a right to fair procedures, which includes the right to be informed of proceedings of fundamental importance affecting her.[14]

These cases clearly indicate that children did have some rights under the Constitution and that the language of certain provisions could be read expansively so that "new" rights could be discovered within the text, or to allow for the extension of existing rights to cover novel situations. As such, they can be read as indicating a newfound rights consciousness among the judiciary. However, this would, first, overstate the matter, due to the relative positioning of children's and parents' interests in the constitutional system. Second, and in light of the

9 [2004] 4 IR 311 (HC). The same judge applied Article 40.3 to another decision affecting children in *Bode v Minister for Justice, Equality and Law Reform* [2006] IEHC 341. Although the substantive judgment was overturned by the Supreme Court, Kilkelly (n 3) 64 states that Denham J did not seem to disagree with the applicability of this constitutional provision to children's rights.

10 Ibid 323.

11 Ibid 322.

12 [2008] IEHC 472.

13 *FN* (n 9)

14 *Z v Y* (n 12) 6.

foregoing point, it does not fully counter the objection raised by the Kilkenny Report that children are effectively invisible within the Constitution. Children could not, following these cases, be properly regarded as rights-bearing subjects in the same way as adults.

The Supreme Court and family intervention

During the 1985 case of *Re JH*, the Supreme Court clearly articulated a presumption that the welfare of a child would be best met by its parents. The balancing of parents' and children's interests nonetheless continued to be problematic, as this presumption clashed with the reality of children experiencing family difficulties, or subject to unwise parental decision-making. The former situation was considered in *Western Health Board v M*,[15] where McGuinness J made clear that in the course of proceedings under the Child Care Act 1991, both the child care authorities and the District Court are "enjoined to observe at all times the paramountcy of the welfare of the child."[16] However, the judgment also warns of the need to consider parental rights, and that any court making a decision on the welfare of a child must consider the constitutional rights of both child and parents.[17] The judgment is carefully phrased and represents an attempt to attain a workable balance between the rights of parents and children. In its decision on the facts, which concerned the foster placement of a child outside the jurisdiction which was opposed by the child's unmarried mother, the welfare of the child was prioritised. However, the fact that the mother was unmarried meant that the presumptions relating to married parents were not canvassed, despite unmarried mothers deriving rights under Article 40.3.[18]

The problem of the interests of children in married families was considered in the Supreme Court judgments of *North Western Health Board v HW and CW*[19] and *N v Health Service Executive*.[20] Each of these decisions builds on the constitutional presumption relating to children's welfare outlined in *Re JH*, arguing that children's rights are recognised and protected within the Constitution, but that children's limited capacities mean that others must act on their behalf. Rather than placing the rights of parents above those of children, these decisions claim the Constitution instead prefers parents, rather than third parties such as social workers, as those responsible for implementing and protecting those rights. Nonetheless, it is difficult to argue against the idea that these two judgments saw children's rights in a more instrumental fashion than had been seen for some time, as in both cases, children's rights were used by the Supreme Court to uphold the

15 [2002] 2 IR 493 (SC).
16 Ibid 507.
17 Ibid 512–513.
18 *State (Nicolaou) v An Bord Uchtála* [1966] IR 567 (SC).
19 *North Western Health Board* [2001] 3 IR 365 (SC).
20 [2006] 4 IR 374.

idea of the integrity of the married family. These judgments, therefore, create significant problems for the ideas of children's agency within constitutional law.

The *North Western Health Board* case related to parental refusal to allow their child to undergo a standard diagnostic procedure known as a PKU test, which involved taking a small sample of blood from a pinprick in a baby's heel. Failure to identify the illness tested for by the PKU test can have serious repercussions for the child, potentially leading to brain damage. The Health Board's argument that the parents were failing in their duty towards the child did not succeed. This was partly due to Hardiman J's assertion that, as the parents took a decision that they believed was in the child's best interests, no failure of duty could be said to have occurred.[21] In other words, there was no objective yardstick against which the parents' decision could be measured. Further, Hardiman J's judgment sought to preclude any kind of intervention in the family falling short of supplanting the place of parents, as this would not properly respect the Constitution or the authority of the family.[22] This effectively cast the shadow of unconstitutionality over less onerous child protection measures such as family support mechanisms. This view appears to be supported by the views expressed by Murray J who held that the threshold for intervention under Article 42.5 would be reached when there existed

> some immediate and fundamental threat to the capacity of the child to continue to function as a human person, physically, morally or socially, deriving from an exceptional dereliction of duty on the parts of parents to justify such an intervention.[23]

The presumption that parents always act in a child's interests was treated more fully in the *N* case. In this case, a child had been placed for adoption by her unmarried parents shortly after her birth. She was placed with a family and had grown attached to them. In the meantime, her natural parents married and sought the return of their daughter, some two years after she had been placed with her prospective adoptive family. The case represented a clash between the birth parents' right to care for their child and the child's right not to have her welfare endangered by removing her from the only family she had known. The Supreme Court unanimously decided that the child had to be returned to the custody of her birth parents. McGuinness J described the test for determining that parents had failed in their duties to such an extent that there were compelling reasons for intervention as "so exacting it would be difficult to see it being met other than in the most extreme circumstances."[24] Hardiman J posited that there must be compelling reasons by which the welfare cannot be achieved in the

21 *North Western Health Board* (n 19) 757.
22 Ibid 758.
23 Ibid 741.
24 *N v HSE* (n 20) 496.

constitutional family,[25] thereby rendering it virtually impossible to satisfy the test. In doing so, he adopted a highly adult-centred approach to questions of child welfare. According to his judgment, the case did not present a question of a clash of rights within a family but was instead about a clash between the family and outsiders. In framing the matter in this way, he stated that: "[t]he Constitution does not prefer parents to children. The preference the Constitution gives is this: it prefers parents to third parties, official or private, priest or social worker."[26]

Hardiman J's decision, therefore, instrumentally aligns parents and children.[27] On the instrumentalist view, there can be no clash of rights because parents exercise their children's rights on their behalf. He held that, because children lack agency, in philosophical and legal terms, their rights need to be exercised by some other person acting in order to secure their rights. The Constitution, Hardiman J argued, chooses parents to perform this task, and preference is given to natural parents, given their biological bond with the child. The "millennia of experience of mankind" and the Book of Kings are cited as authority for the correctness of the Constitutional faith in parents.[28] Children's position in the constitutional order would seem, contrary to the assertions of Hardiman J, to be below that of their parents. Not only that, but children's agency is denied by the decisions in *North Western Health Board* and *N*. While the cases themselves concerned very young children whose capacities would have been limited, there is little in either judgment which recognises the potential for any child to exercise agency. The children's views or interests were not separately represented to the court; children are seen in both judgments as being subject to parental authority save in the most extreme cases when it is for the state to intervene by supplanting the place of the parents.[29]

Children at risk and the Constitution

Children at risk have presented the courts with some difficult legal questions, including what rights these children have, what remedies are constitutionally permissible in order to vindicate these rights and, at a deeper level, how these children should be seen. The phrase "at risk" is here given a wide meaning, covering children at risk of harm due to behavioural issues or psychiatric disturbance or

25 Ibid 511.

26 Ibid 504.

27 See generally, Kilkelly (n 3) 66–71, Mairead Enright, 'Interrogating the Natural Order: Hierarchies of Rights in Irish Child Law' (2008) 11(1) *Irish Journal of Family Law* 3, Mairead Enright, 'Abraham, Isaac, and the North Western Health Board' (2004) 4 *Hibernian Law Journal* 25, Ruth Kelly, 'Baby Ann's Constitutional Rights' (2007) 10(1) *Irish Journal of Family Law* 3, Catherine McLoone, 'Children's Rights within the Constitution and the Proposed Constitutional Reform' (2009) 12(3) *Irish Journal of Family Law* 72.

28 *N* (n 20) 502.

29 Eoin Carolan, 'The Constitutional Consequences of Reform: Best Interests after the Amendment' (2007) 10(3) *Irish Journal of Family Law* 9.

those at risk of sexual abuse. These cases are worth considering together, as they present the courts with dilemmas over the construction of children, and sometimes particular groups of children, as well as the location of those children within the constitutional order. Further, the outcomes of these cases helped to reinforce the idea, mooted in the Kilkenny Report, that the Constitution was somehow lacking in its provision for children. While the good faith/bad decision type of conflict seen in cases such as the *North Western Health Board* case can also present these problems,[30] the cases considered below do not involve the State attempting to intervene in well-meaning families. Rather, they concern children who rely on the State for protection from potential harm posed by themselves or others. In cases where the Constitution seems to prevent necessary child protective actions being taken, it is the Constitution itself, rather than the actions of the State or its agents which can be called into question. As will be outlined later in this chapter, it is the articulation of this kind of argument that led to the emerging consensus that constitutional change was required.

The rights of children at risk have been comprehensively discussed in the context of socio-economic rights jurisprudence.[31] In *FN v Minister for Education*,[32] the question of the interplay between children's rights under Article 40.3 and the state's duties under Article 42.5 was considered. In the context of this particular case, this meant making suitable arrangements for the detention and treatment of the child in question in order to vindicate the child's right to be placed and maintained in secure residential accommodation so as to ensure, so far as practicable, his or her appropriate religious and moral, intellectual, physical and social education. A similar conclusion was reached in *DG v Eastern Health Board*, where it was stated that the courts have jurisdiction to do what is necessary to vindicate constitutional rights.[33] In *DB v Minister for Justice*,[34] Kelly J held that a mandatory order could be granted against the Executive enjoining them to provide a remedy for the child in the form of specific services or accommodation. The matter was revisited in *TD v Minister for Education*.[35] In the High Court, it was

30 Oran Doyle, 'Constitutional Law' in Raymond Byrne and William Binchy (eds) *Annual Review of Irish Law* (Round Hall 2012).

31 On the nature of these rights generally see Philip Alston and Gerard Quinn, 'The Nature and Scope of State Parties' Obligations under the International Covenant on Economic, Social and Cultural Rights' (1987) 9 *Human Rights Quarterly* 156 and Daniel Whelan and Jack Donnelly, 'The West, Economic and Social Rights and the Global Human Rights Regime: Setting the Record Straight' (2007) 29(4) *Human Rights Quarterly* 908.

32 [1995] 1 IR 409 (HC).

33 [1997] 3 IR 511, 522 (SC).

34 [1999] 1 IR 29 (HC).

35 [2000] 3 IR 62 (HC). On the impact of this judgment, see Gerry Whyte, 'Constitutional Litigation and Disability Rights' (2012) 47(2) *Irish Jurist* 303, Marc de Blacam, 'Children, the Constitution and the Separation of Powers' (2002) 37 *Irish Jurist* 113, Gerry Whyte, *Social Inclusion and the Legal System: Public Interest Law in Ireland* (Institute of Public Administration 2002), 177–205 and 340–363, and Conor O'Mahony, 'Education, Remedies and the Separation of Powers' (2002) 24 *Dublin University Law Journal* 57.

found that the child concerned had specific accommodation needs, and a series of injunctions were granted directing the State to provide for these. The Supreme Court overturned this decision due to concerns that the High Court order had breached the separation of powers.[36] This effectively meant that, in the Court's view, the Constitution itself created barriers to the realization of children's rights. Children could now not seek the vindication of their rights by the courts as the granting of mandatory orders against the government would mean violating the constitutional principle of the separation of powers. As a result, it would be difficult to sustain the argument that children were seen in these cases as rights-bearing subjects in a meaningful sense, given that they would have to rely on the willingness of the executive for the means of realising their rights.

The *TD* decision posed concerns for children's rights in one further way. Not only did the judgment have significant detrimental consequences for claims based on, and judicial orders vindicating, socio-economic rights, Keane CJ also cast doubt on the utility of the unenumerated rights doctrine in the context of socio-economic rights by first calling into question the basis on which such rights could be declared, and second, by questioning whether the declaration of such rights was a matter more properly assigned to the courts or to the legislature.[37] While Keane CJ did state that the High Court was correct in *FN* to declare that the right to secure accommodation was one of the unenumerated rights of the child, he urged caution over the declaration of new rights not already established in precedent. Murphy J questioned whether such a right existed at all.[38] While the decision did not prevent the future declaration of new unenumerated rights for children,[39] such as in *FN v CO*,[40] it could be argued that the *TD* decision ushered in a chilling effect on children's rights rhetoric as the relationship between children and the State would now become couched more in terms of protective duties than in terms of rights.

36 [2001] 4 IR 259 (SC). While the High Court could make an award of damages, grant a declaration that the executive was in breach of the Constitution, or even grant a prohibitory injunction preventing the taking of certain action, mandatory orders could not be made. This involved accepting the reasoning developed in *O'Reilly v Limerick Corporation* [1989] ILRM 181 (HC) where Costello J drew a distinction between corrective and distributive justice; it was stated that the courts only had the institutional capacity to deal with the former, while the latter was more appropriately dealt with in the political realm. For a discussion of the influence of the *O'Reilly* case on the later judgments on children's socioeconomic rights, see Aoife Nolan, *Children's Socio-Economic Rights, Democracy and the Courts* (Hart Publishing 2011) 163–170.

37 *TD* (n 36) 281.

38 Ibid 316. On the development of case law on socio-economic rights since this decision see generally, Gerry Whyte, 'Public Interest Litigation in Ireland and the European Convention on Human Rights Act 2003' in Suzanne Egan, Liam Thornton and Judy Walsh (eds), *Ireland and the European Convention on Human Rights: 60 Years and Beyond* (Bloomsbury 2014), and Liam Thornton, 'Socio-Economic Rights and Ireland' in Suzanne Egan (ed.) *International Human Rights: Perspectives from Ireland* (Bloomsbury 2015).

39 Nolan (n 36) 167–170.

40 *FN v CO* (n 9).

Two later Supreme Court judgments had placed the question of protection, as distinct from the rights, of children at risk at the centre of public and political concern. In *CC v Ireland*,[41] section 1(1) of the Criminal Law Amendment Act 1935 was declared to be incompatible with the Constitution. This provision essentially provided that where a person is proven to have had sexual intercourse with a girl under 15, his mental state was irrelevant to a finding of guilt or innocence and so he could be convicted despite his belief that the girl was older than 15. The creation of an offence of absolute liability for such a serious criminal offence was regarded as being repugnant to the constitutional guarantees of fair procedures in criminal trials under Article 38.1. Other sections of the same Act, notably section 2(1) which governed intercourse with girls under 17, were now open to a potentially successful constitutional challenge.

A complicating factor in this case was the rule that pre-1937 laws which are later declared to be constitutional might be deemed to be of no effect from the date of the enactment of the Constitution.[42] In effect, therefore, it was arguable that the 1935 Act had ceased to be operative in 1937, and so no legal basis existed for the prosecution or detention of men charged and convicted under its provisions since that date. This led to a man, Mr A, arguing for his release on this basis, despite having pleaded guilty to a series of offences under the impugned section. In *A v Governor of Arbour Hill Prison*,[43] the High Court initially ordered his release having accepted that there was no legal basis for his detention now that the relevant parts of the 1935 Act had been declared void. However, the State's appeal to the Supreme Court was successful on the basis that there was no rule stipulating that a declaration of unconstitutionality has to have retrospective effect, meaning that not only was Mr A re-arrested, but none of the other six men detained under the impugned section could apply for release.

The decisions in *CC* and *A* are not judgments centred on children's rights per se, being instead concerned with discrete points of constitutional law – in the former case, the constitutionality of absolute liability in criminal law, and in the latter, the effect of a finding that a statute is unconstitutional. Children's rights featured in neither judgment, although they have been treated as such,[44] and the question of whether the State was entitled to adopt an absolute liability regime in the interests of child protection was briefly canvassed in *CC*.[45] Nevertheless, the facts of each case did engage the extent to which children can be protected from the harmful sexual practices of others, and so children's right to protection was a relevant issue even though it did not play a significant role in either judgment. What was most important about each decision was the impact it had, first, on the

41 [2006] 4 IR 1 (SC).

42 See Gerard Hogan and Gerry Whyte, *JM Kelly: The Irish Constitution* (4th edn, Tottel Publishing 2003) 899–900.

43 [2006] 4 IR 88 (HC, SC). The case and reactions to it are discussed further in Chapter 8.

44 Kilkelly (n 3) 266–270.

45 See the discussion in *CC* (n 41) 81–84.

construction of children, and second, on the case for a constitutional amendment dealing with children's issues.

The advancement of children's rights issues following the cases discussed in this section was undertaken by the political branches of government rather than the courts, following sustained public pressure from subpolitical actors, such as survivors of child abuse. The public reaction to child protection scandals will be examined in detail in Chapters 7 and 8, but suffice to say that there was now clear public concern over the need to engage in constitutional reform. An examination of the Oireachtas debates in this period shows how reform was justified on the basis that it would protect innocent children. Individuals charged or convicted under the 1935 Acts were described as "perverts ... manipulative, depraved and cunning",[46] and as "self-confessed beasts",[47] whereas the children concerned were presented as "children of confirmation age ... plied with alcohol".[48] The net effect of the cases was seen as allowing the prison door "off the hinge for sex abusers".[49] Older teenagers who engaged in non-exploitative sexual experimentation with one another were described as lacking "the emotional or psychological maturity necessary to deal with the consequences of sex".[50] As a result, legislation, and indeed constitutional reform was seen as necessary to allay "public fury".[51]

Relatively few political voices offered an alternative approach though Deputy Higgins did point out, in respect of mature teenagers, that many did possess the capacity for mature decision-making.[52] An important contribution, in light of later events, was made by Senator O'Rourke. She asked "whether there are enough safeguards for children in the Constitution", answering her own question by stating "I believe not, but I do not know how one would frame a constitutional referendum to encompass everything that one would need to do."[53] When it was decided that constitutional reform should be pursued, it was Senator O'Rourke, as a Dáil Deputy, who chaired the Committee tasked with considering the wording of any reforming provision.[54]

It is difficult to extract a clear picture of the child from the case law concerning children and their role in the constitutional order. The images of the child presented in these cases and the political debates ranges from children who have rights against the State,[55] to children at risk of abuse by "beasts",[56] and indeed

46 Dáil Debates 30 May 2006, vol 620, col 1035, Enda Kenny TD.
47 Dáil Debates 30 May 2006, vol 620, col 1050, Caoimhghín Ó Caoláin TD.
48 Dáil Debates 30 May 2006, vol 620, col 1035, Enda Kenny TD.
49 Dáil Debates 2 June 2006, vol 621, col 16, Enda Kenny TD.
50 Dáil Debates 2 June 2006, vol 621, col 19, Enda Kenny TD.
51 Ibid. See also, Dáil Debates 2 June 2006, vol 621, col 36, Ciaran Cuffe TD; Seanad Debates 2 June 2006, vol 83, col 1791, Senator Jim Walsh.
52 Dáil Debates 2 June 2006, vol 621, col 45, Joe Higgins TD.
53 Seanad Debates 2 June 2006, vol 83, col 1804, Senator Mary O'Rourke.
54 These issues in relation to decision-making will be returned to in Chapter 8.
55 See the case law on economic and social rights, such as *FN* (n 32) and the High Court decision in *TD* (n 35).
56 See the decision in *A* (n 43) and political commentary that followed.

who require protection from their own risky decision-making.[57] It appears that even in the immediate post-Kilkenny era, there has been no single paradigmatic view of the child or a single approach to children's rights in the courts, as they have been seen as legitimate objects of unwise parental decision-making, subjects capable of participating in important decisions and vulnerable objects in need of extraordinary levels of constitutional protection. The child may even play all three roles simultaneously, depending on the question being considered. Once it was decided that constitutional reform of some kind was necessary, the lack of clarity in legal and political thinking about children expressed in constitutional case law and in parliamentary debates was to bedevil the attempts to frame a constitutional amendment.

Constitutional reform: law and politics

The path to the referendum

Following the Report of the Kilkenny Incest Inquiry, the question of constitutional reform to make better provision for children and children's rights came to public prominence. In the Inquiry's Report, Judge Catherine McGuinness found that, in order to prevent such a case happening again, "consideration [should] be given by the Government to the amendment of Articles 41 and 42 of the Constitution so as to include a statement of the constitutional rights of children".[58] Following this, the matter was considered by two parliamentary bodies – the Constitution Review Group,[59] and the All-Party Oireachtas Committee on the Constitution.[60] Both bodies found that the Constitution ought to be amended so as to provide for children's rights, although they differed over the extent of their proposed reforms.[61]

An interesting insight into how reform was thought about can be gained by examining the submissions of people and organizations who made written submissions and provided oral testimony to these committees, and the All-Party Committee in particular. If Ireland were really undergoing a process of reflexive modernization, one would expect to see a movement away from traditional social structures, and the desire to grant constitutional rights to children as a sign that they were now being considered as agents in a meaningful sense. However, O'Mahony's analysis of the submissions made to the Committee would appear to

57 See the decision in *CC* (n 41) and the political commentary that followed.

58 McGuinness (n 1) 96.

59 Constitution Review Group, *Report of the Constitution Review Group* (Stationery Office 1996).

60 All Party Oireachtas Committee on the Constitution, *Tenth Progress Report: The Family* (Stationery Office 2006) (APOCC).

61 For an analysis of the respective proposals see both Aoife Nolan, 'The Battle(s) over Children's Rights in the Irish Constitution' (2007) 22(4) *Irish Political Studies* 495 and Conor O'Mahony, 'Falling short of expectations: the 2012 children amendment, from drafting to referendum' (2016) 31(2) *Irish Political Studies* 252, 258–265.

undermine this view. He argues that the submissions made to this Committee fit "squarely into the religious-conservative versus secular-liberal cleavage"[62] which is detectable within Irish political discourse. Interestingly for concepts of trust and expertise in late modernity, professional organizations, including organizations working with children, political parties and professional representative groups such as the Law Society of Ireland advocated in favour of a change, while many of those opposing change were drawn from smaller, religiously motivated organizations, and from individuals.[63] Among opponents of reform there was a clear distinction between those organizations such as mainstream religious organizations who recognised that children did have rights and interests, but believed that further constitutional reform would harm these by undermining the family, and those who demonstrated an open hostility to the very idea of children's rights.

The All-Party Committee recommended cautious and limited change in 2006,[64] but this began a process of further political engagement with the issue including a commitment by the then Taoiseach to hold a referendum,[65] a consultation process led by the Minister for Justice,[66] the publication of a proposed amendment in 2007,[67] and the establishment of a new Committee on Child Protection,[68] and the Joint Oireachtas Committee on the Constitutional Amendment on Children.[69] The tenor of the former Committee's debates was set during the opening remark of the Chairman, Deputy Peter Power, who declared that "[t]here can be few issues more important than the protection of the children of the nation against the scourge of predatory sexual abuse and

62 O'Mahony, ibid, 256, drawing on the description of political cleavages outlines by Richard Sinnott, 'Cleavages, parties and referendums: relationships between representative and direct democracy in the Republic of Ireland' (2002) 41 *European Journal of Political Research* 811.

63 The full reports of 49 different organisations advocating both views are reproduced in the Appendix to the Report, APOCC (n 60).

64 O'Mahony (n 61) 258.

65 Speech by An Taoiseach, Bertie Ahern TD, Eve of Ard Fheis Event, City West Hotel, Dublin, 3 November 2006.

66 See Nolan (n 61) 508–509.

67 On which see Carolan (n 29), Ursula Kilkelly and Conor O'Mahony, 'The proposed children's rights amendment: running to stand still?' (2007) 10(2) *Irish Journal of Family Law* 19, Aisling Parkes, 'Children should be seen and not heard: a reflection on the proposed constitutional amendment' (2008) 11(3) *Irish Journal of Family Law* 58.

68 Joint Committee on Child Protection, *Report Joint Committee on Child Protection* (Stationery Office 2006).

69 Joint Committee on the Constitutional Amendment on Children, *First Report – Interim Report on the Twenty-Eighth Amendment of the Constitution Bill 2007* (Stationery Office 2008), Joint Committee on the Constitutional Amendment on Children, *Article 42(A).5.2° – Proposal to give legal authority to create offences of absolute or strict liability in respect of sexual offences against or in connection with children* (Stationery Office 2009) and Joint Committee on the Constitutional Amendment on Children, *Third Report: Twenty-Eighth Amendment of the Constitution Bill 2007: Proposal for a Constitutional Amendment to Strengthen Children's Rights* (Stationery Office 2010).

statutory rape."[70] The work of the Joint Oireachtas Committee was again dominated pro- and anti-reform advocates arranged on similar lines to the earlier All-Party Committee.[71] Its eventual proposal, published in 2010, for a new children's rights provision was welcomed by reform advocates.[72] It contained a strong protection of children's right to have their best interests regarded as the first and paramount consideration,[73] the right to be heard in any judicial or administrative proceedings affecting the child[74] and "the right of the child to such protection and care as is necessary for his or her safety and welfare".[75]

The influence of child protection concerns on the Committee's approach raises a question over how committed it was to children's rights, however. From an examination of the available minutes of the Committee's deliberations,[76] it is evident that a significant amount of time was devoted to discussing the issues of strict and absolute liability for sex offences, and the possibility of introducing soft information-based vetting. This can be partly attributed to the *CC* and *A* cases being the main motivators for the establishment of the Committee. Comparatively little time was, therefore, devoted to the discussion of children's rights (particularly those beyond child protection), although this view was rejected by members of the Committee.[77] Nonetheless, this exact point was put to the Committee by the Ombudsman for Children,[78] by the National Youth Council of Ireland[79] and by the Children's Rights Alliance on two separate occasions.[80] Indeed, the opening statements by Committee members specifically referenced the *CC* decision and the Soham murders in England.[81] At a meeting in January 2009, repeated references were made to various child protection scandals including the Kilkenny

70 Joint Committee on Child Protection Debates, 19 July 2006.
71 O'Mahony (n 61) 260.
72 Ibid 262.
73 Proposed Article 42.1.2° and 42.1.3°. See Ursula Kilkelly, 'Kilkelly on 'Best Interests' and the Proposed Constitutional Amendment' (26 April 2010) available at https://humanrightsinireland.wordpress.com/2010/02/26/kilkelly-on-best-interests-and-the-proposed-constitutional-amendment/, accessed 29 December 2019.
74 Proposed Article 42.2(iii).
75 Proposed Article 42.2(ii).
76 While 15 sittings of the committee were held in public session, the majority, 47, were held in private. No record of the discussions of these private meetings exist in the public domain, and so any conclusions about the views of the Committee, and the legal advice received by it, must remain tentative.
77 Joint Committee on the Constitutional Amendment on Children Debates 13 February 2008, Alan Shatter TD.
78 Joint Committee on the Constitutional Amendment on Children Debates 13 February 2008, Ombudsman for Children.
79 Joint Committee on the Constitutional Amendment on Children Debates 9 September 2008, National Youth Council of Ireland.
80 Joint Committee on the Constitutional Amendment on Children Debates 6 February 2008 and 8 October 2008, Children's Rights Alliance
81 See, in particular, speeches by Deputies Power and Howlin, Joint Committee on the Constitutional Amendment on Children Debates 6 December 2007.

Inquiry.[82] It is, therefore, open to question how the Committee deliberations, which appeared to proceed along the lines that children were regarded as objects in need of protection, resulted in a strong vindication of children's rights, with the consequent recognition of children as agents.

The Children's Rights Amendment: Article 42A

The apparent support for the proposal did not translate into a swift referendum. Further delays resulted in a new wording being proposed, which resulted in a referendum being held in November 2012.[83] The new wording proposed to delete Article 42.5 and insert a new Article 42A, which reads as follows:

> 1 The State recognises and affirms the natural and imprescriptible rights of all children and shall, as far as practicable, by its laws protect and vindicate those rights.
> 2.1° In exceptional cases, where the parents, regardless of their marital status, fail in their duty towards their children to such extent that the safety or welfare of any of their children is likely to be prejudicially affected, the State as guardian of the common good shall, by proportionate means as provided by law, endeavour to supply the place of the parents, but always with due regard for the natural and imprescriptible rights of the child.
> 2.2° Provision shall be made by law for the adoption of any child where the parents have failed for such a period of time as may be prescribed by law in their duty towards the child and where the best interests of the child so require.
> 3 Provision shall be made by law for the voluntary placement for adoption and the adoption of any child.
> 4.1° Provision shall be made by law that in the resolution of all proceedings—
> i. brought by the State, as guardian of the common good, for the purpose of preventing the safety and welfare of any child from being prejudicially affected, or
> ii. concerning the adoption, guardianship or custody of, or access to, any child, the best interests of the child shall be the paramount consideration.
> 4.2° Provision shall be made by law for securing, as far as practicable, that in all proceedings referred to in subsection 1° of this section in respect of any child who is capable of forming his or her own views, the views of the child shall be ascertained and given due weight having regard to the age and maturity of the child.

There was significant legal concern over the extent of change in the constitutional framework which this new wording could bring about. It was closer in tone and

82 See, in particular, speeches by Deputy Howlin and Senator Fitzgerald, Joint Committee on the Constitutional Amendment on Children Debates 28 January 2009. These particular scandals are outlined in Chapters 7 and 8.

83 On the delays between 2010 and 2012, see O'Mahony (n 61) 262–264.

substance to the 2007 All Party Committee's wording than the more expansive approach taken by the 2010 Joint Oireachtas Committee. As O'Mahony notes, the provisions relating to best interests and the right to be heard were watered down from the 2010 proposals,[84] although he did recognise that the intention of the amendment seemed clear in its desire "to reinforce the fact that children have rights as individuals and not merely as a sub-set of the family unit."[85] Nolan highlighted that overall balance of Articles 41 and 42 would "remain resolutely un-child-centric",[86] and while it would represent a step forward for children's rights in Ireland, it would not bring Ireland fully into line with its commitments in international human rights law, and the Convention on the Rights of the Child in particular.[87] Harding's summation of the position of children in the constitutional order following the amendment is damning – "yet again children's interests come second to the political will to uphold the special place of the idealised marital family."[88]

The idea that children, rather than being recognised as subjects and agents within the constitutional order, continued to occupy a more ambivalent position would seem to be supported by polling data from before and after the referendum itself. While opinion polling data is not necessarily as strong an indicator of public feelings on children's place in the Constitution as the final referendum result, it can give us a snapshot of how particular constitutional controversies were thought about at a particular time. The first major surveys on the question of inserting children's rights expressly into the Constitution was conducted in late 2006 by *The Irish Times*, after both of the decisions in the *CC* and *A* cases, and the then-Taoiseach's announcement of his decision to hold a referendum on the question.[89] This poll initially reported that 70% of respondents favoured a constitutional change to provide for children's rights.[90] A further *Irish Times* poll the following month showed a marginal difference, with 68% supporting a referendum, while only 16% opposed constitutional change.[91] It was reported that, when

84 Ibid 264.

85 Conor O'Mahony, 'Legal Analysis of the Children's Referendum: Article 42A.1' (23 October 2012) http://humanrights.ie/constitution-of-ireland/legal-analysis-of-the-childrens-referendum-article-42a-1, accessed 24 October 2019.

86 Aoife Nolan, 'The Children's Referendum: The Children's Referendum is Finally Upon Us' (23 October 2012), http://humanrights.ie/constitution-of-ireland/the-childrens-amendment-is/, accessed 24 October 2019.

87 Ibid. A similar point was made by Ursula Kilkelly, 'Legal Analysis of the Children's Referendum: Article 42A.4.1°' (23 October 2012), http://humanrights.ie/constitution-of-ireland/the-childrens-amendment-is/ accessed 24 October 2019.

88 Maebh Harding, 'Ireland: Constitutional recognition of children's rights and paramountcy of welfare' in Bill Aitken (ed), *International Survey of Family Law* (Jordans Family Law 2013) 196.

89 Stephen Collins, 'Plebiscite on rights of child looks set for March' *The Irish Times* (Dublin, 4 November 2006) 1.

90 Carl O'Brien, 'Poll Shows 70% Favour Change to Constitution on Children's Rights' *The Irish Times* (Dublin, 6 November 2006) 3.

91 Stephen Collins, 'Public Supports Children's Rights Referendum Plan' *The Irish Times* (Dublin, 4 December 2006) 1.

asked about their attitude to the Supreme Court decision the previous month in *N v HSE*,[92] 31% supported the contention that the Court had been "correct to put the rights of natural parents before the rights of adoptive parents", while 46% were opposed to it.[93] This data shows a clear movement towards a broader social recognition of the idea that children do have rights, that these rights ought to be recognised in constitutional law and the public would be prepared to undertake significant constitutional reform in order to achieve this aim.

One issue which raises questions over our ability to draw meaningful conclusions from the public discourse surrounding the referendum is the fact that there was virtual unanimity among even largely conservative bodies and commentators in support of the referendum, meaning that its main opponents were largely fringe organizations.[94] RTÉ, Ireland's national broadcaster, admitted facing a real challenge in its attempt to ensure balanced coverage of both sides of the debate, given that "the No side is just so small and so much on the margins of society."[95] This presents as a significant problem in analysing the referendum because, even though opponents had to be drawn from the margins, they were guaranteed significant media coverage because of the interpretation of case law governing referendum campaigns; in particular, the decision in *Coughlan v Broadcasting Complaints Commissioner* which imposes a fairness requirement on broadcasters, by treating both sides in the campaign equally.[96] This, arguably, led to voter disengagement and a view gradually emerged among reform advocates that the main stumbling block for proponents of the amendment was public confusion rather than opposition. A poll released in the month prior to the referendum showed public support at 58%, and opposition at only 4%, while "don't know" represented one-third of responses.[97] The same survey also demonstrated that while only 10% of respondents felt they had a good understanding of the proposal, a clear majority of the respondents either had only a vague understanding (37%) or did not know what the referendum was about (24%). The confusion was compounded by a Supreme Court finding only two days before the referendum that the government's information campaign had breached constitutional requirements relating the public financing of referendum information campaigns.[98]

92 *N v HSE* (n 20).

93 Collins (n 89).

94 Examples include a range of ad hoc groups, such as Alliance of Parents against the State, and minor organisations of longer standing such as the Christian Solidarity Party. See further, O'Mahony (n 61) 269–272.

95 Deaglán de Bréadún, 'RTÉ Executives to outline Referendum Coverage Plan' *The Irish Times* (Dublin, 26 September 2012) 7.

96 [2000] 3 IR 1 (SC), see also *McKenna v An Taoiseach (No 2)* [1995] 2 IR 10 (SC) and *Hanafin v Minister for the Environment* [1995] 2 IR 321 (SC).

97 Stephen Collins, 'Poll Shows Children's Rights Poll to be Carried' *The Irish Times* (Dublin, 20 October 2012) 8.

98 *McCrystal v Minister for Children and* Youth *Affairs* [2012] 2 IR 726, [2012] IESC 53. See also *Jordan v Minister for Children and Youth Affairs* [2015] 4 IR 232, [2015] IESC 33.

The referendum passed by a margin of 58% to 42%, on a turnout of only 33.5%, the lowest in any referendum since 1996, and the third-lowest figure overall in the state's history.[99] After the referendum, the Referendum Commission undertook research into voting patterns.[100] Analysis of the Commission's research highlights that the level of understanding of the issues played a significant role in voting outcome.[101] It was found that 41% of voters did not understand the children's amendment well or did not understand it at all, while 34% abstained because they felt that they lacked knowledge on the issue. The Commission reported that 67% and 63% of respondents who understood the issue "well" or "to some extent", respectively, gave it their support. On the other hand, 52% of voters with little or no knowledge ticked "no". These figures lend support to the argument that symbolism was a dominant motivation in both the political desire to hold the referendum and in the vote itself.[102]

Effects of reform: Post-2015 case law

It remains to briefly examine the legal effects of the amendment. Relatively few cases have considered Article 42A in detail, and as a result caution must be exercised when drawing conclusions from these decisions. The first point to note is that the first section of Article 42A, whereby the state recognises and guarantees to vindicate the natural and imprescriptible rights of the child, is self-executing. This means that, unlike the remainder of the article, no legislation is necessary to bring it into force. Its scope, however, is unclear. It certainly introduces a principle of non-discrimination between children.[103] Given the relatively broad and non-specific meaning of the provision, it is possible to read it either a rhetorical flourish or, in a mirror of the earlier unenumerated rights provision of Article 40.3, as opening up a ground on which courts can declare that children have certain rights which are inherently contained within the provision. The Supreme Court has determined that it is not "possible to look at Article 42A.1 as creating a standalone provision conferring rights on children",[104] although it must be recognised that this statement was made in the context of determining that the provision did not apply to unborn children. It appears, therefore, that while

99 Claire McGing, 'The Children's Referendum 2012' (2014) 29(3) *Irish Political* Studies 471, 475.

100 Referendum Commission, *B&A: Post Children's Referendum Poll* http://www.refcom.ie/en/Past-Referendums/The-Children-Referendum/Quantitative-Survey.pdf, accessed 24 October 2019. These empirical findings are addressed in the context of referendum theory and voter behaviour by O'Mahony (n 61) 268–274.

101 McGing (n 99).

102 Stephen Collins, 'Low Turnout A Lesson not to Tinker with Constitution' *The Irish Times* (Dublin, 12 November 2012) 16.

103 *Sivsivadze v The Minister for Justice* [2015] IESC 53, [2016] 4 IR 403; *Dos Santos v The Minister for Justice* [2015] IECA 210 and *PH v CFA (leave application)* [2016] IEHC 106, [45].

104 *M (Immigration) v Minister for Justice* [2018] IESC, [11.21].

the courts are presently not minded to engage in a very expansive reading of the provisions, they do seem to be willing to consider Article 42A, and Article 42A.1 in particular, as indicating the beginnings of a new constitutional settlement for children. For instance, the courts have rejected the idea that the amendment imposes a duty on local authorities to provide housing for children,[105] which would be a novel measure. On the other hand, there has been a recognition that a child has a right of access to a parent,[106] which effectively elevates a statutory and common law right to the constitutional level.[107]

One of the most comprehensive statements of the effect of Article 42A is found in *Re JB*.[108] O'Donnell J stated that the amendment was "designed to ensure that the Constitution was more clearly child-centred."[109] Further, he posited that "the amendment as a whole was directed towards a perceived approach of statutory and constitutional interpretation as a matter of history, which was considered to be unsatisfactory in principle, and to give rise to potentially unsatisfactory results."[110] These statements can be read as an acknowledgement that there was at least a perceived need to make a break with the constitutional past. This view is supported by a further statement by O'Donnell J that the new provisions can be "seen as a restating of the balance, acknowledging in explicit terms the individual rights of children", thereby enabling their interests to be placed at the centre of constitutional decision-making. Further, MacMenamin J asked whether the amendment requires courts to

> place greater weight on a more *retrospective* analysis of the applicants' actions and failures, or, rather, a more *prospective* approach, at once taking into account the broader picture, but laying greater weight on the children's *future* legal status?[111]

He held that the latter approach now clearly had to be taken, thereby obliging courts to consider the future prospects of, and consequentially the risks to, the individual child in question. Nonetheless, the court did divide over the question of whether the amendment created a "free-standing" best interests principle which could be applied so as to direct a statutory body to put certain statutory obligations aside in the best interests of the children at the centre of the decision. The majority did direct the Authority to do so, while the minority held that Article 42A cannot be read as creating an external source for the protection of the best interests of a child separate and distinct from statute.

105 *PT and AHT v Wicklow County Council* [2017] IEHC 623.
106 *EE v Child and Family Agency* [2016] IEHC 777.
107 A similar point was made in respect of the strengthening of participation rights in *AO'D v Judge O'Leary* [2016] IEHC 555, [90].
108 *CB and PB v Attorney General* [2018] IESC 30.
109 Ibid 5.
110 Ibid.
111 Ibid 121. Emphasis in the original.

It is also somewhat unclear what effect the new constitutional framework will have on the kinds of issues raised in *North Western Health Board* and *N v HSE.* The relevant sections of Article 42A essentially provide that, in certain cases relating to child welfare, provision shall be made by law for the welfare of the child. As such they appear to be enabling provisions. In order to fulfil these obligations, the Children and Family Relationships Act 2015 and the Adoption (Amendment) Act 2017 have introduced changes to issues such as the eligibility of all children for adoption regardless of parental marital status and introduced a new range of factors for courts to consider when determining best interests. On the wider question of the impact of Article 42A displacing the compelling reasons standards and presumptions contained in older case law, there is some dispute in the limited dicta of the courts. In *PH v Child and Family Agency*,[112] it was stated that the new provisions do not take away from the right of the child to the society of its parents but enhance it, and the presumption that the child's best interests will lie with the parents remains in place. Further, the presumption will continue to apply unless there are

> compelling reasons that the welfare of the child cannot possibly be upheld in the society of its parents, or where proportionate state action becomes necessary in the exceptional case of parental failure of sufficient gravity as to trigger Art. 42A.2. However, as the concept of proportionality itself connotes, the greater the impact on the relationship between parent and child, the greater the need for compelling justification for the interference with that relationship.[113]

As against this, the comments of O'Donnell J in *Re JB*,[114] which refer to Article 42A as restating the balance, and the comments of Clarke CJ in *M v Minister for Justice* about the difficulties over the legal position of children in marital families that arose because of cases such as *Re JH* and *N v HSE*,[115] would appear to imply that the Supreme Court would likely have to consider the entire question of children's rights in the context of family autonomy entirely afresh in the wake of the constitutional amendment.

Conclusion

The Constitution's relationship with children has changed, but it is not clear to what extent. While early cases such as *G v An Bord Uchtála* opened up the possibility that children could begin to enjoy the status of rights-bearing subjects, agents in a meaningful sense, later decisions such as *North Western Health*

112 [2016] IEHC 106.
113 Ibid 45.
114 *CB and PB* (n 108).
115 *M (Immigration)* (n 104) [11.20].

Board and *N v HSE*, despite occurring in a more reflexive social era retrenched towards a more instrumentalist view of children's rights, and hence brought the constitutional relationship to parents and children back to one based on simple modernity. These cases saw children's rights as a means by which the traditional preference for family-based decision-making could be strengthened, even in circumstances which were potentially harmful to children.

Nonetheless, the decisions relating to the age of consent and the consequences for child protection seemed to act as a touchpaper reigniting the debate, which had flickered in the 1970s and 1990s, about a constitutional provision specifically for children. Political will seemed to be behind an amendment, but disagreements over the extent of reform among both parliamentarians and society at large showed how fragile the consensus was. When the referendum did occur, it was marked by apathy and confusion. Though the referendum was successful, and children now enjoy an elevated status within the constitutional framework when compared with the position they previously held, it is difficult to claim that there has been a wholesale shift of public perceptions of children as agents, at least insofar as constitutional law is concerned. The courts have to date been somewhat circumspect over the effect of the amendment. It would, therefore, be going too far to claim radical change in all aspects of the legal system. Children may now be regarded as agents in the constitutional order, but their status seems rather tentative. The position of children in the legislative framework represents a rather different story, and this will be dealt with extensively in the following chapters.

References

All Party Oireachtas Committee on the Constitution, *Tenth Progress Report: The Family* (Stationery Office 2006).

Alston P and Quinn G, 'The Nature of and Scope of State Parties' Obligations under the International Covenant on Economic, Social and Cultural Rights' (1987) 9 *Human Rights Quarterly* 156.

Carolan E, 'The Constitutional Consequences of Reform: Best Interests after the Amendment' (2007) 10(3) *Irish Journal of Family Law* 9.

Collins S, 'Plebiscite on rights of child looks set for March' *Irish Times* (Dublin, 4 November 2006) 1.

Collins S, 'Low turnout a lesson not to tinker with constitution' *Irish Times* (Dublin, 12 November 2012) 16.

Collins S, 'Poll shows children's rights poll to be carried' *Irish Times* (Dublin, 20 October 2012) 8.

Collins S, 'Public supports children's rights referendum plan' *Irish Times* (Dublin, 4 December 2006).

Constitution Review Group, *Report of the Constitution Review Group* (Stationery Office 1996).

de Blacam M, 'Children, the Constitution and the Separation of Powers' (2002) 37 *Irish Jurist* 113.

de Bréadún D, 'RTÉ executives to outline referendum coverage plan' *Irish Times* (Dublin, 26 September 2012) 7.

Doyle O, 'Constitutional Law' in Raymond Byrne and William Binchy (eds), *Annual Review of Irish Law* (Round Hall 2012).
Enright M, 'Abraham, Isaac, and the North Western Health Board' (2004) 4 *Hibernian Law Journal* 25.
Enright M, 'Interrogating the Natural Order: Hierarchies of Rights in Irish Child Law' (2008) 11(1) *Irish Journal of Family Law* 3.
Harding M, 'Ireland: Constitutional Recognition of Children's Rights and Paramountcy of Welfare' in Bill Aitken (ed), *International Survey of Family Law* (Jordans Family Law 2013) 196.
Joint Committee on Child Protection, *Report Joint Committee on Child Protection* (Stationery Office 2006).
Joint Committee on the Constitutional Amendment on Children, *First Report - Interim Report on the Twenty-Eighth Amendment of the Constitution Bill 2007* (Stationery Office 2008).
Joint Committee on the Constitutional Amendment on Children, *Article* 42(A).5.2° - *Proposal to Give Legal Authority to Create Offences of Absolute or Strict Liability in Respect of Sexual Offences Against or in Connection with Children* (Stationery Office 2009).
Joint Committee on the Constitutional Amendment on Children, *Third Report: Twenty-Eighth Amendment of the Constitution Bill 2007: Proposal for a Constitutional Amendment to Strengthen Children's Rights* (Stationery Office 2010).
Kelly R, 'Baby Ann's Constitutional Rights' (2007) 10(1) *Irish Journal of Family Law* 3.
Kilkelly U, *Children's Rights in Ireland: Law, Policy and Practice* (Tottel Publishing 2008).
Kilkelly U, 'Kilkelly on 'Best Interests' and the Proposed Constitutional Amendment' (26 April 2010) <https://humanrightsinireland.wordpress.com/2010/02/26/kilkelly-on-best-interests-and-the-proposed-constitutional-amendment/>.
Kilkelly U, 'Legal Analysis of the Children's Referendum: Article 42A.4.1°' (23 October 2012) <http://humanrights.ie/constitution-of-ireland/the-childrens-amendment-is/>.
Kilkelly U and O'Mahony C, 'The Proposed Children's Rights Amendment: Running to Stand Still?' (2007) 10(2) *Irish Journal of Family Law* 19.
McGing C, 'The Children's Referendum 2012' (2014) 29(3) *Irish Political Studies* 471, 475.
McGuinness C, *The Kilkenny Incest Investigation: Report Presented to Mr Brendan Howlin TD, Minister for Health by South Eastern Health Board* (Stationery Office 1993).
McLoone C, 'Children's Rights within the Constitution and the Proposed Constitutional Reform' (2009) 12(3) *Irish Journal of Family Law* 72.
Nolan A, *Children's Socio-Economic Rights, Democracy and the Courts* (Hart Publishing 2011).
Nolan A, 'The Children's Referendum: The Children's Referendum is Finally Upon Us' (23 October 2012), <http://humanrights.ie/constitution-of-ireland/the-childrens-amendment-is/>.
O'Brien C, 'Poll SHOWS 70% favour change to constitution on children's rights' *Irish Times* (Dublin, 6 November 2006) 3.

O'Mahony C, 'Legal Analysis of the Children's Referendum: Article 42A.1' (23 October 2012), <http://humanrights.ie/constitution-of-ireland/legal-analysis-of-the-childrens-referendum-article-42a-1>.

O'Mahony C, 'Falling Short of Expectations: The 2012 Children Amendment, from Drafting to Referendum' (2016) 31(2) *Irish Political Studies* 252.

Parkes A, 'Children Should be Seen and Not Heard: A Reflection on the Proposed Constitutional Amendment' (2008) 11(3) *Irish Journal of Family Law* 58.

Referendum Commission, *B&A: Post Children's Referendum Poll* <http://www.refcom.ie/en/Past-Referendums/The-Children-Referendum/Quantitative-Survey.pdf>.

Sinnott R, 'Cleavages, Parties and Referendums: Relationships Between Representative and Direct Democracy in the Republic of Ireland' (2002) 41 *European Journal of Political Research* 811.

Whelan D and Donnelly J, 'The West, Economic and Social Rights and the Global Human Rights Regime: Setting the Record Straight' (2007) 29(4) *Human Rights Quarterly* 908.

Whyte G, 'Constitutional Litigation and Disability Rights' (2012) 47(2) *Irish Jurist* 303.

Whyte G, 'Public Interest Litigation in Ireland and the European Convention on Human Rights Act 2003' in Suzanne Egan, Liam Thornton and Judy Walsh (eds), *Ireland and the European Convention on Human Rights: 60 Years and Beyond* (Bloomsbury 2014), and Liam Thornton, 'Socio-Economic Rights and Ireland' in Suzanne Egan (ed), *International Human Rights: Perspectives from Ireland* (Bloomsbury 2015).

7 Child abuse and risk in a new modernity

Child protection law and policy, 1992–2006

Introduction

This chapter charts legislative developments in child protection between the passing of the Child Care Act 1991 and the constitutional crisis sparked by the decision in *CC v Ireland* in 2006.[1] In doing so it brings the concept of reflexivity to the fore. Ireland was now going through the transition from simple, traditional modernity to late modernity in earnest. During the 1990s, the concepts of subpolitical agents and the detraditionalization of social relationships became prominent features of the Irish sociological landscape, as did another facet of reflexive modernity, the development of social and regulatory responses to risk, aiming to manage it rather than eliminate it. Indeed, as it became uncontroversial that children could be recognised as victims of abuse, the focus shifted somewhat away from them and onto the risks children faced. What was regarded as a risk, or risk factor, was, therefore, the subject of reconstruction. Legislators reacted to increased public concern over the spectre of child sexual abuse in a way that prioritised regulation and prevention. Knowledge of this topic, which began to emerge in professional circles in the 1980s, now emerged into the public domain and helped to bring about the disembedding of social relations, a process characteristic of late modernity. This involved the disintegration of traditions of trust based on hierarchies, leading a radicalization of knowledge, a more negotiated concept of trust in social institutions and the rise of subpolitics.[2] These factors reshaped the legal and policy landscape governing child protection work, while the idea that children could be rights-bearers was somewhat absent from social and political discourse.

This chapter will first outline the scandals which occurred during this period. As a result of these, public understanding of child abuse as a phenomenon was radically altered and children were now recognised by the public as meaningful members of the moral community, a step that was essential if children were to transition fully to legal subjects. It will then move to examine two distinct strands

1 [2006] 4 IR 1 (SC).
2 See generally, Ulrich Beck, *World Risk Society* (Wiley Blackwell) 1999, and Anthony Giddens, *The Consequences of Modernity* (Polity Press 1990).

of reform – the revision of the criminal law to accommodate child victims in new ways, and the new focus on information as a means of risk reduction. The chapter will argue that the legal reforms which took place were characteristic of late modernity itself – the recognition of the importance of technological change, the disturbance of traditional understandings and relations of authority, and the realization that risks had to be worked with rather eliminated.

Child abuse scandals and public consciousness

In November 1990, a Catholic priest was convicted of a sexual offence against children for the first time in Ireland. Fr James Doyle pleaded guilty and received a three-month suspended sentence.[3] The case was reported in the local newspaper, the *Wexford People*. However, within one hour of publication, a backlash against the coverage commenced.[4] The newspaper's office was inundated with calls protesting against the story. By that evening, the townspeople had gathered in front of the office building in Wexford's main street and proceeded to burn copies of the newspaper in a mass demonstration. Complaints against the newspaper continued for weeks and there was even a campaign to boycott any product or service which used the People Newspaper group for advertising. Letters were written to the newspaper for many weeks to come; the lead was taken by teachers in local primary schools who complained that the coverage was discriminatory, ill-judged and irresponsible, that it was conducted in an undignified manner, and that it was nothing more than the reaction of the gutter press against a man who had done much for his community.[5]

This account of the public reaction to a confirmed case of case sexual abuse is invaluable for helping to chart the progress of late modernity in Ireland during the 1990s. Significant works of scholarship have examined this process, most especially with respect to the decline of traditionally authoritative institutions like the Catholic Church.[6] This also impacted on child protection. The differences in public reaction seen between the time of the Doyle case and later child protection scandals bear the marks of two distinct but related sociological phenomena – the radicalization of public knowledge and the development of subpolitics. Before

3 Francis D Murphy, Helen Buckley and Laraine Joyce, *The Ferns Report* (Stationery Office 2005) 76, 134.

4 This account is drawn from Fintan O'Toole, 'The strut of power gave them the sense that they could do whatever they liked, whenever they liked' *The Irish Times* (Dublin, 29 October 2005) 110, and Susie Donnelly and Tom Inglis, 'The Media and the Catholic Church in Ireland' (2010) 25(1) *Journal of Contemporary Religion* 1.

5 See Tom Mooney, *All the Bishop's Men* (Collins Press 2011) 60–61, and Peter Guy, 'The Casey Effect: The Collapse of Catholicism in Ireland' in Catherine Rees (ed), *Changes in Contemporary Ireland: Texts and Contexts* (Cambridge Scholars Publishing 2013) 23.

6 Among these works, see in particular Diarmuid Ferriter, *The Transformation of Ireland 1900–2000* (Profile Books 2004), Diarmuid Ferriter, *Occasions of Sin: Sex and Society in Modern Ireland* (Profile Books 2009), Roy Foster, *Luck and the Irish: A Brief History of Change from 1970* (Oxford University Press 2008) and Tom Inglis, *Moral Monopoly: The Rise and Fall of the Catholic Church in Ireland* (2nd edn, University College Dublin Press 1998).

these phenomena are examined, it will be necessary to briefly chart the various child abuse scandals uncovered during this time period.

A brief overview of child abuse scandals, 1993–2006

The early 1990s were watershed years in Irish child protection; major scandals unfolded, bringing child abuse to public attention as never before. A scandal has been defined as what happens "when private acts that disgrace or offend the idealised, dominant morality of a social community are made public and narrativized by the media, producing a range of effects from ideological cultural entrenchment to disruption and change."[7] The first major public scandal involving child protection, and one of the most significant, was the Kilkenny Incest Inquiry of 1993. The Kilkenny Inquiry bears all of the characteristics just mentioned.[8] The matter came to public attention when a man was sentenced to seven years' imprisonment for rape and incest committed against his daughter over a 15-year period. The resulting inquiry report highlighted a number of major concerns over the operation of child protection social work, the weaknesses of the legal framework and the presence of social attitudes that in some ways enabled the abuse to go undetected. Later that year, Kelly Fitzgerald, a 15-year-old girl, died following physical abuse and neglect at the hands of her parents, leading to another well-publicised report.[9]

One major study chronicles 29 separate child protection inquiries that took place between 1993 and 2012.[10] This, however, does not include all child protection scandals encountered in this period, as not all scandals resulted in formal child protection inquiries. One major example of a scandal of this nature was the controversy over the extradition request relating to Fr Brendan Smyth; the only inquiry into this affair was not a child protection inquiry, but an administrative one focused on the handling of the extradition request by the Office of the Attorney General.[11] Nonetheless, its impact was so significant that it is the only child abuse scandal in Ireland to have resulted in the fall of a government. Relations between the two parties in the governing coalition were tense over the proposed appointment of the Attorney General Harry Whelehan as the new President of the High Court. These tensions arose over Whelehan's supposed social conservatism, given that he had sought the injunction against a 14-year-old rape victim in the infa-

7 James Lull and Stephen Hinerman, 'The Search for Scandal' in James Lull and Stephen Hinerman (eds), *Media Scandals: Morality and Desire in the Popular Culture Marketplace* (Polity Press 1997) 3.

8 Catherine McGuinness, *The Kilkenny Incest Inquiry Report* (Stationery Office 1993).

9 Joint Committee on the Family, *Kelly: A Child is Dead* (Stationery Office 1996).

10 Helen Buckley and Caroline O'Nolan, *An Examination of Recommendations from Inquiries into Events in Families and their Interactions with State Services, and their Impact on Policy and Practice* (Government Publications 2013) 51–52.

11 Eoghan Fitzsimons, *Report of Attorney General on Investigation into Fr Brendan Smyth File* (Stationery Office 1994).

mous *X* case,[12] and his attempt to protect a government minister from questioning by a tribunal.[13] It eventually emerged that the Northern Irish authorities had requested the extradition of Fr Brendan Smyth, at the time resident in the Republic, to face trial in relation to historic sexual offences and that the file relating to the extradition request had been in the Attorney General's office for seven months without being acted upon. When Whelehan was eventually appointed to the High Court, Labour ministers resigned from the government, causing its collapse. This was an example of a child abuse scandal as a political, rather than a social work or religious or moral scandal, but the public prominence of the case contributed significantly to both the profile and public understanding of child abuse in Ireland.[14]

The mid- and late-1990s were to see a deluge of disclosures, documentaries and official reports into child abuse. Following the Smyth revelations, details began to emerge of abuse at Madonna House in Dublin,[15] and at Goldenbridge Industrial School, which was the subject of a documentary screened on national broadcaster RTÉ which gave it a particular public prominence.[16] The Joseph McColgan trial, which resulted in his imprisonment for rape and incest,[17] was quickly followed by his children's negligence claim against the North-Western Health Board,[18] the publication of his daughter's account of the abuse,[19] and the official report into the incident.[20] A report into sexual abuse by prominent swimming coaches was also published.[21] In 1999, RTÉ broadcast *States of Fear*,[22] a three-part documentary examining the abuse perpetrated in industrial and reform schools earlier in the century. As the last of the three episodes was to be broadcast, then Taoiseach Bertie Ahern made a public apology on behalf of the State "to the victims of childhood abuse for our collective failure to intervene, to detect their pain, to come to their rescue".[23] In addition, the government agreed to establish a commission of inquiry into the matter, with the Commission to Inquire into

12 *Attorney General v X* [1992] 1 IR 1 (SC).
13 *Attorney General v Hamilton (No. 1)* [1993] 2 IR 250 (SC).
14 Harry Ferguson, 'The Paedophile Priest: A Deconstruction' (1995) 84 *Studies: An Irish Quarterly Review* 247.
15 Department of Health, *Report on the Inquiry into the Operation of Madonna House* (Stationery Office 1996).
16 Louis Lentin (Director), *Dear Daughter* (RTÉ 22 February 1996).
17 Kathy Sheridan, 'Father's Abuse and Beatings Extended over 17 Years' *The Irish Times* (Dublin, 24 May 1995) 5.
18 Carol Coulter, 'McColgans Savour Outcome of Ordeal' *The Irish Times* (Dublin, 24 January 1998) 8.
19 Susan McKay, *Sophia's Story* (Gill and Macmillan 2008).
20 North Western Health Board, *West of Ireland Farmer Case: Report of Review Group, presented to North Western Health Board, July 1998* (North Western Health Board 1998).
21 Joint Committee on Tourism, Sport and Recreation, *First Interim Report of the Joint Committee on Tourism, Sport and Recreation: Protection of Children in Sport: Report of the Independent Inquiry into Child Sexual Abuse in Swimming* (Stationery Office 1998).
22 Mary Rafferty (Director) *States of Fear* (RTÉ, 27 April 1999, 4 May 1999, 11 May 1999).
23 Maol Muire Tynan, 'Inquiry into Child Sex Abuse to Start in September' *The Irish Times* (Dublin, 12 May 1999) 1.

Child Abuse Act 2000 eventually leading to the publication of the Ryan Report in 2009.[24] Later documentaries, such as *Cardinal Secrets*[25] and *Suing the Pope*,[26] led to the establishment of the Ferns Inquiry and the inquiry into child abuse in the Archdiocese of Dublin.[27]

Concerns over child abuse and the effectiveness of child protection law and policy were also evident outside the context of clerical or institutional abuse. In 2002, a Garda investigation into online child pornography known as Operation Amethyst led to the arrest of over 100 suspects, and significant media attention.[28] Particular attention was focused on the case against a Circuit Court judge which collapsed due to the inadmissibility of crucial evidence.[29] In the summer of 2006, two Supreme Court decisions relating to the Criminal Law Amendment Act 1935 caused significant public reaction. In *CC v Ireland*,[30] provisions of the 1935 Act prohibiting unlawful carnal knowledge of a girl under 15 were declared to be unconstitutional due to the unavailability of a defence of reasonable mistake as to the girl's age. Following this, men incarcerated under this law sought their release from prison, resulting in the legally and socially significant case of *A v Governor of Arbour Hill Prison* which saw the High Court uphold the applicant's claim for release, a decision overturned by the Supreme Court.[31]

The impact of scandals on public understanding of abuse

This catalogue of reports and inquiries transformed the understanding of child abuse in the public mind. The Kilkenny Inquiry alone was described as helping to move Ireland "from a society that could not believe these things occurred to one where some people were super-aware of child sexual abuse."[32] The public's understanding of the abuse and its attitude towards traditional relationships of authority were radically altered by the experience of living through these decades. When set against the backdrop of the public reaction to the Fr James Doyle controversy, accounts of public reaction to abuse stories seem scarcely believable. The fact that the Child Care Act 1991 had not been implemented in full became a matter of public concern after the story of the Kilkenny scandal

24 Commission to Inquire into Child Abuse (CICA), *Report of the Commission to Inquire into Child Abuse* (Stationery Office 2009).
25 Mary Rafferty (Producer), *Prime Time: Cardinal Secrets* (RTÉ, 17 October 2002).
26 Colm O'Gorman (Director), *Suing the Pope* (BBC Two, 19 March 2002).
27 Yvonne Murphy, *Report of the Commission of Investigation into the Catholic Archdiocese of Dublin* (Stationery Office 2009).
28 See Ian O'Donnell and Claire Milner, *Child Pornography: Crime, Computers and Society* (Willan Publishing, 2007) 118–136 for an account of the operation and its aftermath.
29 *People (DPP) v Curtin*, *The Irish Times*, 24 April 2004 (CC).
30 *CC v Ireland* (n 1). For more on these, see the discussion in Chapter 6.
31 [2006] 4 IR 88 (SC).
32 Trish Hegarty, 'If Abuse is Suspected, Listen First to the Child' *The Irish Times* (Dublin, 3 December 1994) 9.

broke.[33] The trade union representing healthcare workers refused to cooperate with any further implementation measures until adequate funding was made available.[34] This early radicalization stands in contrast not only to incidents such as the reaction to the Doyle conviction, but social attitudes to children and violence more generally. The Kilkenny Inquiry report focused attention on the social acceptance of domestic violence, which was seen "in a fatalistic way as a relatively normal part of life."[35] A columnist wrote that there was a "punitive attitude to children [that] is so ingrained, and the notion of children having rights so alien, that most people see nothing wrong with child beating."[36] Following acknowledgement of the scandal, however, one priest was to describe the public mood as a "national mea culpa."[37]

The shift in mood was further demonstrated by the public's disquiet over the handling of claims of abuse by clerics. As indicated above, the Smyth controversy gained political currency due to the government decision to appoint the person ultimately responsible for extradition requests to a senior judicial role. Regardless of the fact that this involved points of constitutional practice largely unknown to the populace at large prior to this controversy,[38] there was a strong sense that Whelehan should be held accountable for what was seen as a child protection failure. When his account of events stated that the facts surrounding the extradition request showed no need for urgency, civil society groups criticised this on the basis that it sent a problematic message to victims of sexual abuse.[39] As the controversy dragged on and the government collapsed, polling showed that accountability was a key concern for the public, that 75% of survey respondents now opposed his judicial appointment and that 86% favoured legal changes that would allow him to appear before a Dáil committee to answer questions on the affair, with only 7% opposed to such a move.[40] This was a significant transforma-

33 See Joe Carroll and Mark Brennock, 'Inquiry Ordered into Failure of Health Services in Incest Case' *The Irish Times* (Dublin, 4 March 1993) 6, Maol Muire Tynan, '£40m Needed to Implement Child Care Act' *The Irish Times* (Dublin, 23 April 1993) 6, Kieran McGrath, 'McGuinness Report is a Step forward' *The Irish Times* (Dublin, 15 May 1993) 5.

34 Ella Shanahan, 'Policy against Child Abuse is Needed, Incest Inquiry Told' *The Irish Times* (Dublin, 15 May 1993) 5.

35 McGuinness (n 8) 89.

36 Nuala O'Faolain, 'Next Time There Has to be Someone Who Can Say "Well, I Tried, I Did My Best"' *The Irish Times* (Dublin, 3 June 1993) 11.

37 Canon Denis O'Callaghan, 'Kilkenny Incest Case' *The Irish Times* (Dublin, 10 March 1993) 13.

38 There was supposedly a constitutional convention giving the Attorney General first refusal on judicial appointments. The development of the controversy and the convention's role in it is discussed in Gary Murphy, *Electoral competition in Ireland since 1987: The politics of triumph and despair* (Oxford University Press 2016) 67–69. See also, Harry McGee, 'Path from Attorney General to Judge is well trodden' *The Irish Times* (Dublin, 20 June 2017) 3.

39 Trish Hegarty, 'Concern over AG's Report on Smyth' *The Irish Times* (Dublin, 14 November 1994) 5.

40 Geraldine Kennedy, 'Slump in support for Fianna Fáil over Harry Whelehan' *The Irish Times* (Dublin, 21 November 1994) 1 and the data produced in Table E, Procedures Relating to the Attorney General at 7.

tion in public perception of the importance of dealing effectively with child abuse concerns, a transformation which would continue in later years.

The public disquiet over the Whelehan/Smyth controversy would show itself in a different way when other traditionally powerful social institutions came to be targets of protest over their lack of action to take child abuse seriously. The Catholic Church came to be targeted by protests, such as the one cited in the *New York Times* report of "dozens" of campaigners protesting outside a mass involving Cardinal Desmond Connell to celebrate the bicentenary of the founding of the Christian Brothers,[41] on the grounds that the Cardinal was seen as tacitly endorsing an order embroiled in abuse allegations. By this stage, the new socially significant image of the paedophile priest had been forcefully embedded in the public psyche.[42]

Survivors of abuse and representative associations working with them came to play a key role in the process of shifting public perceptions. The Kilkenny Incest survivor, known as Mary, had part of her story told in the *Irish Times*.[43] Sophia McColgan's account of her childhood abuse by her father became a bestseller. Christine Buckley's narrative shaped the *Dear Daughter* documentary which opened up the public consciousness to institutional abuse; Bernadette Fahy's memoir also highlighted abuse at Goldenbridge,[44] while Colm O'Gorman and John Kelly became well-known public figures in the early 2000s. The organizations to which O'Gorman and Kelly respectively belonged, One in Four and Survivors of Child Abuse, featured prominently over the following decade alongside more traditional civil society and campaigning groups.

The voices of these individuals and groups were crucial in shaping public responses to the scandals. One journalist has asserted that the issue "needed … victims and their families telling their stories to camera" in order to "galvanise public and political will in unprecedented determination to root out this great rot once and for all."[45] They made child abuse a subject on which the Irish people had come to debate their identity.[46] Empirical work has highlighted the importance of the media's discovery of child sexual abuse to victims and survivors of abuse,[47]

41 Brian Lavery, 'Demonstrators in Dublin Protest Abuse by Priests' *The New York Times* (New York, 8 April 2002) available at www.nytimes.com/2002/04/08/us/demonstrators-in-dublin-protest-abuse-by-priests.html, accessed 29 December 2019.
42 On this phenomenon generally, see Ferguson (n 14) 247.
43 Geraldine Kennedy, '"The Less You Struggled, The Less You Got Hit" She Said', *The Irish Times* (Dublin, 19 May 1993) 6.
44 Bernadette Fahy, *The Freedom of Angels: Surviving Goldenbridge Orphanage* (O'Brien Press 1999).
45 Patsy McGarry, 'An Irishman's Diary' *The Irish Times* (Dublin, 9 November 2002) 13.
46 Harry Ferguson, 'States of Fear, Child Abuse, and Irish Society' (2000) 50(1) *Doctrine and Life* 20, 21.
47 See, for example, Jenny Kitzinger, 'Transformations of Public and Private Knowledge: Audience Reception, feminism and the experience of childhood sexual abuse' (2001) 1(1) *Feminist Media Studies* 91.

while also helping to set policy agendas.[48] The increasing flow of memoir-based accounts of child abuse has ensured that the rest of the public know what it felt like to be subject to abuse, in addition to contributing to public anger over the failures of the church and the state to ensure the protection of children. Survivor accounts also helped to drive a narrative of a betrayal of trust by these institutions. Memoirs and survivor stories, therefore, had a "corrective" effect, as public anger engendered by these stories helped to dismantle the atmosphere of secrecy and shame that surrounded such incidents.[49] In effect, it was these accounts of lived experiences that helped to replace the attitude of general complacency that existed over children's issues and to end the politics and culture of denial of child abuse. The public's understanding of child abuse had been radicalised by non-traditional, subpolitical agents, who in previous decades were seen as a social problem.

These changes in social reactions map very clearly onto an understanding of modernity as reflexive and preoccupied with risk. It has been argued that "reflexivity is an expression of the process that happens when we (individuals and institutions) reflect critically on the development we, ourselves, have been a part of creating."[50] This critical reflection led to "individualization", the disentanglement from traditional social institutions, and disembedding from traditional social structures.[51] This means increasing scepticism over the ability of these traditional institutions to cope with the risks people face, and a consequent decline of trust in those institutions. This can lead to two distinct responses – counter-modernization, which seeks a return to more traditional ways of thinking and being so as promote a sense of security, and a more radical subpolitics. This latter response seeks to politicise what was previously unpolitical,[52] thereby opening up new areas of social life for political engagement and debate. This engagement is ad hoc and direct in nature, "shaping society from below".[53]

It was this radical subpolitics driven by those previously excluded from political power which, I argue, shaped the legal framework, bringing with it a new knowledge of risk, sensitivity to its consequences and capacity to mobilize against those perceived consequences.[54] The frameworks of child protection law and social work policy that existed prior to the Kilkenny Inquiry were radically transformed by these social shocks. The claim made by Ferguson in 1995 that "law

48 Michael Breen, 'Through the Looking Glass: How the Mass Media Represent, Reflect and Refract Sexual Crime in Ireland' (2007) 10 *Irish Communications Review* 5 and Michael Breen, Hannah McGee, Ciaran O'Boyle, Helen Goode and Eoin Devereux, '"Suing the Pope" and Scandalising the People: Irish Attitudes to Sexual Abuse by Clergy Pre- and Post-Screening of a Critical Documentary' (2009) 11 *Irish Communications Review* 77.

49 Catriona Crowe, 'On the Ferns Report' (2006) 22 *Dublin Review* 5.

50 Malene Freudendal-Pedersen, *Mobility in Daily Life: Between Freedom and Unfreedom* (Routledge 2009) 29

51 Beck (n 2).

52 Ibid 93.

53 Ibid 39–40.

54 Michael Moran, *The British Regulatory State: High Modernism and Hyper-Innovation* (Oxford University Press 2002) 27, summarising Giddens (n 2) 124–134.

will now play a much greater part in decision-making and monitoring professional practice"[55] has been borne out to such an extent that the law has increasingly regulated parts of what was once within a professional social worker's discretion. The law has now begun to regulate issues like reporting of child abuse concerns and has introduced new rules governing the sharing of information not only between agencies working with children but also between centralised disclosure bodies and private organizations. Many of these rules focus on information relating to questions of how "risky" or dangerous an individual may be, and especially whether they can be said to pose a risk of sexual danger. There has been a "transformation in the relationship between expertise, knowledge and laypeople" due to a "radicalised consciousness of risk" among the general public that simply did not exist prior to the Kilkenny scandal.[56]

New perceptions of risk and the expansion of the criminal law

Following the radicalization of the public understanding of child abuse and risk, it is important to understand how the law reacted to this. As outlined in Chapter 1, Giddens and Beck argue that the nature and understanding of risk is constantly redefined in late modernity; during the 1990s and 2000s, risk was redefined in light of changed perceptions of child abuse, and those who perpetrated it. Significant change has consequentially occurred in Irish child protection law. The substantive criminal law has undergone significant expansion – new modes of behaviour capable of producing risks were brought within its ambit, changes in criminal procedure and the handling of offenders were designed to both uncover and punish more cases of child abuse while simultaneously reducing the risk of abuse, and the processes for managing information about risks has also changed radically. The increased use of regulatory systems of information management was a direct response to the new public awareness of children being seen as continually at risk of harm. Regulation was also a response to the new public awareness of the possibility of system failure – as trust in church and state institutions tasked with protecting children declined following exposure of their failures, the state turned to new means of regulation in order to restore some element of trust. Heightened regulation has been seen as "the counter to risk as an essential basis for sustaining trust in a radically individualised, risk-sensitive society."[57] Law and child protection social work have thus formed a much closer union than was previously the case.

55 Harry Ferguson, 'Child Welfare, Child Protection and the Child Care Act 1991: Key Issues for Policy and Practice' in Harry Ferguson and Pat Kenny (eds), *On Behalf of the Child: Child Welfare, Child Protection and the Child Care Act 1991* (A & A Farmar 1995) 35.

56 Harry Ferguson, 'Protecting Irish Children in Time: Child Abuse as a Social Problem and the Development of the Child Protection System in the Republic of Ireland' (1996) 44(2) *Administration* 5.

57 Michael Clarke, *Regulation: The Social Control of Business between Law and Politics* (Macmillan 2000) 25.

These issues discussed below are of particular interest in the context of the emergence of a late modern, risk society in Ireland. They map different aspects of the reflexive modernization process. The changes in the law of evidence demonstrate a decisive shift away from children as objects and increasingly towards children as subjects. As will become clear, the easier reception of children's evidence is predicated on the recognition that they have a meaningful story to tell, and that story needs to be given due respect and recognition by the legal system. These reforms, therefore, showed a willingness to allow children to participate in the criminal process, continuing the process of their construction as agents. The detraditionalization of Irish society and consequent loosening of social bonds of power and authority was clearly demonstrated in the debates leading to reform of the criminal law relating to offences by people in powerful positions vis-à-vis children. As the debates leading to these reforms show, the very fact that people with responsibilities towards children were now being problematized highlights how the power of previously impervious institutions like religious organizations or even the family itself had now become more diffuse and less solid. In conjunction with the third of these reforms, which relates to technological change, it also highlights the state's attempt to govern and manage risks never previously thought of as risks.

Changes in the reception of children's evidence

The Criminal Evidence Act 1992 made radical changes to the way in which evidential rules operated in prosecutions for child sexual abuse. Much of the legislation was inspired by the Law Reform Commission Report on the matter.[58] During its introduction in the Dáil, the Act was described as a measure largely designed to address evidential difficulties in child abuse cases,[59] with children being described as the state's "most vulnerable" citizens.[60] Child sexual abuse itself was labelled as a "major social problem ... a time bomb in society that has not yet exploded."[61] It was posited that vigilantism against child sex offenders was increasing; while such actions were condemned, they were seen as "signal[ling] the depth of emotion involved" and the reality that there are some things that cannot be restored.[62] Several TDs referred to the need to introduce reform quickly in light of the collapse of an incest prosecution only a matter of weeks previously due to an evidential technicality.[63]

58 Law Reform Commission, *Report on Child Sexual Abuse* (LRC 32-1990), discussed at Chapter 5.

59 Dáil Debates 3 March 1992, vol 416, col 1284, Minister Pádraig Flynn TD.

60 Ibid, col 1293.

61 Dáil Debates 3 March 1992, vol 416, col 1337, Bill Cotter TD.

62 Dáil Debates 5 March 1992, vol 416, col 1710, Joe Jacob TD.

63 See 'Man found not guilty of incest' *The Irish Times* (Dublin, 20 February 1992) 4 and 'Shatter Concerned at Incest Case Collapse' *The Irish Times* (Dublin, 21 February 1992) 7; Dáil Debates 3 March 1992, vol 416, col 1319–1322, Alan Shatter TD, Dáil Debates 3 March 1992, vol 416, cols 1328 and 1330, Michael Bell TD, Dáil Debates 5 March 1992, vol 416, col 1702, Mary Wallace TD.

The 1992 Act, therefore, belongs to a very specific moment in social and legal history – the period when child abuse was coming to be accepted as a real and widespread phenomenon. Children were being accepted not only as victims but as people who deserved to have their voices heard, and perpetrators as men deserving conviction and punishment.[64] Yet this was also before the full disclosures of the Kilkenny, Smyth and McColgan scandals. Children were thus not entirely presented as blameless, and the punitive attitude towards perpetrators which characterised later legislation such as the Sex Offenders Act 2001 was not yet evident. This idea of children not being free of blame is important, as it demonstrates that the construction of children as threats still featured occasionally in legislative debates. A vivid description of children at risk, the very children at whom the legislation was aimed, was provided by Deputy Cotter:

> Children of all ages are wandering the streets of this city every day out of the control of their parents. They are at risk from all sorts of human predators as well as being at risk of abuse. They are learning to be criminals. Children who are sexually abused can suffer the most awful emotional disturbance which, unless appropriate treatment is provided, leaves them as emotionally crippled adults unable to enjoy a normal existence.[65]

This conflation of children being at risk by virtue of being "out of control" and engaging in risky behaviour makes clear the way in which they were seen prior to the scandals emerging – as in need, as deserving, but not without blame. They were deemed deserving of special accommodation as victims of abuse, the impact of which was now being recognised, but they had to undergo significant further reconstruction before they could be regarded as being social and legal subjects. There was also a scrupulous recognition of the need to preserve fairness towards accused individuals. While contemporary rules of evidence were described as "archaic", it was stated in Dáil debates that reform "must not destroy those elements of fairness, due process and other safeguards which have been developed to protect the accused person."[66] When the specific reforms outlined below are viewed in their totality, there is a clear movement towards children being seen as agents. Returning to the idea of children's agency outlined in Chapter 1, the children to whom these reforms would apply had their ability to act in the world enhanced by new facilitatory technologies.[67] The capacity for children to act upon the social structures of the law and change not only their own lives, but the lives of others, by the act of speaking was greatly enhanced by this legislation.

64 One TD made specific reference to the gendered nature of abuse – see Dáil Debates 5 March 1992 vol 416, col 1699, Nuala Fennell TD.

65 Dáil Debates 5 March 1992 vol 416, col 1685, Bill Cotter.

66 Dáil Debates 3 March 1992, vol 416, col 1331, Brian Hillery TD.

67 David Oswell, *The Agency of Children: From Family to Global Human Rights* (Cambridge University Press 2013) 78.

In terms of the legal reforms undertaken by the 1992 Act, three main issues are relevant: the competence and compellability of witnesses, the reception of children's evidence by non-traditional means and the changes in corroboration requirements. The 1992 Act extended the categories of people who were both competent and compellable as witnesses in criminal trials, meaning that more people were deemed legally capable of being called as witnesses and could also be made to testify at a trial. Under the Criminal Justice (Evidence) Act 1924, a person could generally not be called by the prosecution to testify against their spouse, unless that spouse was charged with one of a handful of listed exceptions, which did not include a wide range of possible offences against children, such as rape, incest or indecent assault.[68] These provisions, therefore, militated against the prosecution of sexual abuse by family members where a disclosure had been made, for example, to a mother about abuse by a father. However, in *People (DPP) v JT*,[69] the Court of Criminal Appeal held that the rights accorded to families by Article 41 of the Constitution did not provide constitutional cover for these rules on competence and compellability, as there was no constitutional reason justifying them; further, compellability of witnesses to whom a disclosure of abuse was made was necessary to vindicate the rights of family members who had been victimised.[70] This situation is now governed by section 22 of the 1992 Act, which makes clear that spouses are now compellable at the instance of the prosecution in any trial of an offence involving violence, the threat of violence or a sexual offence against a person under 17 years of age.

The ways in which the evidence of children themselves was to be received and weighted were also substantially reformed by the 1992 Act. Section 27(1) provides that the unsworn evidence of a child under 14 could be heard "if the court is satisfied that he is capable of giving an intelligible account of events which are relevant to those proceedings." This drastically departs from the previous statutory provisions which permitted unsworn evidence of children only where the child was deemed to have "sufficient intelligence" to justify the reception of the evidence, and was deemed to understand the duty to tell the truth; such evidence alone was incapable of grounding a conviction.[71] In addition to the introduction of the new intelligibility test, the rule requiring the unsworn evidence of a child to be corroborated was also abolished,[72] as was the requirement for a warning where the jury was asked to convict based solely on the uncorroborated evidence of a child.[73] The shift to the bare ability to give an intelligible

68 See Schedule. See also *McGonagle v McGonagle* [1951] IR 123 (SC) which recognised a handful of other minor exemptions.

69 (1988) 3 Frewen 141 (CCA).

70 Ibid 158.

71 See section 30 of the Children Act 1908, as amended by sections 28 and 44 Criminal Justice Administration Act 1914.

72 Section 28(1) 1992.

73 Section 28(2) 1992. The constitutionality of this section was upheld in *White v Ireland* [1995] 2 IR 268 (HC), although it appears that the comments relating to this provision at 283 were obiter.

account of events and the reform of corroboration requirements were crucial in making it easier to hear the accounts of child victims, who were now placed in the same position with respect to evidence rules as any other sexual offence complainants.[74] It was a recognition that child abuse occurred in private, that corroboration was often impossible and that when children made allegations of abuse, they should be taken seriously rather than being seen as the product of blackmail or imagination.

New rules were also introduced allowing child sexual abuse complainants to give evidence through facilitatory mechanisms, such as live television link, or an intermediary. Section 13 of the 1992 Act permits a television link system to be used by all witnesses under the age of 17, unless the court "sees good reason to the contrary".[75] Importantly, these provisions require no special trauma or distress to be proven before technological methods are utilised – they apply to all child witnesses, unless the court directs otherwise. When subjected to constitutional challenge as an interference with the right to a fair trial, the Supreme Court held that there was no right to direct confrontation with witnesses, and so it was within the remit of the legislature to accommodate young witnesses as a group without the need for case-by-case assessments.[76] Despite the general desire to ease the burden of testifying on child witnesses, the importance of the solemnity of court attendance and the seriousness of the consequences attending upon a conviction were evident when one TD raised a concern about the introduction of video link evidence:

> It is important that people should go to court in a court atmosphere. After all, this Bill deals with serious crime entailing serious penalties. We must have an atmosphere in which people can get a fair trial, so that they will not be tried by TV or video. They should be tried in the circumstances appertaining to a court.[77]

The final significant accommodation tailored to young and vulnerable witnesses is found in section 14. This provides that evidence from a young person may give evidence through an intermediary if, "having regard to the age or mental condition of the witness, the interests of justice require" it.[78] Any questions put through an intermediary "shall be either in the words used by the questioner or so as to convey to the witness in a way which is appropriate to his age and mental condition the meaning of the questions being asked."[79] This was adopted instead of the "child examiner" advocated in Law Reform Commission report.[80] The

74 Thomas O'Malley, *Sexual Offences* (2nd edn, Round Hall 2013) 407.
75 The age was raised to 18 by section 257(3) of the Children Act 2001.
76 *Donnelly v Ireland* [1998] 1 IR 321 (SC) 357–358.
77 Dáil Debates 3 March 1992, vol 416, col 1327, Michael Bell TD.
78 Section 16(1).
79 Section 16(2).
80 Law Reform Commission (n 58) 76–78.

Commission envisaged this person as acting "as a conduit for all questions from the lawyers and that his or her role would be to establish and maintain rapport and ease of communication with the child witness" on the basis that "too high a price is being paid for the right to conduct a wholly uninhibited and 'direct' cross-examination of a child witness."[81] The fact that the child examiner proposal was not taken up by the legislature shows that there was still discomfort at potentially inhibiting the conduct of a criminal defence. The role of intermediary, therefore, represents a compromise between accommodation of children's needs for a system which was sensitised to their needs as witnesses and a traditional understanding of the procedural needs of an accused person. Nonetheless, the intermediary still attracted some criticism during debate on the Bill. Deputy Shatter saw the role of intermediary as too close to that of the child examiner, and instead proposed "that lawyers should be put under a specific duty in cross-examining somebody who is alleged to be a victim of such an offence to have regard to the tender years of the victim."[82] Despite this objection, the role of intermediary remained in section 14, somewhat enhancing the possibilities for children to participate in the process.

Offences by persons in authority

Given the social scandals which began to emerge following the Kilkenny Report and the revelations of clerical abuse, the criminal law began to treat persons in positions of authority who committed offences against children as deserving of heavier sentences than other offenders. The maximum punishment for incest committed by men was increased twice in the 1990s. Section 1 of the Punishment of Incest Act 1908 had proscribed that a maximum sentence of seven years could be imposed for this offence. This was raised to a maximum of 20 years by the Criminal Justice Act 1993,[83] and to life imprisonment by the Criminal Law (Incest Proceedings) Act 1995.[84] The heavier sentences were seen as justified due to the "abuse of a relationship based on power over vulnerable children who have no capacity to choose or to know the sort of activity in which they are involved" and by the "coercion, threats, betrayals of fundamental trust and, in many cases, distortion of subsequent relationships for the remainder of the victim's life."[85] The Minister for Justice who later introduced the 1995 Act spoke of shedding tears of sympathy for the victim of the Kilkenny scandal, while also shedding tears of "frustration and anger that these horrors can still be perpetrated against an innocent young woman".[86] This presaged a new era of punitive attitudes towards offenders guilty of an abuse of trust, represented by harsh penalties. While there

81 Ibid 77.
82 Dáil Debates 3 March 1992, vol 416, col 1307, Alan Shatter TD.
83 Section 12.
84 Section 5.
85 Dáil Debates 24 May 1995, vol 453, col 1063, Liz O'Donnell TD.
86 Dáil Debates 3 March 1993, vol 427, col 688, Nora Owen TD.

was no substantive opposition in the Dáil or Seanad to the increased penalties, putative opponents were castigated by Brendan McGahon TD as "the bleeding hearts and do-gooders in our society [who] have helped to dismantle the sentencing system" and who helped to bring about a society in which sexual offending was rife, one with "too much law and no order."[87] McGahon on another occasion expressed support for chemical castration of men who abused children, referring specifically to the abuser at the centre of the *X* case, who had raped his daughter's friend.[88]

Some recognition was also accorded to the need to reassess how a relationship of trust could develop, with amendments to the 1908 Act proposed which would have made it possible to prosecute step-parents who had procured consent for intercourse from their step-children who were over the age of consent by a process of grooming. This more sophisticated understanding of the abuse of trust concept did not find support, and the amendments were rejected.[89] The Children Act 2001 revisited the question of abuse by family members. Part XII of the Act contains a series of provisions aimed at strengthening child protection through criminal law. Section 246 essentially replaces section 12 of the 1908 Act by criminalising cruelty to children. The new provision states that it is an offence for

> any person who has the custody, charge or care of a child wilfully to assault, ill-treat, neglect, abandon or expose the child, or cause or procure or allow the child to be assaulted, ill-treated, neglected, abandoned or exposed, in a manner likely to cause unnecessary suffering or injury to the child's health or seriously to affect his or her wellbeing.

This was to be punishable by a maximum sentence of £10,000 or imprisonment for a term not exceeding 7 years or both, signifying the severity of the offence.[90] O'Malley characterises the offence as one designed to criminalise the "ill-treatment of children by the infliction of violence or by neglecting to provide a child with food, clothing or other necessities for their survival."[91] In this sense, it largely mirrors the earlier provisions, and its main use may well be to provide an alternative charge in circumstances where parental behaviour does not readily fall within the ambit of other offences.[92]

Section 249 goes a considerable way further in criminalising exploitative conduct however, introducing a new offence of causing or encouraging a sexual offence with a child. It provides that a person may be convicted

87 Dáil Debates 24 May 1995, vol 453, col 1078, Brendan McGahon TD.
88 Ibid, col 1079. See *AG v X* (n 12).
89 Dáil Debates 28 June 1995, vol 455, col 402, Liz O'Donnell TD.
90 Section 246(2)(b). This is the maximum for conviction on indictment; the maximum sentence on summary conviction is £1,500 or imprisonment for a term not exceeding 12 months or both as provided for in section 246(2)(a).
91 O'Malley (n 74) 146.
92 Ibid.

> if, having the custody, charge or care of a child, he or she causes or encourages unlawful sexual intercourse or buggery with the child or causes or encourages the seduction or prostitution of, or a sexual assault on, the child.[93]

The maximum sentence for this offence is £25,000 or imprisonment for a term not exceeding 10 years or both.[94] Importantly, the term "child" is defined by reference to the age of consent, 17 years of age,[95] rather than the age of majority of 18 which is used for criminal legislation targeting commercial exploitation as well as being the age at which the state's child protection duties cease.[96]

As Gillespie notes, this section is not targeting physical contact with a child, but instead "criminalises a person who should be responsible for the welfare of a child."[97] The aim would appear to be to ensure that any person entrusted with responsibility for a child, and not merely a child's parent, is guilty of an offence if they facilitate the commission of a sexual offence. This significantly expands the remit of criminal responsibility and appears to be predicated on a shift in the understanding of what constitutes harmful conduct towards children as well as a shift in attitudes towards who can be regarded as responsible for a child's safety. The section is worded in such a way that it is applicable to a person who has temporary care or control of a child, such as in an education or sporting context, as well as parents, step-parents or others fulfilling a child care role. There is limited evidence for these propositions, however, as these provisions were not subjected to any parliamentary examination. Nonetheless, the attempt to criminalise a wider range of conduct, coupled with harsh punishments for those who exploited a position of trust and authority, would be consistent with a regulatory–preventative framework characteristic of a risk society.

Emerging threats and new technology

The final strand of criminal law reform in the years after the Kilkenny Inquiry was a concern over modern technology's role in child abuse. Two main statutes enacted during this period demonstrate this concern – the Sexual Offences (Jurisdiction) Act 1996 and the Child Trafficking and Pornography Act 1998. In their own ways, these Acts present information technology and the possibility of easier global travel as potential risks to children. These risks were new and had no historical precedent in Ireland. These concerns mirror the understanding of risk advocated by Beck, which holds that modern technologies reinforce cultural change by creating new kinds of risk. As he argued in *Risk Society*, "[i]n advanced

93 Section 249(1).
94 Section 249(2).
95 Section 249(4).
96 See Child Trafficking and Pornography Act 1998, s 2(1), as amended by Criminal Law (Sexual Offences) Act 2017, s 9 and Child Care Act 1991, s 2.
97 Alisdair A Gillespie, *Sexual Exploitation of Children: Law and Punishment* (Round Hall 2008) 90.

modernity, the social production of wealth is systematically accompanied by the social production of risk."[98] As an increasingly wealthy Tiger economy, temporally situated within a period of rapid technological progression, Irish society had indeed produced new risks to be regulated.

The 1996 Act effectively extends the jurisdiction of Irish criminal law to offences committed overseas. Its main provision is that a person who is a citizen or ordinary resident of the State and who does something outside the State which (a) is an offence in the place where the act is done, and (b) would be an offence if committed inside the State, is guilty of the latter offence, and may be tried and punished within the State.[99] The legislation was largely prompted by concern over child prostitution and sex tourism, the seriousness of which was outlined by John O'Donoghue TD, the opposition Justice spokesman and later Minister, who described the offences as "the ultimate form of exploitation, a terrible crime against the most vulnerable in society, a crime against humanity."[100] Nora Owen TD, then Minister for Justice, accepted that Irish people were now implicated in child sex tourism; recognising the possibility that there was a very small number of people were engaged in the practice, she posited that "[e]ven if only a handful of Irish people are so involved, it is incumbent on us as legislators to take action."[101] Consequentially, section 3 makes it an offence to knowingly arrange, or authorise the arrangement of, transport so that a person can commit a sexual offence, while section 4 criminalises the publication of information which is intended or is likely to promote the commission of an offence.

Further important points were raised during the Dáil debates which deepen our understandings of why this legislation came about. First, it was linked to the recent uncovering of paedophilia.[102] Second, the State's international legal obligations under the UN Convention on the Rights of the Child were also cited as a reason for introducing the legislation.[103] This reference to the Convention was underpinned by an increasing recognition that children were now coming to be recognised as rights-holders. The Convention, which obliges States Parties to take measures to protect children from abuse and exploitation,[104] was was apparently understood as providing a right for a child "to freedom from sexual abuse"

98 Ulrich Beck, *Risk Society: Towards A New Modernity* (Polity Press 1992) 19.
99 Section 2. The Schedule to the Act lists the offences to which the 1996 Act may be applied. See the commentary in Gillespie (n 97) 20–30 and O'Malley (n 74) 262–266.
100 Dáil Debates 14 November 1995, vol 458, col 354, John O'Donoghue TD.
101 Dáil Debates 14 November 1995, vol 458, col 370, Minister Nora Owen TD.
102 Dáil Debates 14 November 1995, vol 458, col 358, Eoin Ryan TD.
103 Ibid.
104 United Nations Convention on the Rights of the Child (adopted 20 November 1989, entered into force 2 September 1990) 1577 UNTS 3, Article 19. See also Optional Protocol to the Convention on the Rights of the Child on the Sale of Children, Child Prostitution and Child Pornography (adopted 25 May 2000, entered into force 18 January 2002) G.A. res. 54/263, Annex II, 54 U.N. GAOR Supp. (No. 49) at 6, U.N. Doc. A/54/49 (2000).

which necessitated bringing offenders to justice through the imposition of new criminal legislation.[105]

The 1998 Act introduced a range of new offences, varying from the trafficking of a child into or out of the State for the purpose of sexual exploitation,[106] to the production, distribution[107] and possession of child pornography.[108] O'Donnell and Milner trace the first mention of child pornography in the Dáil to 1984, with the next reference occurring in 1991, leading them to claim there was a lack of sustained interest in legislating on the issue.[109] However, an exchange in the Dáil in 1995 indicated that child pornography was not at the time illegal[110]; in order for a ban on particular material to be issued, it first had to come to the attention of the Censorship of Publications Board.[111]

The legislation was introduced, it was claimed, "despite there being no obvious child pornography problem in Ireland prior to 1998".[112] This legislation was largely designed to deal with the proliferation of child abuse imagery through the internet,[113] and by concern over the possible existence of paedophile rings.[114] As with the 1996 Act, the pornography legislation represents a clear attempt to regulate new risks. The recognition that children could be victimised in new ways, or perhaps that a whole new range of people could access abusive imagery as a result of technological change represents a major deviation from the view current throughout the earlier twentieth century that children were most at risk from moral dangers associated with parental conduct.[115] A further important feature of the 1998 Act was the recognition that children could be victimised or endangered by people with whom they had not had direct contact. The idea that the lack of physical proximity between a child and another person was no barrier to that person being regarded as a risk was carried to its logical conclusion in those aspects of law reform which sought to manage information about risk in a preventative fashion. It is to these reforms that we now turn.

Changing perceptions of risk and information management

Perhaps the strongest indicator that the frequency of attempts to regulate the risks children faced had come to characterise a risk society is provided by the desire to use information and data to guide child protection work. This is distinctly

105 Dáil Debates 15 November 1995, vol 458, col 633 Liz O'Donnell TD.
106 Section 3.
107 Section 5.
108 Section 6.
109 O'Donnell and Milner (n 28) 112–113.
110 See the exchange between Minister for Justice Nora Owen TD and John O'Donoghue TD at Dáil Debates 26 October 1995, vol 457, col 1706.
111 O'Donnell and Milner (n 28) 115.
112 Ibid 117.
113 Dáil Debates 18 December 1996, vol 473, col 487, Liz McManus TD.
114 Dáil Debates 17 December 1996, vol 473, col 136, Minister Austin Currie TD.
115 See the discussion in Chapter 4.

late modern phenomenon – the ease with which information could be gathered, stored and communicated was simply not the same in earlier periods. There was also a growing trend towards the belief that information about individuals who had proven to be a danger in the past could be used to determine what level of risk they posed in the future.[116] This need not take the form of a near-actuarial determination, and so be characteristic of historical approaches to risk, but rather was the basis for a new management of risks in broader terms.[117] Further, the use of information would no longer be a matter solely of discretion or informal decision-making, but would now take place in a structured way, and would increasingly be mandated by law.

While increased legal regulation of social work practice by law will be examined more in the following chapter, the material discussed here represents the early stages of this process, which manifested itself in through three distinct mechanisms. These were the reform of the child protection guidelines in order to facilitate greater interagency cooperation, legislative change designed to ensure that information about risky individuals was at the state's disposal and the development of the new administrative practice of vetting to assist employers and voluntary organizations in undertaking a safeguarding function. The courts also began to interpret the Child Care Act 1991 in a way which facilitated interagency communication about risks as a means of furthering children's interests.

Reform of child protection guidelines

The Kilkenny Incest Inquiry had highlighted major flaws in the implementation of the 1987 Child Abuse Guidelines; for instance, when a victim reported a physical assault by her father to a doctor who, instead of reporting the matter to the health board as envisaged under the 1987 Guidelines, sought to admonish the father directly.[118] Indeed, the Report concluded that:

> Constraints on the flow of information within the health care system, within hospitals and between hospitals, GPs and Community Care, derive from a deeply held tradition of respect for the privacy of family related information, coupled with professional practices in relation to confidentiality especially where adults were concerned.[119]

In the wake of the Kilkenny Scandal, the Department of Health's 1987 Guidelines were supplemented by the *Notification of Suspected Cases of Child Abuse between*

116 See generally, Robert Castel, 'From Dangerousness to Risk' in Graham Burchell, Colin Gordon, Peter M Miller, *The Foucault Effect: Studies in Governmentality* (Harvester Wheatsheaf 1991).
117 See generally the discussion of risk and law in Chapter 1.
118 McGuinness (n 8) 81.
119 McGuinness (n 8) 87.

the Health Boards and An Garda Síochána document issued in 1995.[120] The 1995 guidelines were designed to ensure that the health board and the Gardaí notified each other of any suspected cases of child abuse and were described in the Ferns Report as being "administratively mandatory".[121] Despite the "administratively mandatory" nature of the guidelines, there were significant weaknesses in their implementation. Significantly, many Gardaí were unaware of their existence and many social workers were reticent about reporting suspected abuse to the Gardaí for fear that it would undermine their child protection role.[122] The guidelines themselves were short-lived, however, as they were then subsumed into the more comprehensive *Children First Guidelines.*

Children First: National Guidelines for the Protection and Welfare of Children was published in 1999.[123] Writing in 1996, Buckley highlighted that

> publicity and consequent public reaction to revelations of maltreatment of children … have highlighted the subject of child abuse and focussed on the need for 'certainty' in combating it, to a point where procedures will have a dominant role to play in child care agencies.[124]

Children First was effectively a response to this need and represents a significant point in the process of the increasing juridification of child protection social work. The Guidelines established a comprehensive framework for the definition, reporting and assessment of child abuse and neglect. The Guidelines dealt with the four main categories of abuse – physical, emotional, sexual and neglect – and for the first time provided definitions of each.[125] In particular, the needs of children and families were put at the centre of child care work.[126] This becomes especially clear when the principles guiding the drafting of *Children First* are examined.[127] The welfare of children is described as being of "paramount importance". The guidelines also state that "[a] proper balance must be struck between protecting children and respecting the rights and needs of parents/carers and families; but where there is conflict, the child's welfare must come first."[128] This is

120 Department of Health, *Guidelines on the Identification and Management of Non-Accidental Injury to Children* (Stationery Office 1987), Department of Health, *Notification of Suspected Cases of Child Abuse between the Health Boards and An Garda Síochána* (Stationery Office 1995).

121 Murphy, Buckley and Joyce (n 3) 55.

122 Helen Buckley, 'Child Abuse Guidelines in Ireland: For Whose Protection?' (1996) 44(2) *Administration* 37, 43. See also Helen Buckley, 'Children First: Implications for Practice' (2000) 3 (4) *Irish Journal of Family Law* 10.

123 Department of Health and Children, *Children First: National Guidelines for the Protection and Welfare of Children* (Stationery Office 1999). Referred to hereafter as *Children First.*

124 Buckley (n 122) 39.

125 *Children First* (n 123) 31.

126 Ibid 17.

127 Ibid 22–23.

128 Ibid 22.

an innovative statement but it is important to note that there is no mention of children's rights of any kind, merely that children have welfare interests.

One of the key points emphasised throughout *Children First*, a point vital to understanding the now dominant view that child abuse was a risk for a much wider range of children than previously thought, is that child abuse and neglect is a societal problem and that it is, therefore, everyone's responsibility to report any suspicions they may have.[129] The exact nature of this responsibility at the time was unclear. The guidelines themselves were addressed to a wide audience – health board staff, teachers, Gardaí and other professionals who may come into professional contact with children and the general public. While professionals may be contractually obliged to report suspicions of abuse by their employers or professional associations, no equivalent legal obligation then existed for members of the public. Indeed, the duty to report abuse suspicions has been described elsewhere as "a duty of society" without the possibility of criminal sanction.[130] The standard procedure for the reporting of child abuse outlined in the Guidelines seemed more suited to the reporting of concerns by professionals rather than by the public at large.[131]

Other problems emerged with the operation of *Children First*, and the evidence of its inconsistent implementation in various parts of the country in particular. Concern over the implementation of these guidelines represents a further shift in the perception of children as having interests which required further risk management strategies to be adopted; concerns over implementation, therefore, created the conditions of possibility in which further measures could be taken. Significant regional variations were identified by the Social Services Inspectorate (SSI) who noted that by the end of 2001, some two years after the Guidelines were published, only seven out of ten regional health boards had distributed them to all relevant staff.[132]

One of the consequences of these varying levels of awareness about the Guidelines was the inability of health boards to agree on standardised advanced training, as had been envisaged, because each health board was at a different stage of awareness-raising and implementation of the Guidelines. The SSI report also identified significant differences between health boards when it came to using the standardised child abuse notification system and the formal procedure for cooperation with the Gardaí. It was found that informal procedures were used by several health boards and that there was confusion as to the nature and purpose of the procedures outlined in *Children First*.[133] The National Children's Advisory

129 Ibid 37.

130 Ombudsman for Children, *A Report Based on an investigation into the implementation of Children First: National Guidelines for the Protection and Welfare of Children* (Ombudsman for Children 2010) 6.

131 See generally, *Children First* (n 123) ch 4.

132 Social Services Inspectorate, Social Service Inspectorate, *Report on the Monitoring of Implementation of Children First: National Guidelines for the Protection and Welfare of Children* (Stationery Office 2003) 6–7.

133 Ibid 7–9. The SSI Report was critical, at 8, of the reliance placed on informal lines of communication between relevant bodies.

Council was also concerned by the lack of a coherent medium- to long-term strategy to ensure the continued implementation of the Guidelines.[134] The Council also criticised the speed at which reforms aimed at increasing interagency cooperation were taking place.[135] These weaknesses highlighted the need for the Guidelines to have greater legal force and for reporting and information management to be placed on a statutory footing, a question which was addressed by the debate over the introduction of mandatory reporting.

Mandatory reporting and vetting

While child protection information sharing and notification guidelines were being updated, the introduction of mandatory reporting was being considered. The Law Reform Commission and the Kilkenny Incest Report both recommend that mandatory reporting be introduced, although each had a slightly different emphasis. The Law Reform Commission recommended that certain professionals be under an obligation to report cases where they knew or had good reason to believe that a child had been sexually abused.[136] The Kilkenny Report, however, recommended that a wider range of professionals be obliged to report suspicions of all forms of child abuse.[137] The introduction of the 1995 Notification Guidelines discussed above were later described as "administratively mandatory", indicating a gradual drift towards a mandatory reporting system.[138] Following this, *Putting Children First*,[139] a government discussion document, was published in 1996, and asked for submissions from interested parties

> to consider whether developing our services to protect children from abuse, improving existing arrangements for the notification of child abuse and co-ordinating action in response to such abuse would better serve the interests of children than the introduction of mandatory reporting.140

Mandatory reporting was then promised in the agreed programme for government underpinning the coalition government formed in the wake of the 1997 general election.[141] Clearly, mandatory reporting was now seen as an

134 National Children's Advisory Council, *Advice to the Minister on the Implementation of Children First and Vetting* (Stationery Office 2003) 4.
135 Ibid 5.
136 Law Reform Commission (n 58) 8–10. The professions placed under an obligation to report would have been doctors, psychiatrists, psychologists, health workers, social workers, probation officers and teachers.
137 McGuinness (n 8) 97.
138 Murphy, Buckley and Joyce (n 3) 55.
139 Department of Health, *Putting Children First* (Stationery Office, 1996).
140 Ibid 4.18.
141 Department of the Taoiseach, *Action Plan for the Millennium* (Department of the Taoiseach, 1998) 9, available at www.taoiseach.gov.ie%2Feng%2FPublications%2FPublication

effective and desirable response to child protection concerns; one of the prime reasons used in justifying its introduction was that it would provide a clear signal that the state was now taking child protection seriously.[142] The belief had therefore begun to take hold that the state now needed to have access to a wider range of information about child abuse suspicions in order to better manage risk.

This desire to see mandatory reporting as both a substantive contribution to the child protection system and as a signal that child protection was a political priority is interesting given how it encapsulates how children were thought about. It has been argued that when mandatory reporting was introduced in the United States throughout the 1960s and 1970s, the main aim of reporting statutes was not to enhance children's rights but to construct a system that was essentially medical in nature – to identify parents whose disturbed behaviour indicated that they suffered from a syndrome.[143] It was also claimed the early mandatory reporting advocates, in part because of their medicalised view of child abuse, grossly underestimated its prevalence.[144] Harries and Clare go so far as to say that "[m]any of the arguments are polemical and most of the 'evidence' is inferential and presumptive."[145]

Despite the increasing political appetite for a mandatory reporting system, Ferguson highlighted that there was "little reason to be optimistic" about the introduction of the policy in Ireland.[146] O'Tighearnaigh argued that "the debate on mandatory reporting to date has been about adult, system and professional fear".[147] This characterization of mandatory reporting demonstrates how the desire for its introduction was not based on an understanding that it was needed to improve child welfare services, but that it would allow greater focus on children at risk. The proposals did not progress, partly due to the fear of over-reporting, a deluge of too much information about risky situations. However, a move in the direction of encouraging reporting was taken with the passage of the Protection of Persons Reporting Child Abuse Act 1998, section 3 of which exempted people

---

s_Archive%2FPublications_for_1998%2Factionmillennium1.pdf&usg=AFQjCNFXk-DAc6RPiTsTp_lJ4Zbi8OtQzrw&sig2=lUTZ1YWlkeJ2UIfD9gh5mw, accessed 24 October 2019.

142 Law Reform Commission, *Consultation Paper on Child Sexual Abuse* (LRC CP-2 1989) 23–24, and Department of Health (n 139) 2.1.

143 Gary B Melton, 'Mandated Reporting: A Policy without Reason' (2005) 29 *Child Abuse & Neglect* 9.

144 Kieran McGrath, 'Mandatory Reporting of Suspected Child Abuse—Would the Drawbacks Outweigh the Benefits for Irish Children? (1996) 2(2) *Medico-Legal Journal of Ireland* 44.

145 Maria Harries and Mike Clare, *Mandatory reporting of child abuse: Evidence and options. Report for the Western Australian Child Protection Council* (Department for Community Development 2002) 31, available at www.sph.uwa.edu.au/__data/assets/pdf_file/0009/1102131/MRFinalReport.pdf, accessed 29 December 2019.

146 Ferguson (n 55) 26. See also Helen Buckley, 'Reforming the Child Protection System: Why We Need to be Careful What We Wish For' (2009) 12(2) *Irish Journal of Family Law* 27.

147 Cian O'Tighearnaigh, 'The Reporting of Child Abuse – The Contribution of Mandatory Reporting' (1996) 3(2) *Journal of Child Centred Practice* 95.

who reported suspected child abuse from legal liability if they had acted reasonably and in good faith in both forming the opinion that a child was endangered and in reporting it. While not as strong a measure as a mandatory reporting law, it did mark the first occasion when legislation designed to protect the interests of children, as well as those reporting concerns, was accorded priority over other interests.

During this period, a way of utilising more targeted information began to emerge when vetting also came to be seen as a means by which information could be used as a child protection mechanism. In essence, it is a means of pre-employment screening for people seeking to work with children, whereby an organization – usually an employer or voluntary agency – made a vetting request about a named individual to the Gardaí. The Gardaí would search for and disclose to the requesting organization details of "all convictions and/or prosecutions, successful or not, pending or completed, in the State or elsewhere".[148] This is what is known as "hard" information, information that a person has been convicted or prosecuted for an offence, as distinct from "soft" information which consists of any other information, held by any other agency, such as information about concerns known to a health board that a person may be abusive towards their own children.

The process seems to have begun in 1987,[149] when the Gardaí began to vet both prospective adoptive parents and Irish people applying for jobs in the United Kingdom which would give them substantial access to children. Vetting arrangements were extended to cover new staff seeking work in children's residential centres in 1994,[150] and in 1995 they were extended again to cover staff in the health services and in external agencies receiving public funds.[151] All of this occurred in the absence of any legislative basis. Following a review of vetting arrangements, the Garda Central Vetting Unit (GCVU) was established in 2002 to deal with all aspects of vetting in Ireland. A further Garda Working Group was established and in 2004 it set out its vision of what the vetting system should entail.[152] The Working Group operated from two premises – first, that the safety of vulnerable children must be protected as part of the corporate duty of any organization providing services to children, and that ultimate responsibility for ensuring safety rested with the organization itself; vetting is merely one part of safe recruitment practices. The Group was well aware of the lack of legislative backing for vetting and advised that this be rectified.[153] More

148 Garda Síochána, 'Garda Vetting/Data Protection FAQ' available at http://www.garda.ie/FAQ/Default.aspx?FAQCategory=36, accessed 24 October 2017.

149 Department of Justice, *Working Group on Garda Vetting Report* (Stationery Office 2004) 8.

150 Department of Health Circular, 'Recruitment and Selection of Staff to Children's Residential Centres Operated by Voluntary Bodies' (1994).

151 Department of Health Circular, 'Recruitment and Selection Procedures' (1995). See National Children's Advisory Council (n 134) 12.

152 Department of Justice (n 149).

153 Ibid 29–32.

substantially, however, they argued that only those people who would have substantial, unsupervised access to children should be vetted. No definition of this term is given by the Group, inevitably introducing a wide element of subjectivity as to what counts as substantial and unsupervised, with this question ultimately to be resolved by the organization seeking disclosure.[154] They also called for the inclusion of "allegations and complaints involving alleged criminal activity" within the vetting disclosure,[155] thereby calling for the introduction of soft information-based vetting.

This Report represents a very clear validation of the some this chapter's core claims – first, that modern awareness of child abuse had progressed to the point where previously trusted professionals were now seen as potential sources of threat and risk to children and that traditional social relations were disturbed and public understanding and awareness of abuse radically altered. This is a clear example of the arguments developed by Giddens and Beck about shifts in the perceptions and role of risk in reflexive modernity. Second, it was recognised the information about these risks could, and should, be collated. Third, that the collation of this information and its effective management could be used as part of a risk reduction strategy. Finally, it accorded a central place to law in this process, as the previously informal and unregulated system of disclosure was recognised as requiring replacement by legislation.

Attempts were made in the mid-1990s to develop a legislative basis for pre-employment screening of an individual's sexual history in order to protect children. In the original version of the Employment Equality Bill 1996, section 16(4) provided that a person

> who engages in or has a propensity to engage in any form of sexual behaviour to which an employer or any of the employer's employees, clients, customers or other business contacts might be at risk of exposure or might reasonably object will not be protected from discrimination in this legislation.

During the passage of this legislation, the provision was amended significantly. Opposition and backbench TDs supported the clause in principle if it was designed to combat paedophilia,[156] but it was also recognised that it cast the net too wide. As Helen Keogh TD pointed out,

> [i]ts sweeping terms lay it open to constitutional challenges which could damage its overall intent. By encompassing non-criminal sexual behaviour and personal relationships of adult women and men, to which the public may object, it detracts from the intent of protecting minors from the criminal

154 National Children's Advisory Council (n 134) 13, 14.
155 Department of Justice (n 149) 17 and 30.
156 See the contributions at Dáil Debates 22 October 1996, vol 470, col 737, Helen Keogh TD, and vol 470, col 744, Eric Byrne TD.

and predatory actions of paedophiles. It threatens to open a major loophole based on reasonable customer or client preference, which could translate into prejudice against homosexual people.

By the time the Bill was passed through both Dáil and Seanad, it had been amended to reflect these concerns. The provisions permitting a person to be dismissed on the basis of lawful sexual behaviour to which a person associated with a business could object was instead replaced with a provision permitting a person to be dismissed for criminal sexual behaviour, with a specific reference to sexual offending against children. The new clause stated that:

> (4) Nothing in this Act shall be construed as requiring an employer to recruit, retain in employment or promote an individual if the employer is aware, on the basis of a criminal conviction of the individual or other reliable information, that the individual engages, or has a propensity to engage, in any form of sexual behaviour which is unlawful.
> (5) Without prejudice to the generality of subsection (4), that subsection applies in particular where the employment concerned involves access to minors or to other persons who are vulnerable.

In the course of a review of this legislation to test its constitutionality, the Supreme Court held that these provisions did not violate the Constitution.[157] Concern was raised that the language used in section 16(4) – in particular the phrases "reliable information" and "propensity" – was unconstitutionally vague.[158] An earlier decision had held that the meaning of the phrase "reputed thief" was too vague and certain to form the basis of a criminal offence, and so the legislation at issue in that instance was deemed to be unconstitutional.[159] In the *Employment Equality Bill* decision, however, the Supreme Court was not dealing with the imposition of criminal liability, but with an exemption from a general protection against non-discrimination, and found that the meaning of the relevant phrases could be examined by a future court in light of the particular circumstances of a case and applying the constitutionally required standards of fair procedures.[160]

Moreover, the Court reasoned that the decision to enact such measures was driven by a policy choice that the Oireachtas was entitled to take. Specifically, the Court stated that section 16(5) indicated that the Oireachtas was "conscious of the higher dangers of recidivism with regard to sexual crimes as well as the addictive character of certain sexual offences involving minors".[161] Legislation such as this could not be unconstitutional as it was "justifiable on the grounds of

157 *In re Article 26 and the Employment Equality Bill 1996* [1997] 2 IR 321 (SC).
158 Ibid 374–375.
159 *King v Attorney General* [1981] IR 223 (SC).
160 *In re Article 26* (n 157) 376.
161 Ibid.

prudence and safety."[162] The construction of child sex offenders as near-inevitable recidivists by a Supreme Court that, unlike political figures, could afford to take a more circumspect view of public perceptions of the risks faced by children is striking. While section 16 did not provide a full legislative basis for vetting, it was clear the Court was conscious of the public policy aspects of the legislation, and hence left matters for future courts to determine in light of particular circumstances. Even so, it provided a hint as to how such a case might be determined. The Court was clear in its view that fair procedures could not be compromised; it stated that "it is not every idle word that should be heeded by an employer" and that it would effectively be a "value judgment" for employer's in each case.[163] Nonetheless, "if that judgment is exercised *bona fide* the employer should not be faulted just because it turns out to be wrong."[164] This final statement indicates that a person challenging their dismissal in circumstances where sections 16(4) and 16(5) were relevant would face an onerous task. The Supreme Court here came as close as it possibly could in the circumstances to agreeing with views of Eric Byrne TD who posited that "[i]f there is any doubt, the interests of the children must be paramount."[165]

The 1996 Bill was, however, deemed unconstitutional on other grounds. When the revised legislation was again presented to the Dáil, the sections relating to sexual offending were exactly the same as those considered by the Supreme Court. Some concern was again raised, however, that the phrase "reliable information" was still too vague. Frances Fitzgerald TD, a former social worker and future Minister for Children and Minister for Justice, sought to replace the phrase "reliable information" with the phrase "information from a reliable and verifiable source", with the intention of providing "extra protection to employers when they get extra information".[166] It is not clear from the debates exactly which different sources would have fallen within the scope of this amendment, but it may be that it sought to protect employers who had received information from a health board or other organization which was aware of a risk. The Minister of State defended the present drafting, stating that the "very special danger of paedophilia in society and the potential injury to children prompted the drafting of this subsection. We felt that with sexual contact we must make sure extraordinary caution is required, having regard to the way paedophiles operate", and that it should be left to a court to delineate the exact contours of the provision.[167] As a result, the version of the provisions upheld by the Supreme Court eventually became sections 16(5) and 16(6) of the Employment Equality Act 1998.

162 Ibid.
163 Ibid.
164 Ibid.
165 Dáil Debates 22 October 1996, vol 470, col 744, Eric Byrne TD.
166 Dáil Debates 28 May 1998, Select Committee on Justice, Equality and Women's Rights Debate, Frances Fitzgerald TD.
167 Ibid, Minister of State Mary Wallace TD.

The decision in MQ v Gleeson

As outlined in Chapter 5, section 3 of the Child Care Act 1991 imposes duties on the state to promote the welfare of children not receiving adequate care and protection.[168] This includes a duty to gather, share and coordinate information relating to these children.[169] The first case since the passage of the 1991 Act to assess the level of information-sharing that was required in order to fulfil the duties imposed on the state was *MQ v Gleeson*.[170] The applicant had been enrolled on a social studies course operated by a local education committee.[171] This course involved a placement at a children's play centre. Unbeknownst to the course provider, the local Health Board had received numerous complaints of a "grievous nature" about his behaviour towards his own children over a 19-year period.[172] These complaints covered the entire spectrum of child abuse from emotional neglect to sexual abuse, leading the Health Board to believe that the applicant was unsuitable for work with children.[173] However, no action was ever taken under either the 1908 Act or the 1991 Act, none of the complaints was referred to the Gardaí and none of the allegations was brought to the attention of the applicant. Once the Health Board learned of the applicant's enrolment on the course, they notified the course provider of their concerns, leading to his suspension from the course. As a result, he sought to judicially review both the Health Board's communication of their concerns and the decision to suspend him from the course.

Barr J upheld both the decision to disclose the information and to use the information to suspend the applicant. He noted that the 1991 Act was silent on the extent of the Health Board's obligations to protect children put at risk by preventing unsuitable people seeking to enter child care professions.[174] However, he held that despite this uncertainty, the Board was bound under section 3 to protect not only children known to be presently at risk, but also unidentified children who "by reason of a potential situation in the future are liable to require protection at that time from a prospective danger the nature of which is presently known to or reasonably suspected by a health board".[175] On the facts of the case, it was held that the Board was perfectly entitled to take pre-emptive action; it did not have to wait for children to be abused in order to communicate to another agency that it had concerns over a particular individual's possible propensity to

168 See generally Chapter 5: The Child Care Act 1991: The nature of the state's child protection duties.

169 Section 3(2)(a).

170 [1998] 4 IR 85 (HC).

171 It should be noted that the VEC, which operates on a regional basis, was a state body established by the Vocational Education Act 1930, thus making its decisions susceptible to judicial review.

172 *MQ* (n 170) 89.

173 Ibid.

174 Ibid 99.

175 Ibid.

harm children. The threshold for triggering interagency communication in this context is not the criminal, or indeed civil standard of proof, but when "a significant doubt in the minds of competent experienced health board or related professional personnel that there has been abuse by a particular person."[176] When this threshold is reached, the Health Board has an obligation to take appropriate action. In the context of this particular case, appropriate action consisted of notifying another agency of their concerns. The underlying rationale is that other agencies should be notified of concerning information and a coordinated response formulated in order to ensure that the aim of effective child protection is fulfilled. Overall, *MQ* represents a judicial statement that highlights the need for the state to take preventative measures based on information-sharing if it is to fulfil the section 3 obligations.

The judgment demonstrates the new importance of risk management in child protection, and indeed, a new construction of risk. There was clearly an impression that the applicant posed a risk to children and that this impression necessitated the release of information in order to fulfil the obligations imposed by the 1991 Act. Yet there were also risks to the applicant that had to be carefully managed. The applicant's constitutional rights to a good name and his presumption of innocence could be jeopardised by the communication of alleged criminal activity.[177] Given that the decision to suspend him was taken by a public body, his rights to natural and constitutional justice in administrative decision-making were also compromised. As a result of these significant dangers to legal rights, the various public bodies involved owed him the opportunity to defend himself. Barr J summed up the obligations to the alleged abuser as follows:

> [There is] a duty to take all reasonable steps to interview the [alleged abuser]; to furnish him before interview with notice of the allegations against him in short form; to give him a reasonable opportunity to make his defence and to carry out such further investigations as might appear appropriate in the light of information furnished by him in response to the complaints. No opinion as to the weight to be attached to each complaint should have been formed until the foregoing investigations relating to the [alleged abuser] had been made and information derived therefrom had been carefully assessed.[178]

These procedural protections are regarded as vital if the information-gathering and sharing obligations imposed by section 3 are to be supported by the courts; nonetheless, child protection can legitimately be used as a reason for according a lower priority to the rights of alleged abusers. This was made clear in another decision by Barr J, *Eastern Health Board v Fitness to Practice Committee of the*

176 Ibid 101.
177 For a fuller discussion of the rights, see Geoffrey Shannon, *Report of the Special Rapporteur on Child Protection: A Report Submitted to the Oireachtas* (Stationery Office 2006) 11–17.
178 *MQ* (n 170) 102.

Medical Council.[179] Here, it was stated clearly that when determining whether to disclose information about a particular individual to third parties, a public interest "such as the protection of vulnerable children" takes priority over the interests of such a person.[180] The courts can, therefore, be seen to be reflexively engaging in the further development of guidelines in parallel to those established by child protection experts, reacting to the new awareness of risk by asking how risk could be managed, rather than eliminated.

The management of sex offenders

The Sex Offenders Act 2001 shows more than most legal developments the new ways in which childhood and risk were perceived. Calls for the introduction of some form of sex offender registration system had been made by civil society groups, and the ISPCC and Barnardos in particular, for several years.[181] The legislation introduces a notification requirement for people convicted of most sexual offences.[182] This is commonly referred to as a "register", but instead comprises an obligation imposed on convicted persons to notify the Gardaí of certain details for set periods of time, depending on the length of sentence they received upon conviction. Within seven days of conviction, the Gardaí must be notified by the convicted person of their name, date of birth and address, and they must update the Gardaí any time they change address, or leave the state for longer than seven days, as well as their location while outside the State.[183] According to section 8, this requirement lasts for a period of between five years and life.[184] Failure to comply with these requirements is an offence in itself, liable to a maximum punishment of a €10,000 fine and five years' imprisonment.[185]

The Act also provides for post-release supervision or disclosure requirements.[186] *People (DPP) v Muldoon* provides an example of the kind of requirements contemplated by the legislation.[187] The Court of Criminal Appeal refused the applicant leave to appeal a decision to prevent him from having a computer

179 [1998] 3 IR 399 (HC).
180 Ibid 429.
181 See Catherine Clery, 'Register of Abusers and Children at Risk Sought by ISPCC' *The Irish Times* (Dublin 20 August 1996) 7, Carol Coulter, 'Demand grows for a Paedophile Register' *The Irish Times* (Dublin 18 August 1997) 10, Padraig O'Morain, 'Register of All Sex Offenders Sought as List is Decided' *The Irish Times* (Dublin 31 December 1997) 4, Terry Thomas, 'Protecting the Public: Some Observations on the Sex Offenders Bill 2000' (2000) 10(2) *Irish Criminal Law Journal* 12.
182 See section 3 and Schedule 1 which outlines the offences subject to notification.
183 Section 10.
184 This section also outlines the rules applicable to suspended and consecutive sentences, as well as the rules for juvenile offenders.
185 On summary conviction, the maximum penalty is currently a Class A fine or 12 months' imprisonment, or both – see section 12(3), as amended by section 13 of the Criminal Law (Human Trafficking) Act 2008.
186 See generally Part V of the Act.
187 *Ex tempore* CCA 7 July 2003.

or internet access for 11 years following his conviction for child pornography offences. While O'Malley questions whether such an order could be upheld today given that an internet ban would, as he contends, amount "to a kind of social exile",[188] as well as the success of constitutional challenges to similar sentences in the United States,[189] the intent to manage an individual's risk in a rather punitive way is clear. A particularly important aspect of the legislation from a child protection perspective is found in the provisions limiting the ability of offenders to seek certain types of employment.[190] Section 26 of the Act provides that if an offender seeks employment of which a necessary and regular part consists of having unsupervised access to, or contact with, children or vulnerable adults, they must disclose their convictions.[191] Gillespie makes the point that a sex offender is not prevented from working with children, merely that if they wish to do so, they must disclose their convictions.[192]

Legislation of this nature has been characterised as marking a turn away from welfarism in the criminal justice system and towards a new concern with risk, variously described as a "new risk penology",[193] policy based on precautionary logic,[194] risk-averse policy,[195] and policies of radical prevention,[196] or alternatively as representing a change in emphasis "from dangerousness to risk".[197] The nature and extent of the risks posed by people convicted of sexual offences were constructed within a climate where "law and order" issues had significant political currency and where punitiveness characterised much of the political rhetoric of the time.[198] Originally regarded as a means of addressing women's rights to protec-

188 O'Malley (n 74) 706.

189 See *United States v Holm* 326 F 3d 872 (2003), *United States v Scott* 316 F 3d 733 (7th Cir. 2003) and *United States v Freeman* 316 F 3d 386 (7th Cir. 2003), discussed in O'Malley (n 74) 706–707.

190 Sex Offenders Act 2001, Part IV.

191 Sex Offenders Act 2001, s 26. It should be noted that there are a variety of ways in which offences can be committed under the Act – by applying to be employed, entering into a contract of employment, applying to do relevant work and entering into a contract for services. See generally, Gillespie (n 97) ch 9 and Thomas (n 181).

192 Gillespie (n 97) 327.

193 David Garland, *The Culture of Control: Crime and Social Order in Contemporary Society* (Oxford University Press 2001).

194 Richard V Ericson, *Crime in an Insecure World* (Polity Press 2007).

195 Adam Crawford, 'Contractual Governance of Deviant Behaviour' (2003) 30 *Journal of Law and Society* 479, Ian Loader and Neil Walker, *Civilizing Security* (Cambridge University Press 2007).

196 Bill Hebenton and Tony Seddon, 'From Dangerousness to Precaution: Managing Sexual and Violent Offenders in an Insecure and Uncertain Age' (2009) 49 *British Journal of Criminology* 343.

197 Castel (n 116). See generally, Anne-Marie McAlinden, 'Vetting Sexual Offenders: State Over-Extension, The Punishment Deficit and the Failure to Manage Risk' (2010) 19(1) *Social and Legal Studies* 25.

198 Martin Quigley, 'The Genesis and Origin of the Sex Offenders Act 2001' (2013) *UCD Working Papers in Law, Criminology and Social Studies Research Paper No 2/2013*, 20 http://ssrn.com/abstract=2263262, accessed 29 December 2019.

tion from sexual offending,[199] it was introduced in the Dáil by Minister for Justice John O'Donoghue TD as a means of protecting "the vulnerable, those unable to defend themselves and, of course, our children" from those who would "prey" on them in pursuit of their "vile activities".[200] Opposition TDs focused more closely on paedophilia, with one opposition justice spokesman claiming that the legislation was necessary due to a recidivism rate of 95% among child sex offenders.[201] This necessitated a punitive turn, away from rehabilitation and towards containment and control.[202] Underpinning these sentiments was the Department of Justice's own Discussion Paper on Sexual Offences which viewed the terms "sex offender register" and "paedophile register" synonymously.[203] Nonetheless, the Discussion Paper also recognised that there was no empirical evidence for a recidivism rate of over 90% and that there was "a danger that a public belief of almost certain re-offending by sex offenders could be re-inforced."[204] Ironically, in the face of rapid detraditionalization and the reconstruction of the sources of risk to children, the construction of offenders in these debates shows a relative lack of focus on intra-familial abuse, which had been so heavily problematized in reports from the Kilkenny and McColgan inquiries.

It was clear that there was a political consensus that even if the legislation may impact negatively on those convicted of offence, it is an acceptable imposition in order to ensure that the rights of children were given priority,[205] or that the rights of the local community were protected.[206] This belief in zero-sum trade-offs between the interests of offenders and the interests of the wider community or victims dominated the political discourse. Quigley points out that there were no less than six separate references during the Dáil debates to the need to redress the balance in the criminal justice system in favour of victims and community.[207] Further evidence of the lack of nuance and the adoption of a totalising narrative underpinning the construction of risk was the claim that all sex offenders share three common characteristics: "low self-esteem, low sense of self-worth and little understanding of their victim's position."[208] The desire to construct images of predators posing a constant "stranger-danger" type risk provides evidence for the claim made by McGrath that the measures like this only provided "a safety valve for adult anxiety, rather than a safety measure for children."[209]

199 See its inclusion in the Fianna Fáil–Progressive Democrat programme for government under the heading of women's rights, Department of the Taoiseach (n 141) 8.
200 Dáil Debates 6 April 2000, vol 517, col 1081, Minister John O'Donoghue TD.
201 See also Department of Justice, Equality and Law Reform, *The Law on Sexual Offences — A Discussion Paper* (Stationary Office 1998) ch 10.
202 Dáil Debates 6 April 2000, vol 517, col 1087, Dan Neville TD.
203 Department of Justice (n 201) 79.
204 Ibid.
205 Dáil Debates 6 April 2000, vol 517, col 1088, Dan Neville TD.
206 Dáil Debates 17 May 2000, vol 519, col 599, John Dennehy TD.
207 Quigley (n 198) 20.
208 Dáil Debates 6 April 2000, vol 517, col 1091, Dan Neville TD.
209 Kieran McGrath, 'Registering Sex Offenders' *The Irish Times* (Dublin, 28 January 1998) 17.

Conclusion

The years between the Kilkenny Inquiry and the decisions in the *CC* and *A* cases saw radical reform of child protection law. In reforming the law of evidence and the substantive criminal law in ways that were designed to make the detection and prosecution of child abuse easier, children's interests were recognised and used to justify significant change. Children's interests in an effective protection system also played a significant role in the increased use of information management and risk assessment strategies pioneered during these years. However, what were perhaps the most important changes occurred in public and political attitudes towards children and child abuse. Child abuse was accepted as a real social phenomenon, a real risk that children faced. This was in large part due to the individuals and groups mentioned in the early part of this chapter who engaged in subpolitics, and to whom I will return in the following chapter. This chapter also traced how it came to be recognised that the risk of abuse presented itself both inside the home and outside it, and that people in a position of trust or authority were potential sources of risk.

More fundamentally, these risks were seen as legitimate targets of a new regulatory–preventive way of handling risk. These changes from earlier decades are crucial to understanding not only how child protection changed in the years under examination in this chapter, but also in the following chapter. In the following chapter, further substantive law reforms initiated, and the increased juridification of social work practice by legal rules would be radically furthered by, among other measures, the development of mandatory reporting legislation and a more expansive vetting system.

References

Anonymous, 'Man found not guilty of incest' *Irish Times* (Dublin, 20 February 1992) 4.

Anonymous, 'Shatter concerned at incest case collapse' *Irish Times* (Dublin, 21 February 1992) 7.

Beck U, *Risk Society: Towards A New Modernity* (Polity Press 1992).

Beck U, *World Risk Society* (Wiley Blackwell 1999).

Breen M, 'Through the Looking Glass: How the Mass Media Represent, Reflect and Refract Sexual Crime in Ireland' (2007) 10 *Irish Communications Review* 5.

Breen M, McGee H, O'Boyle C, Goode H and Devereux E, '"Suing the Pope" and Scandalising the People: Irish Attitudes to Sexual Abuse by clergy Pre- and Post-Screening of a Critical Documentary' (2009) 11 *Irish Communications Review* 77.

Buckley H, 'Child Abuse Guidelines in Ireland: For Whose Protection?' (1996) 44(2) *Administration* 37.

Buckley H, 'Children First: Implications for Practice' (2000) 3(4) *Irish Journal of Family Law* 10.

Buckley H, 'Reforming the Child Protection System: Why We Need to be Careful What We Wish For' (2009) 12(2) *Irish Journal of Family Law* 27.

Buckley H and O'Nolan C, *An Examination of Recommendations from Inquiries into Events in Families and their Interactions with State Services, and their Impact on Policy and Practice* (Government Publications 2013).

Carroll J and Brennock M, 'Inquiry ordered into failure of health services in incest case' *Irish Times* (Dublin, 4 March 1993) 6.

Castel R, 'From Dangerousness to Risk' in Graham Burchell, Colin Gordon, Peter M Miller (eds), *The Foucault Effect: Studies in Governmentality* (Harvester Wheatsheaf 1991).

Clarke M, *Regulation: The Social Control of Business between Law and Politics* (Macmillan 2000) 25.

Clery C, 'Register of abusers and children at risk sought by ISPCC' *Irish Times* (Dublin, 20 August 1996) 7.

Commission to Inquire into Child Abuse (CICA), *Report of the Commission to Inquire into Child Abuse* (Stationery Office 2009).

Coulter C, 'Demand grows for a Paedophile Register' *Irish Times* (Dublin, 18 August 1997) 10.

Coulter C, 'McColgans savour outcome of Ordeal' *Irish Times* (Dublin, 24 January 1998) 8.

Crawford A, 'Contractual Governance of Deviant Behaviour' (2003) 30 *Journal of Law and Society* 479.

Crowe C, 'On the Ferns Report' (2006) 22 *Dublin Review* 5.

Department of Health, *Guidelines on the Identification and Management of Non-Accidental Injury to Children* (Stationery Office 1987).

Department of Health, *Notification of Suspected Cases of Child Abuse between the Health Boards and An Garda Síochána* (Stationery Office 1995).

Department of Health, *Putting Children First* (Stationery Office, 1996).

Department of Health, *Report on the Inquiry into the Operation of Madonna House* (Stationery Office 1996).

Department of Health and Children, *Children First: National Guidelines for the Protection and Welfare of Children* (Stationery Office 1999).

Department of Health, Circular, 'Recruitment and Selection of Staff to Children's Residential Centres Operated by Voluntary Bodies' (Stationary Office 1994).

Department of Health, Circular, 'Recruitment and Selection Procedures' (Stationary Office 1995).

Department of Justice, Equality and Law Reform, *The Law on Sexual Offences — A Discussion Paper* (Stationary Office 1998).

Department of Justice, Equality and Law Reform, *Garda Working Group on Garda Vetting Report* (Department of Justice and Equality 2004).

Department of Justice, Equality and Law Reform, *Working Group on Garda Vetting Report* (Stationery Office 2004)

Department of the Taoiseach, *Action Plan for the Millennium* (1998).

Donnelly S and Inglis T, 'The Media and the Catholic Church in Ireland' (2010) 25(1) *Journal of Contemporary Religion* 1.

Ericson RV, *Crime in an Insecure World* (Polity Press 2007).

Fahy B, *The Freedom of Angels: Surviving Goldenbridge Orphanage* (O'Brien Press 1999).

Ferguson H, 'Child Welfare, Child Protection and the Child Care Act 1991: Key Issues for Policy and Practice' in Harry Ferguson and Pat Kenny (eds), *On Behalf*

of the Child: Child Welfare, Child Protection and the Child Care Act 1991 (A and A Farmer 1995) 35.
Ferguson H, 'The Paedophile Priest: A Deconstruction' (1995) 84 *Studies: An Irish Quarterly Review* 247.
Ferguson H, 'Protecting Irish Children in Time: Child Abuse as a Social Problem and the Development of the Child Protection System in the Republic of Ireland' (1996) 44(2) *Administration* 5.
Ferguson H, 'States of Fear, Child Abuse, and Irish Society' (2000) 50(1) *Doctrine and Life* 20.
Ferriter D, *The Transformation of Ireland 1900–2000* (Profile Books 2004).
Ferriter D, *Occasions of Sin: Sex and Society in Modern Ireland* (Profile Books 2009).
Fitzsimons E, *Report of Attorney General on Investigation into Fr Brendan Smyth File* (Stationery Office 1994).
Foster R, *Luck and the Irish: A Brief History of Change from 1970* (Oxford University Press 2008).
Freudendal-Pedersen M, *Mobility in Daily Life: Between Freedom and Unfreedom* (Routledge 2009).
Gardaí Síochána, 'Garda Vetting/Data Protection FAQ'. <http://www.garda.ie/FAQ/Default.aspx?FAQCategory=36>.
Garland D, *The Culture of Control: Crime and Social Order in Contemporary Society* (Oxford University Press 2001).
Giddens A, *The Consequences of Modernity* (Polity Press 1990).
Gillespie AA, *Sexual Exploitation of Children: Law and Punishment* (Round Hall 2008).
Guy P, 'The Casey Effect: The Collapse of Catholicism in Ireland' in Catherine Rees (ed), *Changes in Contemporary Ireland: Texts and Contexts* (Cambridge Scholars Publishing 2013).
Harries M and Clare M, *Mandatory Reporting of Child Abuse: Evidence and Options. Report for the Western Australian Child Protection Council* (Department for Community Development 2002). www.sph.uwa.edu.au/__data/assets/pdf_file/0009/1102131/MRFinalReport.pdf.
Hebenton B and Seddon T, 'From Dangerousness to Precaution: Managing Sexual and Violent Offenders in an Insecure and Uncertain Age' (2009) 49 *British Journal of Criminology* 343.
Hegarty T, 'Concern over AG's report on Smyth' *Irish Times* (Dublin, 14 November 1994) 5.
Hegarty T, 'If abuse is suspected, listen first to the child' *Irish Times* (Dublin, 3 December 1994) 9.
Inglis T, *Moral Monopoly: The Rise and Fall of the Catholic Church in Ireland* (2nd edn, University College Dublin Press 1998).
Joint Committee on the Family, *Kelly: A Child is Dead* (Stationery Office 1996).
Joint Committee on Tourism, Sport and Recreation, *First Interim Report of the Joint Committee on Tourism, Sport and Recreation: Protection of Children in Sport: Report of the Independent Inquiry into Child Sexual Abuse in Swimming* (Stationery Office 1998).
Kennedy G, '"The less you struggled, the less you got hit" she said', *Irish Times* (Dublin, 19 May 1993) 6.

Kennedy G, 'Slump in support for Fianna Fáil over Harry Whelehan' *Irish Times* (Dublin, 21 November 1994) 1.

Kitzinger J, 'Transformations of Public and Private Knowledge: Audience Reception, feminism and the experience of childhood sexual abuse' (2001) 1(1) *Feminist Media Studies* 91.

Lavery B, 'Demonstrators in Dublin protest abuse by priests' *New York Times* (New York, 8 April 2002).

Law Reform Commission, *Consultation Paper on Child Sexual Abuse* (LRC CP-2 1989).

Law Reform Commission, *Report on Child Sexual Abuse* (LRC 32-1990).

Lentin L (Director), *Dear Daughter* (RTÉ 22 February 1996).

Loader I and Walker N, *Civilizing Security* (Cambridge University Press 2007).

Lull J and Hinerman S, 'The Search for Scandal' in James Lull and Stephen Hinerman (eds), *Media Scandals: Morality and Desire in the Popular Culture Marketplace* (Polity Press 1997).

McAlinden A-M, 'Vetting Sexual Offenders: State Over-Extension, The Punishment Deficit and the Failure to Manage Risk' (2010) 19(1) *Social and Legal Studies* 25.

McGarry P, 'An Irishman's diary' *Irish Times* (Dublin, 9 November 2002) 13.

McGee H, 'Path from Attorney General to Judge is well trodden' *Irish Times* (Dublin, 20 June 2017) 3.

McGrath K, 'McGuinness report is a step forward' *Irish Times* (Dublin, 15 May 1993) 5.

McGrath K, 'Mandatory Reporting of Suspected Child Abuse—Would the Drawbacks Outweigh the Benefits for Irish Children? (1996) 2(2) *Medico-Legal Journal of Ireland* 44.

McGrath K, 'Registering sex offenders' *Irish Times* (Dublin, 28 January 1998) 17.

McGuinness C, *The Kilkenny Incest Inquiry Report* (Stationery Office 1993).

McKay S, *Sophia's Story* (Gill and Macmillan 2008).

Melton GB, 'Mandated Reporting: A Policy without Reason' (2005) 29 *Child Abuse & Neglect* 9.

Mooney T, *All the Bishop's Men* (Collins Press 2011).

Moran M, *The British Regulatory State: High Modernism and Hyper-Innovation* (Oxford University Press 2002).

Murphy FD, Buckley H and Joyce L, *The Ferns Report* (Stationery Office 2005).

Murphy G, *Electoral Competition in Ireland Since 1987: The Politics of Triumph and Despair* (Oxford University Press 2016).

Murphy Y, *Report of the Commission of Investigation into the Catholic Archdiocese of Dublin* (Stationery Office 2009).

National Children's Advisory Council, *Advice to the Minister on the Implementation of Children First and Vetting* (Stationery Office 2003).

North Western Health Board, *West of Ireland Farmer Case: Report of Review Group, presented to North Western Health Board, July 1998* (North Western Health Board 1998).

O'Callaghan D, 'Kilkenny incest case' *Irish Times* (Dublin, 10 March 1993) 13.

O'Donnell I and Milner C, *Child Pornography: Crime, Computers and Society* (Willan Publishing, 2007).

O'Faolain N, 'Next time there has to be someone who can say "well, I tried, I did my best"' *Irish Times* (Dublin, 3 June 1993) 11.

O'Gorman C (Director), *Suing the Pope* (BBC 2, 19 March 2002).
O'Malley T, *Sexual Offences* (2nd edn, Round Hall 2013).
O'Morain P, 'Register of All Sex Offenders Sought as List is Decided' *Irish Times* (Dublin, 31 December 1997) 4.
O'Tighearnaigh C, 'The Reporting of Child Abuse – The Contribution of Mandatory Reporting' (1996) 3(2) *Journal of Child Centred Practice* 95.
O'Toole F, 'The strut of power gave them the sense that they could do whatever they liked, whenever they liked' *Irish Times* (Dublin, 29 October 2005) 110.
Ombudsman for Children, *A Report Based on an investigation into the implementation of Children First: National Guidelines for the Protection and Welfare of Children* (Ombudsman for Children 2010).
Oswell D, *The Agency of Children: From Family to Global Human Rights* (Cambridge University Press 2013) 78.
Rafferty M (Director) *States of Fear* (RTÉ, 27 April 1999, 4 May 1999, 11 May 1999).
Rafferty M, (Producer), *Prime Time: Cardinal Secrets* (RTÉ, 17 October 2002).
Shanahan E, 'Policy against child abuse is needed, incest inquiry told' *Irish Times* (Dublin, 15 May 1993) 5.
Shannon G, *Report of the Special Rapporteur on Child Protection: A Report Submitted to the Oireachtas* (Stationery Office 2006).
Sheridan K, 'Father's abuse and beatings extended over 17 years' *Irish Times* (Dublin, 24 May 1995) 5.
Social Services Inspectorate, Social Service Inspectorate, *Report on the Monitoring of Implementation of Children First: National Guidelines for the Protection and Welfare of Children* (Stationery Office 2003).
Thomas T, 'Protecting the Public: Some Observations on the Sex Offenders Bill 2000' (2000) 10(2) *Irish Criminal Law Journal* 12.
Tynan MM, '£40m needed to implement child care act' *Irish Times* (Dublin, 23 April 1993) 6.
Tynan MM, 'Inquiry into child sex abuse to start in September' *Irish Times* (Dublin, 12 May 1999) 1.

8 Agents of change

Children and risk in reflexive modernity, 2006–2017

Introduction

The pace of child protection reform quickened significantly from 2006 onwards. While the Kilkenny Inquiry ushered in a range of new ways of thinking about children, how to protect them from risk and even what those risks were, it marked only the beginning of the end of traditional ways of thinking about these issues. In the period after 2006, the sociological forces of risk, detraditionalization and individualization commonly associated with late modernity came to real prominence and were accompanied by a new political zeal for reform, sparked by a quite different kind of child protection scandal. Whereas the Kilkenny Inquiry and many of the reports that followed in the next decade concerned families and individuals failed by the operation of the child protection system, the touchpaper for this new period was lit by the recognition of a specific weakness within child protection law concerning the age of consent. Two significant legal cases involving age of consent legislation renewed public and political interest in children's issues. They were quickly followed by the publication of comprehensive reports unveiling the systematic abuse which had historically characterised the state's child protection system. These scandals were followed by reports again focusing on the failures of the contemporary system, acting as a constant reminder of the need to take children's rights seriously.[1]

This chapter first outlines the ways in which child abuse concerns were continually kept at the forefront of public consciousness from 2006 onwards. In doing so, it seeks to continue the examination of the issues introduced in the previous chapter, whereby subpolitics and individualization played a significant role in reconstructing abuse and victims of abuse in the public mind. Survivor narratives were again central to this process of cultural transformation, a process which was demonstrated very clearly by the holding of the referendum on children's rights in 2012.[2] The subsequent sections of the chapter again pick up themes introduced in Chapter 7 by showing the various ways in which concern

1 Michael Freeman, 'Why it Remains Important to Take Children's Rights Seriously' (2007) 15 *International Journal of Children's Rights* 5.
2 See Chapter 6.

about abuse by people in authority was one of the key driving forces in the reform of the criminal law infrastructure governing child protection, while perceptions of the risk of abuse, and the risk of exploitation in particular, drove the reform of the law and policy framework governing child protection social work. In this context, the introduction of legal mechanisms providing for new mandatory reporting and vetting systems will be analysed from a risk perspective. Finally, the chapter will address the role of children's rights in all of this. Within the Irish legal system, the development of stronger legal rights for children went hand-in-hand with children being recognised as agents. New legislative and policy initiatives highlight how children have finally come to be thought of as active agents, with greater control over their own biographies than ever before.

Child abuse in the public consciousness

The previous chapter demonstrated that the public awareness of child abuse underwent a radical change during the 1990s. This process of cultural transformation was continued in subsequent years, as the scandals surrounding historic abuse inquiries and current system failures continued. As will be seen in this chapter, scandals continued to play an important background role, shaping public and political responses to child protection crises, and playing a significant role in the 2012 referendum on children's constitutional rights.

In 2006, the legislation governing the age of consent was deemed to be unconstitutional, creating both public anger and legislative panic.[3] In 2007, reports emerged of the death of a family of four in a murder–suicide in Monageer, Co. Wexford, which raised concerns over the adequacy of social work structures.[4] A 2008 report highlighted the failure of the HSE to properly implement the *Children First* guidelines.[5] In 2009, a Roscommon woman was sentenced to the maximum seven years for incest offences committed against her children.[6] That same year, the results of two major historic inquiries became known – the Ryan Commission of Inquiry into conditions in industrial and reformatory schools run by religious orders,[7] and the Murphy Inquiry into sexual abuse by priests of the Dublin Archdiocese.[8] The report into the Monageer tragedy was also published in 2009, criticising the response of both Gardaí and social work services.[9]

3 *CC v Ireland* [2006] 4 IR 1 (SC) and *A v Governor of Arbour Hill Prison* [2006] 4 IR 88 (SC), detailed below.

4 Kate Brosnan, *Monageer Inquiry: A Report Presented to Ms Mary Harney TD, Minister for Health and Mr Dermot Ahern TD, Minister for Justice, Equality and Law Reform* (Stationery Office 2007).

5 Review Inquiry Team, *Review Inquiry on any matter pertaining to Child Protection Issues touching on or concerning Dr A* (Stationery Office 2008).

6 Marese McDonagh, 'Mother Gets Seven Years in Jail for Abuse of Children' *The Irish Times* (Dublin, 23 January 2009) 6.

7 Commission to Inquire into Child Abuse, *Report of the Commission to Inquire into Child Abuse* (Stationery Office 2009).

8 Yvonne Murphy, *Report into the Catholic Archdiocese of Dublin* (Stationery Office 2009).

9 Brosnan (n 4).

2010 saw the publication of the report into the Roscommon scandal,[10] and the disclosure that almost 200 children in care or in contact with the child protection agencies had died during the previous decade.[11] In 2011, failures to report child sexual abuse concerns in the diocese of Cloyne were discovered; what made this report particularly shocking was the failures were not decades-old but took place during the 1990s.[12] The publication of the report into the operation of the Magdalene laundries in 2013, although not a child protection report per se, contributed to the public anger and concern over how the state discharged its responsibilities to vulnerable citizens via religious organizations.[13] A significant number of the women in these laundries were children – the youngest girl admitted to a laundry was nine years old;[14] the laundries operated closely with the industrial and reform school system and received admissions under the Children Acts 1908 and 1941.[15] The anger and concern were deepened by reports that the remains of children had been discovered at the site of a Mother and Baby home run by nuns in Co. Galway.[16] This prompted the establishment of a Commission of Inquiry into Mother and Baby Homes which has confirmed the existence of children's remains.[17] In 2016, a report emerged of sustained sexual abuse at a foster home, including a finding that allegations were not promptly investigated, meaning that a woman with intellectual disabilities was left there for 20 years despite concerns that she had been sexually abused. In May 2017, an audit of the operation of the emergency child protection system found it to be structurally inadequate.[18]

This necessarily brief overview of the child protection controversies which took place over an 11-year period only tells part of the story – the official part, recorded in governmental publications. What is crucial is the transformation that took place within not just within official discourse, but within public consciousness. The beginnings of this transformation were detailed in the previous chapter and began to crystallise in the wake of the age of consent controversy. One of the most telling indicators of the level of public feeling over an issue is the

10 Roscommon Child Care Inquiry, *Roscommon Child Care Case Report of the Inquiry Team to the Health Service Executive* (Stationery Office 2010).

11 Carl O'Brien, 'Child deaths in care or in contact with services now at 188' *The Irish Times* (Dublin, 5 June 2010) 1, Jamie Smyth, 'HSE revises figures for deaths of children' *The Irish Times* (Dublin, 9 December 2010) 3.

12 Yvonne Murphy, *Commission of Investigation Report into the Catholic Diocese of Cloyne* (Stationery Office 2011).

13 Martin McAleese, *Report of the Inter-Departmental Committee to Establish Facts of State involvement with the Magdalen Laundries* (Stationery Office 2013).

14 Ibid xiii.

15 See generally, ibid, chapter 10.

16 Alison O'Reilly, 'A Mass Grave of 800 Babies' *Irish Mail on Sunday* (Dublin, 25 May 2014) 1. On the scandal generally, see PM Garrett, 'Excavating the Past: Mother and Baby Homes in the Republic of Ireland' (2017) 47(2) *British Journal of Social Work* 358.

17 Mother and Baby Homes Commission of Investigation, *Second Interim Report* (Stationery Office 2017). The work of this Commission is ongoing and will not conclude until at least 2020.

18 Geoffrey Shannon, *Audit of the Exercise by An Garda Síochána of the provisions of Section 12 of the Child Care Act 1991* (An Garda Síochána 2017).

presence of public protest in response to particular scandals. As mentioned earlier, in May 2006, the Supreme Court deemed that section 1 of the Criminal Law Amendment Act 1935 was unconstitutional as it did not permit a man charged with unlawful carnal knowledge of a girl under 15 to claim that he had made a reasonable mistake as to her age.[19] This created the possibility that men convicted under this section would be released from prison. As a matter of constitutional law, a statute which predates the 1937 Constitution and which is deemed to be incompatible with the Constitution is effectively declared to have ceased to have legal effect as of 1937.[20] As a result, men who were already imprisoned under this provision were now seeking their release, as the Act under which they were convicted was potentially retrospectively invalidated, meaning that there may no longer have been legal basis for their continued detention.

This led to the decision in *A v Governor of Arbour Hill Prison*,[21] in which the High Court released the applicant from custody on this basis before the Supreme Court overturned this decision several days later. The case of Mr A was particularly troubling from a child protection perspective – he had pleaded guilty to the offence, and the defence of reasonable mistake would not realistically have been open to him, given that the victim was his daughter's 12-year-old friend to whom he had given alcohol.[22] As such, it would appear that he was engaged in clearly exploitative conduct, and could legitimately be characterised as an abuser seeking to take advantage of the fortuitous opening of a legal loophole. The Supreme Court ordered his re-arrest on the basis that he was seen as mounting a 'collateral attack' on the verdict in his case, on the basis that at no stage prior to, or in the course, of his prosecution did he seek to impugn the lawfulness of his prosecution or conviction by highlighting a potential constitutional flaw in the legislation. According to Murray CJ, the constitutional question was settled in favour of the state on the basis of Mr A's inactivity in raising a challenge earlier. He posited that

> where the State relies in good faith on a statute in force at the time and the accused does not seek to impugn the bringing or conduct of the prosecution ... before the case reaches finality, on appeal or otherwise, then the final decision in the case must be deemed to be and to remain lawful notwithstanding any subsequent ruling that the statute, or a provision of it, is unconstitutional.[23]

The Supreme Court decision in *A* closed conclusively any potential loophole created by the *CC* decision, but the construction of both children and the risks they

19 *CC v Ireland* (n 3).
20 See generally Gerard Hogan and Gerry Whyte, *JM Kelly: The Irish Constitution* (4th edn, Butterworths 2003) 895–912; for pre-1937 laws and amending legislation in particular, see 899–900. On the role of delay in seeking a declaration of unconstitutionality, see 902–905.
21 *A* (n 3).
22 *A* (n 3) 168.
23 Ibid 143.

faced was largely defined by a mood of outrage. During the course of political debate, then-opposition leader Enda Kenny TD made reference to an offender as a "pervert",[24] while specifically and repeatedly referring to the victim of Mr A as a girl of Confirmation age who had been plied with alcohol in an attempt to portray the victim as young and innocent, contrasted with a manipulative abuser.[25] Other deputies used similar language – "self-confessed beast who preyed on a 12-year old child".[26] Government backbenchers spoke of the fear of being "crucified" by constituents if they were seen to have acted slowly to close any legal loopholes which could be exploited,[27] indicating a high level of public, as well as political, discontent. This way of framing sexual offending has continued unabated. In 2015, one senator described sexual abuse of children as "on par with murder".[28]

The public approach to the controversy can be most clearly seen in the protests organised in the wake of the High Court's decision in *A*. The mother of Mr A's victim spoke of her distress on a popular radio show, prompting a member of the public to organise protests showing solidarity with victims of sexual abuse and against the government handling of the matter.[29] Demonstrations took place nationwide, attracting around 4,000 people.[30] One woman attending a protest in Dublin spoke of her reasons for attending: "we're here to fight for our children, to fight for the rights of our children."[31] A newspaper report of the demonstrations carried the reaction of Colm O'Gorman, an abuse survivor and then-director of the abuse survivor organization One in Four, where he described the period between the *CC* and *A* decisions as "one of the most 'astounding' weeks in Irish political life. The founder of a charity established to support victims of child sex abuse said he had never dreamt that such solidarity could be shown by ordinary people."[32]

Protests against what were regarded as institutional failures relating to child abuse continued in the aftermath of the publication of both the Ryan and Murphy Reports. The former, officially entitled the *Report of the Commission to Inquire into Child Abuse*,[33] made clear the full scale of abuse in institutions

24 Dáil Debates 30 May 2006, vol 620, col 1035, Enda Kenny TD.

25 Ibid and col 1038.

26 Dáil Debates 30 May 2006, vol 620 col, 1050, Caoimhghín Ó Caoláin TD.

27 Mark Hennessy, 'Backbenchers Briefed on Plan' *The Irish Times* (Dublin, 1 June 2006) 6.

28 Seanad Debates 6 October 2015, vol 242, Daily Book Unrevised 311, Senator Mary White.

29 See in particular, Kate Holmquist, 'Flower Power' *The Irish Times* (Dublin, 3 June 2006) 107.

30 Conor Lally, 'Thousands Gather with White Flowers at Short Notice' *The Irish Times* (Dublin, June 3 2006) 8.

31 Luke O'Neill, 'Protesters Ready to Express Anger at Leinster House' *The Irish Times* (Dublin, 2 June 2006) 8.

32 Seán McCárthaigh, Jimmy Woulfe and Gordon Deegan, 'White Flower Day: Thousands across the country' *Irish Examiner*, http://www.irishexaminer.com/ireland/icrime/white-flower-day-thousands-across-the-country-5104.html, accessed 2 November 2017.

33 CICA (n 7).

operated by religious orders, a role facilitated by successive governments. This commission was established in 2000 with three central aims – to provide a forum where survivors of abuse could tell of their experiences, to investigate allegations of abuse and to publish a report on foot of these findings. The Report was the largest investigation of child abuse conducted in the history of the state. Having heard from some 1,700 witnesses, the Commission concluded that physical and emotional abuse and neglect were common in children's residential institutions, with sexual abuse a common feature especially in institutions for boys.[34] The system as a whole was criticised – the manner in which the institutions were run, the manner in which they were inspected, the manner in which they were financed. These last two criticisms make clear the degree of state culpability – when a problem arose, the structures which the state had imposed and the policies underlying the system meant that there was little, if any, chance of remedial action being taken due to deference to the religious orders and a lack of any appropriate enforcement or disciplinary mechanisms.[35] The findings of the Murphy Report into child abuse by clergy again make clear the systematic nature of this abuse, and its cover-up. The following paragraph illustrates the findings of the report succinctly:

> The Dublin Archdiocese's pre-occupations in dealing with cases of child sexual abuse, at least until the mid 1990s, were the maintenance of secrecy, the avoidance of scandal, the protection of the reputation of the Church, and the preservation of its assets. All other considerations, including the welfare of children and justice for victims, were subordinated to these priorities. The Archdiocese did not implement its own canon law rules and did its best to avoid any application of the law of the State.[36]

Child victims, as found by both Inquiries, were denied recognition as victims by church institutions and by the state. Central to this was the denial of a voice to children, as any complaint was met with disbelief or indifference – children had no means of expressing themselves, or of influencing their surroundings. In the era of traditional, simple modernity, children were predominantly denied agency. One of the central criticisms made by the Commission was the lack of recognition afforded to children as having any story to tell – Department of Education inspectors rarely spoke to the children in schools.[37] An indicator of the reluctance to hear children who did attempt to discuss conditions in the school is provided by an incident reported by Rafferty and O'Sullivan – when Minister for Justice Brian Lenihan visited the Artane Industrial School in 1968, he was approached by a 15-year-old boy who implored him to get the Christian Brothers who ran the

34 Ibid, Volume 5, 451.
35 See in particular, ibid, Volume 4, chapter 6.
36 Murphy (n 8) 4.
37 CICA (n 7) Volume 5, 452.

school to stop beating them; Lenihan's reported response was to ask his driver to "Get me out of this fucking place."[38]

In contrast to this attitude, the testimony of survivors took a central role in the Commission's Report, with a specific Confidential Committee being established for the purposes of allowing abuse victims to recount their experiences.[39] In empirical work with victims, Moriarty found that they tended to view their experiences through the prism of the denial of their human rights and that the ultimate goal of participation in the Inquiry was to be heard and believed.[40] This increased use of memoir and survivor stories, in the context of published survivor accounts, testimony to inquiries and media interviews, represents not only a new desire to hear victims, and treat them as credible,[41] but also helps to explain the reaction to the inquiry reports. They provided the public at large with the "imaginative ability to see strange people – those who are oppressed by humiliation, cruelty and pain – as fellow sufferers."[42] In response to the reports, thousands gathered for a march through Dublin to show solidarity with victims of clerical abuse.[43] During an Easter Mass in April 2010, one thousand pairs of children's shoes were left outside Dublin's Pro-Cathedral, while some protestors entered the cathedral and placed children's shoes on the altar during the service.[44] The previously abused and marginalised victims' stories now served a discovery function, allowing the rest of the community to discover just which rights really mattered.[45] To this end, the use of shoes in the protests is powerful symbol pointing to the newfound ability to imaginatively feel oneself "in the shoes of the despised and oppressed".[46]

38 Mary Rafferty and Eoin O'Sullivan, *Suffer the Little Children: The Inside Story of Ireland's Industrial Schools* (New Island Books 1999) 380.

39 This was not, however, without criticism – see Anne-Marie McAlinden and Bronwyn Naylor, 'Reframing Public Inquiries as "Procedural Justice" for Victims of Institutional Child Abuse: Towards a Hybrid Model of Justice' (2016) 38 *Sydney Law Review* 277, 287.

40 Niamh Moriarty, '"Telling My Story": An Analysis of How Disclosure to the Irish Commission to Inquire into Child Abuse is Constructed' (PhD Thesis, University of East London 2013).

41 Diarmaid Ferriter, 'Suffer Little Children? The Historical Validity of Memoirs of Irish Childhood' in Joseph Dunne and James Kelly (eds) *Childhood and its Discontents* (The Liffey Press 2002).

42 Richard Rorty, *Contingency, Irony, and Solidarity* (Cambridge University Press 1989) xvi.

43 Carl O'Brien, 'Tears and Fury as institutional abuse victims march on Dáil' *The Irish Times* (Dublin, 10 June 2010) 1 and Carl O'Brien, 'Profound moment of validation for forgotten children' *The Irish Times* (Dublin, 11 June 2009) 6.

44 Gladys Ganiel, *Transforming Post-Catholic Ireland: Religious Practice in Late Modernity* (Oxford University Press 2016) 41. See also Caroline O'Doherty, 'Abuse victim's brother plans altar protest during Easter Sunday Mass', *Irish Examiner* (Cork, 30 March 2010).

45 Jurgen Habermas, 'The Concept of Human Dignity and the Realistic Utopia of Human Rights' (2010) 41(4) *Metaphilosophy* 464, 469.

46 Richard Rorty, 'Human Rights, Rationality and Sentimentality', in Stephen Shute and Susan Hurley (eds), *On Human Rights: The Oxford Amnesty Lectures 1993* (Oxford University Press 1994) 126–127.

The new voice for victims represents a continuation of the movement towards subpolitics, initially engendered in the wake of the Kilkenny Inquiry. Individual survivors of abuse like Christine Buckley, Colm O'Gorman and John Kelly who had been leading voices in this context in the earlier decade,[47] maintained a high public profile during this period. As mentioned in the previous chapter, the public's understanding of child abuse was radicalised by non-traditional, subpolitical agents who had once been understood as part of a moral problem. Christine Buckley, in particular, came to represent a new way of seeing abuse and abuse victims; once institutionalised and abused in an industrial school, she later co-founded the Aislinn Centre, which provides therapeutic and educational support to abuse survivors. She met and campaigned with President McAleese,[48] and her funeral was attended by President Higgins, as well as former and serving government ministers.[49] She was described by one commentator as having helped to shift Ireland's cultural axis.[50] Moreover, the organizations and civil society groups who advocated on behalf of abuse victims, such as the Rape Crisis Centre and One in Four, played a significant role in the development of many of the legislative initiatives described below.[51] Colm O'Gorman played a very visible role in legal and political processes, first as the founder of One in Four, then as a senator, and finally as director of Amnesty International's Irish section. For Beck, marginalised groups take centre stage when subpolitics emerges.[52] The transformation of some of these individuals, from abused, silenced objects treated like "moral dirt"[53] to agents capable of contributing significantly to social and legal change is the epitome of subpolitics. After the exposure of child protection scandals, not only did a new knowledge of risk inform the shaping of new legislative responses, but those harmed and previously marginalised by their experience of risks played a central role.

Age, authority and exploitation in the criminal law

The most significant changes in the substantive criminal law which occurred in the years after the *CC* case were driven by two factors: an attempt to combat sexual exploitation of children, and a concern that people in positions of trust or authority had the potential to exploit that position for the purpose of sexual gratification. These trends had begun in the previous decade and mirror the

47 See Chapter 7.
48 Patsy McGarry, 'President Tells Abuse Survivors of Heartfelt Sorrow' *The Irish Times* (Dublin, 29 June 2009) 1.
49 Patsy McGarry, 'A Woman of Extraordinary Courage' *The Irish Times* (Dublin, 14 March 2014) 10.
50 Patsy McGarry, 'Christine Buckley Helped Shift Ireland's Cultural Axis on Child Abuse' *The Irish Times* (Dublin, 12 March 2014) 14.
51 Dáil Debates 27 June 2012, vol 770, col 340, Seán Kyne TD.
52 Ulrich Beck, *World Risk Society* (Polity Press 1999).
53 Harry Ferguson, 'Abused and Looked After Children as "Moral Dirt": Child Abuse and Institutional Care in Historical Perspective' (2007) 36(1) *Journal of Social Policy* 123.

detraditionalization of social relations that are an inherent part of late modernity, as well as the increasing awareness of risk. The attempt to regulate and govern personal relationships based on hierarchies of power through the medium of criminal law can be seen as a reflexive response to the abuse inquiries and other scandals which came to light during these years, but recent legislation shows the emergence of a new idea – that young people had not only an entitlement to protection, but had at least some agency over their own sexual decision-making. The limits of this idea have yet to be fully tested in the courts, but legislation passed in early 2017 has made clear that children are no longer merely passive objects, but active subjects.

Following the Supreme Court's decision in *CC v Ireland*,[54] new legislation was required to effectively recriminalise sexual intercourse with a young person. Although the decision did not remove the possibility of charging a person with the offences of rape, sexual assault or incest, the absence of an offence where liability could be imposed largely or solely on the age of the victim was regarded as unsatisfactory.[55] This is because a charge of incest would only be available in the limited circumstances of familial, and indeed blood, relationships, while the other two offences effectively criminalise sexual acts committed in the absence of consent. This thereby necessitated that the prosecution establishes the absence of consent beyond a reasonable doubt, opening up the possibility that a young victim could be cross-examined so as to demonstrate consent on their part, or at least raise a possibility that consent was not absent.[56] The proposed Sexual Offences (Age of Consent) (Temporary Provisions) Bill 2006 would have simply restored the *status quo ante* with the addition of the reasonable mistake defence, but this was rejected.

The Criminal Law (Sexual Offences) Act 2006 did not, however, do much more than this, but has provided the basis for subsequent legislative reform.[57] Mirroring the now-defunct 1935 provisions, it contains separate rules governing offences against children under 15 years of age and those between 15 and 17. In essence, the age provisions of the legislation provide that 17 is the age of consent for sexual intercourse or buggery, but that a person can consent to other sexual activity at 15. Offences against children under 17 were now covered by the concept of a sexual act with a child, although the marginal notes of the Act refer to the concept of "defilement", echoing the language of legislation dating back to 1885. Defilement is defined as sexual intercourse, buggery, aggravated sexual assault or rape under section 4 of the Criminal Law (Rape) (Amendment) Act 1990.[58] The consent of a young person is no defence to a charge,[59] but a

54 *CC* (n 3).
55 Dáil Debates 1 June 2006, vol 620, col 1762, Brendan Howlin TD.
56 Dáil Debates 2 June 2006, vol 621, col 2, Minister Michael McDowell TD.
57 Katie Stevens, 'An Overview of the Law Governing the Age of Consent for Sexual Activity in Ireland with a View to Reform' (2015) 25(4) *Irish Criminal Law Journal* 90, 91.
58 See generally Thomas O'Malley, *Sexual Offences* (2nd edn, Round Hall 2013) 124–137.
59 Section 2(5) and Section 3(7).

court may consider whether reasonable grounds exist for an allegedly reasonable mistake as the victim's age.[60] Section 2 of the 2006 Act criminalises conduct against a child under 15 and imposes a maximum sentence of life imprisonment. Offences against victims aged between 15 and 17 were governed by section 3 of the 2006 Act; the section is broadly similar to section 2 in terms of the availability of defences.

One of the few important innovations contained in the 2006 Act is the development of the concept of "person in authority". If a person in such a position, such as a parent, someone *in loco parentis*, or a person charged with the supervision, education or welfare of the victim is convicted of an offence, a harsher sentencing regime applies.[61] The aim is to ensure that individuals in a position to exploit a power imbalance are treated more harshly through specific sentencing rules. In effect, committing an offence while in a position of authority exposed a person to up to double the sentence they would otherwise face.[62] The change in the cultural and legal perception of authority figures on the part of lawmakers and society more generally is striking. Whereas the failure to intervene on behalf of abused children highlighted by the Kilkenny Incest case and the McColgan case were due in part to the desire to collectively explain away problematic behaviours by traditional authority figures (in both cases, fathers in married families), this legislation was designed to mark out exactly these authority figures as deserving of especially severe treatment in terms of both liability and sentencing for abusive behaviour.

The idea of targeting authority figures played a central role in subsequent legislative initiatives. In 2012, it was proposed that the maximum penalty for incest be increased to life imprisonment.[63] This was eventually done by section 28 of the Criminal Law (Sexual Offences) Act 2017, although only in respect of incest committed by a man. This was only one of the 2017 Act's measures against authority figures. It also increased the penalties for offences committed against children aged between 15 and 17 under section 3 of the 2006 Act to a maximum

60 Section 2(3) and 2(4), and section 3(5) and 3(6). The Criminal Law (Sexual Offences) Act 2017 now stipulates that the presence of a reasonable mistake as to age must be proved to the balance of probabilities standard – see sections 2(5) and 3(5) of the 2006 Act, as inserted by sections 16 and 17 respectively of the 2017 Act.

61 Section 1 of the Act defined a person in authority as (a) a parent, step-parent, guardian, grandparent, uncle or aunt of the victim (b) any person who is, for the time being, in *loco parentis* to the victim, or (c) any person who is, for the time being, responsible for the education, supervision or welfare of the victim. See also O'Malley (n 58) 129 for a discussion of the difficulties that may be encountered in interpreting the phrase "for the time being". Section 1 has been amended by section 15 of the Criminal Law (Sexual Offences) Act 2017 to include current or former guardians, step-parents and foster-parents and current or former partners of a parent of the child who lives or has lived in an enduring family relationship with the parent.

62 Compare section 3(1)(b) with section 3(1)(a), and section 3(2)(b) with section 3(2)(a). See also increased penalties for subsequent offences – section 3(3)(b) and section 3(4)(b).

63 Criminal Law (Incest) (Amendment) Bill 2012, s 1(b).

possible sentence of 15 years, which is more than double the maximum available in other cases.[64] It also created a new offence whereby 17-year-olds are specifically protected from sexual acts by authority figures. Section 18 of the 2017 Act inserts a new section 3A into the 2006 Act, which makes it an offence for a person in authority to engage in a sexual act with a 17 year old, subject to the now-usual provisions relating to reasonable mistake as to age, while providing an additional defence for the defendant if they can prove "that he or she has reasonable grounds for believing that he or she was not a person in authority in relation to the child against whom the offence is alleged to have been committed."[65]

While authority is usually understood in terms of trust or power deriving from a familial or professional relationship, legislation enacted after 2006 also shows an appreciation for the more subtle ways in which trust between adults and children can be built and then exploited in a process commonly known as grooming.[66] This represents an approach and understanding of risk very much in tune with reflexive modernity. Grooming a child, the process by which an abuser prepares a child to acquiesce to inappropriate sexual activity through gaining trust or bribery has had a complex legislative history. Section 6 of the Criminal Law (Sexual Offences) Act 1993 criminalised the soliciting or importuning of a child to commit a sexual offence under the Criminal Law (Amendment) Act 1935 as part of the growing awareness of child sexual abuse committed by neighbours and family friends.[67] However, a drafting error in the Criminal Law (Sexual Offences) Act 2006 failed to revive the offence after the relevant sections of the 1935 Act were declared unconstitutional. Therefore, the Criminal Law (Sexual Offences) (Amendment) Act 2007 was introduced, which achieved two distinct aims with respect to grooming – it restored the solicitation offence by inserting a new section 6 into the 1993 Act, and also created new offences based around grooming a child through prior contact for the wider purpose of sexual exploitation.[68]

The 2017 Act has sought to tighten the legislative position on grooming. It leaves section 6(1) of the 1993 Act in place and repeals the grooming offences from the 1998 Act.[69] In their place, it provides for a range of new offences designed "to target at the earliest possible point any intention to exploit a child".[70] To this

64 See section 3(1) and 3(2) as inserted by section 17 of the 2017 Act.

65 Section 3A(6) of the 2006 Act, as inserted by section 18 of the 2017 Act.

66 See generally, Anne Marie McAlinden, *'Grooming' and the Sexual Abuse of Children: Institutional, Internet and Familial Dimensions* (Oxford University Press 2012) especially chapters 4 and 5.

67 See comments at Dáil Debates 23 June 1993, vol 432, col 1979, Minister Máire Geoghegan-Quinn TD, and Dáil Debates 6 March 2007, vol 633, col 70, Minister Michael McDowell TD. See also the unsuccessful Private Members Criminal Law (Child Grooming) Bill 2014, debated at Dáil Debates 10 July 2015, vol 886.

68 Section 6 of the 2007 Act inserted new sections 3(2A) and 3(2B) into the Child Trafficking and Pornography Act 1998.

69 See section 10 of the 2017 Act.

70 Seanad Debates 6 October 2015, vol 242, Daily Book Unrevised 307, Minister Frances Fitzgerald TD.

end, section 5 of the 2017 Act creates a new offence of committing a sexual act in the presence of child, while section 6 criminalises causing a child to watch sexual activity, as it was felt that "[f]amiliarising children with such activity or material can take place during the early stages of the predatory process leading to more serious forms of child sexual exploitation."[71] The following sections criminalise meeting a child for the purpose of sexual exploitation,[72] and using information and communication technology to facilitate exploitation, including by sending sexually explicit material to a child.[73]

The focus on individuals in positions of authority is made even clearer when the attitude to sexual relationships among young people are examined. As will be discussed in greater detail below, a consultation exercise with young people undertaken in 2006 highlighted that they were concerned that the law did not create any exemptions for peer relationships that were not exploitative.[74] This view was recognised in the Oireachtas debates on the 2017 Act which recognised that the criminal law ought not to intervene in such circumstances. The Act now provides for a defence where a sexual act can be characterised as "consensual and non-exploitative", so as to provide "recognition ... of underage, consensual peer relationships".[75] In inserting the new section 3(8) into the 2006 Act,[76] it states that it shall be a defence to a charge under section 3 if the defendant is (a) younger, or less than two years older than the complainant, (b) was not at the time of the alleged offence a person in authority in respect of the complainant and (c) was not at the time in a relationship which was intimidatory or exploitative of the complainant.

One of the most striking features of the passage of this legislation is the overwhelmingly positive response it attracted. One TD described it as "a most welcome new provision which more accurately and honestly reflects the real lives of young adults and teenagers",[77] while another highlighted that the "inclusion of a proximity test regarding the age of consent ensures the focus of our criminal law legislation remains the protection of children and sexual assault rather than interfering in consensual sexual activity between young people."[78] Although referring to another aspect of the legislation, one senator spoke of ensuring that it was important to respects "the sexual agency of all actors, while criminalising all sexual

71 Dáil Debates 5 October 2016, vol 923, Daily Book Unrevised 116, Minister Frances Fitzgerald TD.
72 Section 7.
73 Section 8(1) and 8(2).
74 Office of the Minister for Children, *Report on consultations with teenagers on issues to be considered by the Minister for Children when examining the age of consent for sexual activity* (Stationery Office 2006).
75 Seanad Debate 6 October 2015, vol 242, Daily Book Unrevised 308, Minister Frances Fitzgerald TD.
76 As inserted by section 17 of the 2017 Act.
77 Dáil Debates 3 November 2016, vol 927, Daily Book Unrevised 29, Catherine Connolly TD.
78 Dáil Debates 2 November 2016, vol 927, Daily Book Unrevised 67, Josepha Madigan TD.

acts that are not agreed on or understood by all parties."[79] This perfectly summarises the intention of the consultation process, as well as the tone of the legislative debate. The recognition that young people had some agency over their own sexual decision-making, coupled with the continued emphasis on the criminalization of exploitative conduct reflects the gradual recognition of children as subjects.

The extension of information and risk management legislation

The movement to make information usage and risk assessments central to child protection reached its peak in the period following 2006. The concern evident in the reform of substantive criminal law discussed in the previous section was in effect mirrored in the reform of the legal framework governing child protection work and associated areas. The trends discussed in the previous chapter of facilitating greater information-sharing between state agencies, of encouraging the reporting of child abuse concerns, and the assessment of the suitability of individuals working with children on the basis of prior conduct moved from the realm of social work practice to law, representing the continued juridification of social work in the form of reduction of professional discretion over the handling of certain situations and its replacement by new modes of legal regulation. There were two distinct aspects to this – the first relates to the gradual entrenchment of both mandatory information-sharing and mandatory reporting into legal duties, while the second relates to the now mandatory vetting and risk assessment of individuals who, through employment or otherwise, would come to occupy the kinds of positions of authority that had in recent years come to be recognised as sources of risk.

Mandatory reporting and information-sharing

The previous chapter outlined the path to the publication of the *Children First Guidelines* in 1999.[80] While intended to provide comprehensive, national guidance on how child abuse concerns would be handled by the various authorities in this area, it became evident that there were significant gaps in its application, as exposed by a number of reviews into its operation. The Office of the Minister for Children[81] and the Ombudsman for Children[82] commented critically on the implementation of the Guidelines, and in particular on the continued reliance on local practices instead of the supposedly national Guidelines. The ministerial

79 Seanad Debates 6 October 2015, vol 242, Daily Book Unrevised 38, Senator Katherine Zappone.

80 Chapter 7.

81 Office of the Minister for Children and Youth Affairs, *National Review of Compliance with Children First: National Guidelines for the Protection and Welfare of Children* (Stationery Office 2008).

82 Office of the Children's Ombudsman, *Investigation into the implementation of Children First: National Guidelines for the Protection and Welfare of Children* (Stationery Office 2010).

review highlighted two main issues arising from the local implementation of the Guidelines:

> the absence of consistency in the delivery of child welfare and protection services across the country and, more importantly, the absence of any standards against which delivery of services can be benchmarked and monitored.[83]

Not only were difficulties in the delivery of child protection services identified, but a lack of consistency in the level of information-sharing, envisaged as a central part of child protection policy by *Children First*, was also noted.[84] A number of factors contributed to these difficulties, including constitutional and legal difficulties with the sharing of information, communication difficulties between different professional groups, logistical difficulties in relation to designing and maintaining databases to store information, inconsistent terminology and definitions, and access to and use of information technology.[85] Ultimately the review concluded that the problems in child protection could not be traced back to problems with the *Children First Guidelines* themselves or their legal status, but with the way in which they were implemented.

The Ombudsman for Children's review proved to be much more critical. First, the Guidelines were described as not being drafted with sufficient clarity.[86] This required the production by the HSE of clarification documents, which undermines the claim of *Children First* to be considered the sole source of practice guidance in this area.[87] As with the ministerial review, the problem of regional variation in implementation was evident. Even basic matters such as the definitions of child abuse outlined by *Children First* were not implemented nationwide.[88] Such regional variations were seen as having a serious impact on the effectiveness of child protection work. There was also a lack of clarity and consistency regarding the basis on which child abuse complaints were investigated[89] and the extent of cooperation between the HSE and the Gardaí.[90] Even in HSE areas which were described as proactive in their efforts at implementation of *Children First*, worrying lapses in administrative practice were identified, such as the failure to record outcomes of child protection assessments.[91] The Ombudsman concluded that, as of 2010, the desire to actively implement *Children First* in its entirety

83 OMCYA (n 81) 14.
84 Ibid 3.
85 Ibid 6.
86 OCO (n 82) 17.
87 Ibid 29.
88 Ibid 54.
89 Ibid 78.
90 Ibid.
91 See for example, ibid 30, where the Review draws on the findings of an internal audit of the Cork and Kerry local health offices. For example, *Children First* requires that the outcome of all child protection assessments be recorded but 75% of assessments in this region had no outcome recorded.

had lost momentum.[92] Nonetheless, a revised version of *Children First* was published in 2011.[93] Although broadly similar to the original 1999 Guidelines, there were some important differences, one of the most important of which was their explicit extension to cover voluntary, sporting and religious organizations having contact with children, thereby mirroring the criminal law's concern with potentially exploitative sexual conduct arising from an abuse of power in a relationship formed in a community context.[94]

The main concerns remaining with regard to the Guidelines were the questions of their legal status and the extent of the legal obligations they imposed in terms of the reporting of concerns and the handling of information once reporting had taken place. Administrative decisions reached by a minister, such as guidelines without a statutory basis, cannot create obligations equivalent to those which can be imposed by either primary or secondary legislation, and may be legally unsound.[95] As a result, while many professionals involved in child protection work felt obliged to follow and implement *Children First*,[96] there was no legal duty to do so. This was underscored by an industrial dispute over an agreement within the HSE which led some staff to believe that they were not obliged to fully comply with the Guidelines.[97] This led to calls to place *Children First* on a statutory basis from, among others, the Special Rapporteur on Child Protection.[98] The Minister for Children also pledged that this would form part of the government response to the Ryan Report.[99] When introducing the new Guidelines in 2011, Minister for Children Frances Fitzgerald also adverted to this problem, stating that a new statutory system would be introduced, as the "days of voluntary compliance are over when it comes to child protection".[100] It was becoming apparent that there was an increased role for regulation in how child protection work was

92 OCO (n 82) 43.

93 Department of Children and Youth Affairs, *Children First: National Guidance for the Protection and Welfare of Children* (Stationery Office 2011). For a discussion of the definition of sexual abuse found in the Guidelines, see *EE v Child and Family Agency* [2017] IEHC 777.

94 See OCO (n 82) 7.

95 *O'Neill v Minister for Agriculture* [1998] 1 IR 539 (SC).

96 Ursula Kilkelly, 'Learning Lessons from the Past: Legal Issues Arising from Ireland's Child Abuse Inquiries' (2012) 12(1) *Irish Journal of Applied Social Studies* 8.

97 Ibid 16.

98 Shannon, *Third Report of the Special Rapporteur on Child Protection* (Stationery Office 2009) x; see also Children's Rights Alliance, 'Response to the Report by the Office of the Ombudsman for Children, Children First: National Guidelines for the Protection and Welfare of Children', available at www.childrensrights.ie/index.php?q=knowledgebase/child-protection/response-report-office-ombudsman-children-children-first-national-gui, accessed 29 December 2019.

99 OMCYA, *Implementation Plan for the Commission to Inquire into Child Abuse* (Stationery Office 2009) 55–56.

100 OMCYA, 'Press Statement by Ms Frances Fitzgerald TD, Minister for Children and Youth Affairs – Launch of Children First 2011 – National Guidance for the Protection and Welfare of Children, 15 July 2011', available at https://www.dcya.gov.ie/viewdoc.asp?DocId=1595&CatID=11&mn=&StartDate=01+January+2011 accessed 24 October 2019.

done. As this regulation came increasingly from the imposition of new legal rules, and the influence of legal processes on child protection work, it is possible to speak of child protection work as an increasingly juridified space.

The extension of MQ v Gleeson *and information-sharing obligations*

The previous chapter discussed the decision of *MQ v Gleeson*,[101] which saw the High Court approve the use of information-sharing by the statutory child protection agency as a legitimate way of exercising its duty to promote the welfare of children, imposed by section 3 of the Child Care Act 1991. This gave legal sanction to the ability of the relevant bodies to share information about child protection concerns, and about potentially dangerous individuals, once procedural safeguards were followed. While the discussion about *Children First* in the previous section outlined the weaknesses of that particular framework document, two High Court decisions from 2010 provided clear evidence that, regardless of *Children First*, the reporting of concerns, even if not supported by evidence such as a criminal conviction, was consistent with obligations under the Child Care Act 1991.[102] Taken together these judgments demonstrate a clear recognition that risk reduction and management was a corollary of the duty to promote the welfare of children, and of the importance of exchanging information as means of fulfilling this duty.

In *I v Health Service Executive*,[103] the applicant had been accused of sexually abusing a 13-year-old girl. He sought to quash the HSE's decision to investigate whether any child protection concerns arose from the allegation and to prevent any such HSE investigation taking place until criminal proceedings against him were resolved. He also sought to prevent the dissemination of any information about the allegation. Hedigan J reviewed the *MQ* decision and summarised the decision into four principles. These are

(1) The respondent … has a duty to investigate in the circumstances here. There may be a risk and that risk must be assessed.
(2) The respondent must afford the applicant fair procedures.
(3) If the respondent comes to the conclusion that there is a risk, it is under a duty to communicate that to an appropriate party.
(4) The respondent's role in conducting this investigation is not an administration of justice. It does not make any determination of guilt or innocence. Its role is quite distinct from that of the Director of Public Prosecutions. Its role is the protection of vulnerable children. The Director of Public Prosecutions' role is the detection and conviction of criminals, including child abusers.

101 [1998] 4 IR 85 (HC).
102 *I* v *Health Service Executive* [2010] IEHC 159, *PDP v A Secondary School* [2010] IEHC 189.
103 [2010] IEHC 159.

Applying these principles to the present case, Hedigan J pointed that not only was there a duty on the HSE to investigate a complaint but that "such an investigation should always occur at the earliest possible time after the risk to a vulnerable child is apprehended and before the risk crystallises into actual harm."[104] The dissemination of information was seen as a valid means of exercising this child protection duty.

It is interesting that the concept of fair procedures, whether stemming from administrative law or constitutional law, was not discussed to any significant extent. The court ruled that the HSE may communicate information to third parties once it is "minimal and only to the extent necessary to protect children who may be at risk. Such communication should be targeted in a context of specific child protection concerns."[105] The reason for caution was to ensure that the applicant's constitutional and administrative rights are protected. Yet this statement, which effectively reiterates the more general proportionality principle,[106] was the only real mention of fair procedures in the judgment. Instead, Hedigan J was more concerned with ensuring the relative autonomy of the HSE in how they undertook this type of investigation. He pointed out that the HSE ought not to be "looking over its shoulder" fearing intervention by the courts, nor should judicial review be anything other than "very rare and limited to points of principle being established".[107] Yet it was also notable that the policy framework supplementing the duty to investigate abuse allegations was not mentioned. At no point were the *Children First* guidelines mentioned or did they form any part of the court's analysis. This would have been helpful in outlining the exact nature of the HSE's obligations to investigate and to share information with other relevant agencies.

PDP v A Secondary School also concerned allegations of sexual abuse, this time against a secondary school teacher.[108] The response to the allegations by various state authorities was extremely problematic.[109] O'Neill J agreed that the decision of *MQ v Gleeson* was correct in establishing that the duties under section 3 extend to children who may be placed at risk in the future based on a reasonable suspicion of potential harm. He also stated that the duty to investigate complaints implied by section 3 is triggered when a credible complaint of child sexual abuse is made.[110] He went somewhat further in stating that

104 Ibid [6].
105 Ibid [7].
106 On the status of this principle in Irish administrative law, see Gerard Hogan and David Gwynn Morgan, *Administrative Law in Ireland* (4th edn, Round Hall 2010) 772–775. The principle is also important in the application of the European Convention on Human Rights in Ireland, on which see Fiona de Londras and Cliona Kelly, *European Convention on Human Rights Act: Operation, Impact and Analysis* (Round Hall 2010) 156–159.
107 Ibid [6]. This view was repeated in *FA v Child and Family Agency* [2018] IEHC 806.
108 [2010] IEHC 189.
109 The factual history is set out in detail in section 1 of the judgment.
110 Ibid [5.5]

> If the allegation is found to be established after appropriate investigation, it is then a matter for the statutory authority in whom s.3(1) powers are vested to select the appropriate means to protect any children it finds to be at risk from the predatory behaviour of the abuser in question.[111]

This decision vests the HSE with a wide discretion in how it carries out its child protection function, meaning that it has discretion to communicate relevant information to appropriate authorities if doing so facilitates achieving a child protection aim.

The only limitation placed on this discretion is that the investigation must "observe the norms of natural justice and fair procedures."[112] The conduct of the HSE in this case was regarded by the court as highly inappropriate in that it did not protect the rights of the applicant. Yet despite the HSE conceding that procedures to date had not always respected the applicant's procedural rights, O'Neill J was adamant that he could not prohibit any further investigations as this would inhibit the HSE from carrying out its statutorily conferred protective duties. It would appear, therefore, that while the courts are willing to declare that procedures adopted prior to the hearing have not complied with the principles of natural and constitutional justice, they are not willing to prevent future investigations, or incidents of information-sharing, which are designed to prevent a risk of future harm coming to fruition. The later decision in *Cooke v HSE* also applies the principles established in *MQ v Gleeson* to the compilation of a report following a complaint of inappropriate contact and the subsequent notification of this to the Gardaí.[113] This decision again made clear that there was no statutory or other basis upon which the court would be entitled to restrain the HSE from communicating their findings to the Gardaí even if their initial report was compiled in the absence of fair procedures.[114]

The concept of risk management underpins each of these judgments. They are collectively concerned with the possibility that a particular individual may pose a risk to as yet unidentified children. This concept of future risk, initially found in *MQ* and heavily supported in *PDP*, represents a major change in the way that courts expect child protection work to be carried out. It is no longer enough that reports of child abuse be investigated; action must now be taken to discharge an obligation to prevent future risks. They also provided indirect support for the introduction of some form of mandatory reporting legislation, or at least, the placing of *Children First* on a statutory basis; by largely ignoring the Guidelines, the courts highlighted the wide legal gap concerning information sharing. Each of the cases essentially relates to a quite specific point of administrative law: given

111 Ibid. The wording implies that the court is discussing the constitutional aspects of fair procedures, on which see Hogan and Gwynn Morgan (n 106) 582–593.
112 Ibid.
113 [2010] IEHC 503.
114 Ibid [71].

that the HSE must fulfil statutory obligations to promote children's safety (and it has discretion as to how to fulfil this duty), was the sharing of information about, and subsequent investigation of, child protection concerns a lawful exercise of this discretion in furtherance of the HSE's statutory obligation? None of the judgments referred to *Children First*, though the *PDP* judgment refers to the Department of Education and Science Child Protection Guidelines.[115] The exact nature and status of these guidelines, and their relationship with *Children First* remained unclear, and in the absence of clarity and binding regulations governing the exercise of social work discretion over-reporting or communication of concerns, it was becoming clear that reliance on guidelines was becoming untenable.

The introduction of mandatory reporting: criminal law and social work responses

To this end, two legislative initiatives have clarified the roles of individuals and organizations who may come into contact with child protection concerns. The first was the Criminal Justice (Withholding of Information on Offences Against Children and Vulnerable Persons) Act 2012, while the second was the Children First Act 2015. Together, these Acts provide for a mandatory reporting system while also establishing a statutory basis for interagency cooperation and information-sharing. As already indicated, the weak status of *Children First* consigned it to the realm of professional discretion. Inquiry reports advocated the introduction of mandatory reporting of child abuse, but the governmental response continued to favour leaving reporting and dissemination of concerns as "a matter of discretion, although the exercise of that discretion is governed by the framework of national policy and interagency protocols".[116] By the end of 2015, any semblance of discretion was effectively removed, as these two statutes, when taken together, formed the basis of a mandatory reporting system.[117] Many earlier calls for the introduction of this approach did not address fundamental organizational questions including who would be obliged to report, to whom concerns would be reported and what standard of proof would be required before the obligation to report would be triggered.[118] The 2012 and 2015 Acts now provide comprehensive and clear rules on when, and how, the obligation to report is triggered.

115 Department of Education and Science, *Child Protection Guidelines 2001* (Stationery Office 2001) since replaced by Department of Education and Science, *Child Protection Guidelines 2006* (Stationery Office 2006).
116 Kilkelly (n 96) 16.
117 Ibid, 17.
118 See also Isla Wallace and Lisa Bunting, *An examination of local, national and international arrangements for the mandatory reporting of child abuse: The implications for Northern Ireland* (NSPCC 2009) and Lisa Bunting, Anne Lazenbatt and Isla Wallace, 'Information Sharing and Reporting Systems in the UK and Ireland: Professional Barriers to Reporting Child Maltreatment Concerns' (2010) 19(3) *Child Abuse Review* 187.

The 2012 Act provides in section 2 that it is an offence for any person to withhold information about an offence committed against a child, defined as a person under the age of 18. This includes any sexual offence, as well as offences involving violence or exploitation.[119] The offence is committed where (a) a person knows or believes that an offence had been committed against a child, (b) has information which he or she knows or believes might be of material assistance in securing the apprehension, prosecution or conviction of that other person for that offence and (c) fails without reasonable excuse to disclose that information as soon as it is practicable to do so to a member of the Garda Síochána.[120] Any information acquired after the passage of the 2012 Act, whether it relates to an offence committed before or after that time, must be disclosed.[121] The offence carries a maximum penalty of up to ten years' imprisonment.[122] A victim is not under an obligation to disclose information,[123] and the Act does not displace existing legal privilege which would prevent a person from disclosing information they received about an offence.[124]

Certain defences are available under the Act, with one of the most important provided for in section 4(1). This states it shall be a defence for a person charged to show that the child victim made it known that they did not wish the offence to be reported and that they both knew of and relied upon that wish. However, there is a presumption that a child under the age of 14 does not have the capacity to form such a view, and so a person charged under the 2012 Act cannot rely on this defence unless they first rebut the presumption relating to the child's capacity.[125] If the child is under 14, a parent or guardian may form the view that no disclosure is to be made, thereby providing a defence both to person that they tell about the offence,[126] and to the parents themselves.[127] Professionals working with victims also have limited defences, even where abuse by a family member is suspected.[128] The 2012 Act is further limited by fact that the person who committed the underlying offence must be alive.[129]

Parliamentary debates on the legislation make clear that it was expressly inspired by the reports into clerical and religious abuse.[130] There was a

119 See Schedule 1 as amended. Buckley also makes the point that the 2012 Act also criminalises information relating to offences committed in other jurisdictions by Irish citizens or residents, an important issue in light of certain findings of the Murphy Report. See Lydia Buckley 'Can the Criminal Law Put an End to the "Cover-Up" of Clerical Sexual Abuse?' (2014) 24(2) *Irish Criminal Law Journal* 98, 102.
120 Section 2(1).
121 Section 2(2).
122 Section 7.
123 Section 2(3).
124 See Section 2(4) and the discussion in O'Malley (n 58) 293.
125 Section 4(2)
126 Section 4(4).
127 Section 4(5). For the defences established under subsections (4) and (5), see the limitations imposed by subsections (6) and (7).
128 Section 4(8) – 4(11).
129 Buckley (n 119) 102.
130 Seanad Debates 10 May 2012, vol 215, Daily Book Unrevised 337, Minister Alan Shatter TD.

recognition that the Ryan, Murphy and Cloyne Reports demonstrated that there had been a culture of secrecy and silence about child abuse, and a culture of deference towards the Catholic Church.[131] This marks a clear departure from earlier decades when the social position and power of the Church would have militated against this kind of criticism, as well as the belief that child abuse by clerics, and others in positions of responsibility, was not possible. Yet the introduction of new reporting obligations was seen not only as possible, but as inevitable,[132] and necessary to allay public misgivings over whether concerns should be reported.[133] In the discussion of the relationship between reporting obligations and religious privilege, one TD made clear that he did

> not believe the general community, nor our courts in this day and age, would take the view that the damage done to the church was of far greater concern than the likely damage done to the children who might be the victims of perpetrators of abuse.[134]

Furthermore, the legislation was taken to be symbolic of a changed value system, as a signal that would "make it clear to everybody, including the church, that children's rights and the laws of the land come first".[135] This linking of children's rights to the new way of thinking about traditional attitudes, as with the constitutional changes undertaken at this time that were discussed in Chapter 6, is further evidence of the detraditionalization and individualization processes. The introduction of mandatory reporting was only possible through the continued emphasis on survivor narratives, the detraditionalization of social structures and the recognition of children as subjects that are part of a reflexive approach to modernity.

The *Children First Guidelines* were effectively given statutory force by the Children First Act 2015. The 2011 Guidelines are deemed, by virtue of section 6(3), to be ministerial guidelines issued for the purpose of providing practical guidance on the fulfilment of the obligations imposed by the Act. As such, this provides them with a legal status superior to guidelines that do not have a statutory basis, as it means that they are now an essential part of how discretion in providing child protection services is to be exercised, while avoiding the potential constitutional pitfalls that could arise if they were instead regarded as

131 Seanad Debates 10 May 2012, vol 215, Daily Book Unrevised 346, Senator Jillian van Turnhout and Seanad Debates 10 May 2012, vol 215, Daily Book Unrevised 364, Minister Alan Shatter TD.

132 "We must go down this road. We must give confidence that protection is available and that people's stories will be heard properly. We cannot avoid this": Dáil Debates 26 June 2012, vol 770, col 75, Dara Calleary TD.

133 Dáil Debates 27 June 2012, vol 779, col 392, Seámus Healy TD.

134 Dáil Debates 27 June 2012, vol 779, col 880, Minister Alan Shatter TD.

135 Seanad Debates 12 June 2012, vol 215, Daily Book Unrevised 39, Senator David Cullinane.

comparable to secondary, or delegated, legislation.[136] The 2015 Act also provides for obligatory risk assessments to be completed by child care service providers.[137]

Crucially, the 2015 Act complements the 2012 Act by obliging "mandated persons" to report child protection concerns in specified circumstances. This obligation arises whenever such person "knows, believes or has reasonable grounds to suspect, on the basis of information that he or she has received, acquired or becomes aware of in the course of his or her employment or profession" that a child is being, has been, or is at risk of being harmed.[138] This obligation is imposed upon the wide range of professionals to whom the label of "mandated person" is applied; Schedule 2 of the 2015 Act provides an extensive and exhaustive list of such professionals, and includes doctors, nurses, physical and psychological therapists, dentists, teachers, social workers, clergy and members of religious orders, social workers and probation officers, among others. The 2015 Act only permits limited exemptions from this obligation, such as the exemption created to avoid duplication of reports.[139]

The more substantive exemption arises where a mandated person knows or believes that a person under the age of consent is involved in sexual activity. Section 14(3) provides that where a mandated person is aware that a child between the ages of 15 and 17 is involved in a sexual relationship, there is no obligation to report this when the person with whom the child is involved is not more than two years older than the child, the mandated person knows or believes that there is no material difference in capacity or maturity between the young people concerned, there is no indication of exploitation or intimidation and it has been made clear by the child concerned that they do not wish a disclosure to be made. Where a report is made, an obligation is also imposed on mandated persons to cooperate in inquiries,[140] while the disclosure of information by the Child and Family Agency, who had now taken over child protection responsibilities from the HSE, to other parties is permitted in limited circumstances.[141]

The Children First legislation, first proposed in 2012,[142] passed the Oireachtas with virtual unanimity. The Dáil debates show that the spectre of abuse inquiries hung over the legislation, showing the extent to which the scandals generated by these inquiries had radicalised the way in child abuse was seen.[143] It was argued

136 On which, see Hogan and Gwynn Morgan (n 106) 37.
137 See Part 2 of the Act.
138 Section 14(1).
139 See section 14(4)
140 Section 16.
141 Section 17.
142 For more on the development of the legislation, see Joint Committee on Health and Children, *Report on Children First (Heads of) Bill 2012* (Houses of the Oireachtas 2012).
143 See the comments at Dáil Debates 30 April 2014, vol 839, Daily Book Unrevised 68, Robert Troy TD, and Seanad Debates 21 July 2015, vol 241, Daily Book Unrevised 848, Senator Aideen Hayden.

that the legislation was "about bringing an end to any remaining attitudes which may choose to ignore child abuse and neglect."[144] It was therefore seen as having a consciousness-raising effect, and of moving the issue of doing something about child abuse "from one of good intentions to one of concrete obligations. It moves the issue from vagueness to precision and it moves from a culture of 'should report' to one of 'must report'."[145] The only question to cause significant controversy was whether criminal sanctions should be imposed for failure to report. Head 20 of the original Bill had provided for a maximum sentence of 5 years imprisonment to be available where a person was convicted of such an offence, but criminal liability was removed from the final draft of the Bill, and its reinsertion was resisted, despite pressure from some TDs.[146] The exemption created for non-exploitative sexual conduct by young people also demonstrates an increased awareness of the agency of young people, as it passed through the Oireachtas without contention.

The two Acts represent two distinct kinds of response to the information-sharing problem. The 2012 Act is firmly situated within a criminal law context, providing penalties for the failure to report relevant information without a lawful excuse. The 2015 Act, on the other hand, specifically moved away from the use of criminal penalties, and is targeted more towards ensuring a comprehensive and coordinated social work response to child protection concerns. The provision of specific guidance on how cases involving technically illegal but non-exploitative sexual behaviour by young people should be handled, and the ability of children over the age of 14 to prevent the disclosure of information about abuse acknowledges that children are recognised as having decision-making capacity and as possessing agency over how sensitive matters will be handled. In this way, the two Acts navigate a course through the late modern child protection system – they demonstrate an awareness of risk, and an awareness that it cannot be eliminated, but may be managed and worked with. They also demonstrate a concern for individualization through the recognition that young people will make their own life choices while permitting legal intervention where there is a possibility of exploitation. Finally, they recognise the need for regulation of what was previously discretionary practice, and that this requires a displacement of discretion in favour of legal regulation.

The formalization of the vetting system

As outlined in the previous chapter, the use and role of information management have extended far beyond interagency cooperation and the management of reporting to encompass risk assessments based on the suitability of individuals

144 Dáil Debates, 1 May 2014, vol 839, Daily Book Unrevised 93, Jerry Buttimer TD.
145 Dáil Debates 30 April 2014, vol 839, Daily Book Unrevised 61, Minister Frances Fitzgerald TD.
146 Dáil Debates 30 April 2014, vol 839, Daily Book Unrevised 68–69, Robert Troy TD.

seeking to work with children in a process known as vetting.[147] While this began in the late 1980s, it again came to public prominence in the wake of *CC* and *A* cases, despite those cases having nothing whatsoever to do with vetting of employees or volunteers. Much like issues relating to reporting and interagency cooperation, vetting had operated as an administrative practice, and calls were made for the practice to be enshrined in legislation, while also permitting more extensive vetting to take place. The introduction of such a framework was supported by bodies established as a direct consequences of the age of consent controversies such as the *Report of the Joint Oireachtas Committee on Child Protection*,[148] the *First Interim Report of the Joint Oireachtas Committee on the Constitutional Amendment on Children*,[149] and the *First Report of the Special Rapporteur on Child Protection*.[150] Each of these proposed a vetting statute which would allow for the collection and disclosure of "soft" information to approved bodies and for a limited purpose. This information, it will be recalled, extends beyond information pointing to a conviction or prosecution for a criminal offence relevant to child protection, but also to concerns or investigations relating to a person's suitability for work in an environment where they would be in a position of responsibility towards children. These proposals for the "institutionalisation of vetting"[151] represent a very clear move towards the precautionary logic which seeks to govern risky conditions.[152] A similar scheme had also been introduced in the United Kingdom, based on a similar set of principles.[153]

This desire for access to a wider range of information represents what Buckley sees as the determination to reduce risk in child care settings,[154] a desire which led to the development of a range of employment-based restrictions designed to prevent people seen as risks to children from working with them. The previous chapter outlined how the Employment Equality Act 1998 made clear that employers were exempt from liability if they failed to hire, or retain in employment, a person who had engaged in, or was believed to have a propensity to

147 See Chapter 7.

148 Joint Oireachtas Committee on Child Protection, *Report of Joint Oireachtas Committee on Child Protection* (Houses of the Oireachtas 2006) 87–88.

149 Joint Oireachtas Committee on the Constitutional Amendment on Children, *First Interim Report of the Joint Oireachtas Committee on the Constitutional Amendment on Children* (Houses of the Oireachtas 2008) 4.

150 Geoffrey Shannon, *First Report of the Special Rapporteur on Child Protection* (Stationery Office 2007) 11–17.

151 Frank Furedi and Jennie Bristow, *Licensed to Hug: How Child Protection Policies are Poisoning the Relationship between the Generations* (Civitas 2008) xii.

152 Pat O'Malley *Risk, Uncertainty and Government* (Glasshouse 2004) 318–319.

153 On this, see Anne-Marie McAlinden, 'Vetting Sexual Offenders: State Over-Extension, The Punishment Deficit and the Failure to Manage Risk' (2010) 19(1) *Social and Legal Studies* 25.

154 Helen Buckley, 'Duty to Care: Reducing Risk in Childcare Settings' 2006 9(3) *Irish Journal of Family Law* 3.

engage in, unlawful sexual conduct.[155] Section 176 of the Criminal Justice Act 2006 exposes employers to criminal sanctions by creating the offence of reckless endangerment of a child. This allows a person who has control over an abuser, defined as a person believed to have harmed or abused a child, to be prosecuted for recklessly permitting a child to be left in a situation which creates a substantial risk of harm or for failing to take reasonable steps to protect a child. Hiring a convicted offender to work with children would likely be considered to be recklessly exposing a child to a substantial risk of harm. This is another example of risk aversion informing legislation – by creating the risk of criminal penalty for an employer,[156] it attempts to control the possibility of an offender being hired by introducing a disincentive.

Further use of conviction-based, or hard, information has been sanctioned by the Criminal Justice (Spent Convictions and Certain Disclosures) Act 2016. This Act provides that, in most circumstances, a person is under no obligation to disclose that they have been convicted of an offence once seven years have passed since that conviction.[157] One of the exceptions to this rule is in respect of convictions for sexual offences, including offences against children,[158] reflecting the view that "there are certain convictions that can never become spent,"[159] given that "[t]he highest level of protection must apply when those who have committed serious offences seek employment that involves contact with children".[160] Recent sexual abuse scandals again featured as part of the justification for the exemption, despite its scope being significantly wider than offences against children,[161] while the recidivism rate for sexual offenders was also used as a justification, in a manner similar to that deployed in the debates on the Sex Offenders Act 2001.[162] Each of these measures represents a move towards a precautionary or prophylactic approach towards individuals suspected of posing a risk to children.[163] Not only that, but they also provide for the criminalization of those who are seen not to take risk reduction sufficiently seriously.

The centrepiece of the vetting and risk assessment system, however, is the National Vetting Bureau Act 2012. This provides that certain organizations

155 See section 16(4) and 16(5) of the Employment Equality Act 1998, and the discussion at Chapter 7.
156 The offence is punishable by an unlimited fine or imprisonment of up to ten years, or both: section 176 (4).
157 See section 5 and 6 of the 2016 Act.
158 See the cumulative effect of section 4, section 5(1)(c) and section 10(2).
159 Dáil Debates 7 March 2013, vol 795, Daily Book Unrevised 66, Minister Lucinda Creighton TD.
160 Dáil Debates 14 March 2013, col 796, Daily Book Unrevised 686, Tom Fleming TD.
161 See Dáil Debates 12 March 2013, vol 796, Daily Book Unrevised 88, John O'Mahony TD.
162 Dáil Debates 12 March 2013, vol 796, Daily Book Unrevised 92, Paul J Connaughton TD.
163 Carol S Steiker, 'Foreword: The Limits of the Preventative State' (1998) 88(3) *Journal of Law and Criminology* 771, Nigel Parton, *Safeguarding Childhood: Early Intervention and Surveillance in a Late Modern Society* (Palgrave Macmillan 2006) 164–165.

may not hire a person unless vetting disclosure has been obtained in respect of that person[164]; again, developing beyond a merely prophylactic model, failure to obtain such a disclosure is a criminal offence.[165] These provisions apply to those organizations and individuals engaged in a wide range of work and social activities, including education, cultural and sporting activities, religious observance and practice, and medical work.[166] Once an application for a vetting disclosure is made, the Vetting Bureau will assess whether the person to whom it relates has any convictions, or if there is "specified information" relating to the vetting subject. Specified information is, in effect, soft information, and is defined as information concerning a finding or allegation of harm to another person received by the Vetting Bureau from either the Gardaí or a "scheduled organisation" which could reasonably give rise to a bona fide concern that the person may harm a child.[167] Such information shall not be disclosed, according to section 15(3)(b), unless it is deemed to be "necessary, proportionate and reasonable in the circumstances for the protection of children". Section 15(4) stipulates the factors that must be taken into account in making such a determination, including whether the rights of the person have been considered and taken account of in a manner that is consistent with fairness and natural justice.[168] Once a disclosure is made to the organization who sought it, it "may consider and take into account all the information disclosed to it … when assessing the suitability of the person who is the subject of the disclosure to do relevant work".[169] The 2012 Act further strengthens mandatory reporting requirements by stipulating that the organizations listed in Schedule 2, including professional regulatory bodies such as the Teaching Council and the Medical Council, are obliged to notify any concerns they have about a person which have been established following an investigation to the Vetting Bureau.[170] Where exercising its functions under the Child Care Act 1991, the Child and Family Agency is mandated to notify such information "as soon as may be", thereby avoiding the need for a child protection inquiry to be completed.[171]

The 2012 Act is a clear example of not only the increased role played by risk in child protection law but also of the kind of disturbances in social relations and attitudes towards risk which are commonly found in late modernity. The legislation was seen as essential due to the belief that "paedophiles and sex abusers will not go away",[172] and that they will continually work around obstacles designed

164 Section 12(1).
165 Section 12(2).
166 See Part 1, Schedule 1.
167 See section 1 and section 19.
168 Section 15(4)(f). This mirrors the requirements outlined in the decisions following *MQ v Gleeson* and the subsequent information sharing cases discussed earlier in this chapter.
169 Section 16(2).
170 Section 19 (1).
171 Section 19(2).
172 Dáil Debates 18 September 2012, vol 774, Daily Book Unrevised 91, Finian McGrath TD.

to stop them from abusing children.[173] The legacy of abuse scandals was evident, with Soham murderer Ian Huntley[174] and convicted swimming coach Derry O'Rourke[175] both mentioned as people who may have been prevented from having access to children if soft information vetting had been available.[176] One TD expressed the view that their perception of their local community had changed in response to abuse scandals:

> When I studied the Bill, I found myself considering that this level of vetting would probably not be required in tight-knit rural communities such as the one in which I grew up. However, I realised that was the wrong assumption because there have been many incidents in what we felt were very protected communities. This is about challenging ourselves and challenging the way we feel. Vetting is a reality and something that must be done.[177]

This change in how child abuse was perceived represents an abandonment of traditional modes of social interaction characterised by tight community bonds, bonds which have been replaced by belief in pervasive, ever-present risks. This is also seen in the calls to make the legislation more widely applicable, such as the proposal to include child-minders and private nannies within its remit.[178] The way in which it represents social change is further underscored by the recognition that children not only live with continual risks but also that they are viewed differently. One TD encapsulated part of the argument of this and the preceding chapter by simply stating, "[i]n 20 years our view of children has changed significantly",[179] while another stated that "we recognise that the children of Ireland have a right to – and are entitled to – the highest standards of protection."[180] These simple acknowledgements of a changed societal view, expressed using the language of rights and concomitant obligations, may seem unimportant by themselves, but in the context of the then-referendum on children's rights and the framing of other child protection reforms including mandatory reporting as a children's rights

173 Ibid.

174 Ian Huntley was convicted of the murder of two schoolgirls in Soham, England. He first encountered the girls through his employment at a neighbouring school, despite having been investigated, but not charged in connection with, earlier sexual offences against children. See generally, Michael Birchard, *The Birchard Inquiry: Report* (The Stationery Office 2004).

175 Derry O'Rourke was a former Irish national and Olympic swimming coach convicted of a series of sexual offences against girls under 15.

176 Dáil Debates 19 September 2012, vol 775, Daily Book Unrevised 35, Catherine Murphy TD, and Dáil Debates 19 September 2012, vol 775, Daily Book Unrevised 27, Patrick O'Donovan TD.

177 Dáil Debates 20 September 2012, vol 775, Daily Book Unrevised 282, Tom Barry TD.

178 Dáil Debates 18 September 2012, vol 774, Daily Book Unrevised 83, Niall Collins TD.

179 Dáil Debates 19 September 2012, vol 775, Daily Book Unrevised 30, Jerry Buttimer TD.

180 Dáil Debates 18 September 2012, vol 774, Daily Book Unrevised 86, Pádraig Mac Lochlainn TD.

issue, indicate that children were finally emerging as legal subjects possessing agency, rather than passive recipients of welfare or concern.[181]

The vetting system is grounded in an approach to risk that recognises that it cannot be eliminated, but must be managed and controlled. On the introduction of the legislation, it was stated that "is essential to ensure that employers can make informed decisions in instances where persons are seeking employment which involves access to children or vulnerable persons."[182] This links very closely with the idea found in criminal law that people in positions of authority in respect of children are now a central focus of child protection legislation. It also represents the attitude towards the interaction between risk, private decision-making and public administration taken by Fisher and Steele. Fisher understands law's role in respect of risk as being to limit the power of public bodies tasked with risk regulation,[183] while Steele recognises public agencies as increasingly being employed in presenting information about risks, information which is often inconclusive, but with decisions on risk-based activity delegated to individuals.[184] The 2012 vetting legislation does precisely this – a public body is established to provide information to individuals who must then take responsibility for how to use it. The public body's role is thereby limited to that of a curator, selecting the relevant information and presenting it in such a way as to allow its consumer to make links and draw conclusions for themselves, conclusions which may be inaccurate, but justifiable on the basis that a future child's interests take priority.

Children's rights and children's agency in child protection legislation

The earlier sections of this chapter made clear that during the last decade, child protection had become a significant legislative concern and the courts had interpreted legislation in a way which seeks to ensure that protective mechanisms are effective. However, that does not necessarily translate into children being regarded as agents or rights-holders. Such an approach could mean that children were still being regarded as merely having interests, or recognised as victims deserving of sympathy and protection. It would deny children the very substance of being agents – the ability to participate and influence the direction of their lives.[185] While the constitutional reforms initiated following the 2012 referendum,

181 For more detail on the referendum itself, see Chapter 6.
182 Dáil Debates 18 September 2012, vol 774, Daily Book Unrevised 79, Minister Alan Shatter TD.
183 See generally, Elizabeth Fisher, *Risk Regulation and Administrative Constitutionalism* (Hart Publishing 2007).
184 Jenny Steele, *Risk and Legal Theory* (Hart Publishing 2004).
185 On the question of substance in children's rights adjudication, see John Tobin, 'Justifying Children's Rights' (2013) 21(3) *International Journal of Children's Rights* 395 and John Tobin, 'Courts and the Construction of Childhood: A new way of thinking' in Michael Freeman (ed) *Law and Childhood Studies* (Oxford University Press 2012).

discussed in detail in Chapter 6, point to a certain level of public ambivalence over children as agents and rights-holders, it appears that at the political and legislative levels, the acceptance of these concepts has been more thoroughly entrenched, making clear that the individualization aspect of late modernity has come to be fulfilled.

While the wording of the constitutional amendment placed certain obligations on the state to legislate so that both a child's best interests and views would play a significant role in certain legal proceedings,[186] it did not provide for a more thorough entrenchment of the idea of children as agents, such as through a wider understanding of child participation outside the narrow confines of legal disputes. Therefore, it has fallen to legislation and social policy to actualise children's agency, giving it a more substantive effect. In the period after the *CC* and *A* cases, it became evident that legislative change was being increasingly justified by reference to children's rights; this was particularly true of the use of rights rhetoric to justify mandatory reporting and vetting. References to rights as a justification for more extensive protection does not, however, do anything to reposition children from being victims receiving protection from a benevolent legal and political system. It is instead the ability to actually play a meaningful part in the legal process, through the creation of conditions of possibility for such participation that represents the transition to agency.

Throughout this book, the discussion of participation has been largely been limited to mechanisms designed to increase young people's participation in the investigatory process and on court-based procedures relating to children's evidence. However, participation has a much wider meaning than this, one aspect of which is consultation in policy design.[187] This approach has begun in Ireland, signalling greater acceptance of the rights of children to participate in and have their views heard on issues affecting them, in line with the requirements of Article 12 of the UN Convention on the Rights of the Child.[188] The National Children's Strategy, adopted in 2000, made clear that "children will have a voice in matters which affect them and their views will be given due weight in accordance with

186 Articles 42A.4, discussed in detail in Chapter 6.

187 The model of participation used in the Irish context is drawn from Laura Lundy, '"Voice" is not enough: conceptualising Article 12 of the United Nations Convention on the Rights of the Child' (2007) 33(6) *British Educational Research Journal* 927. See further, Roger Hart, *Children's participation. The theory and practice of involving young citizens in community development and environmental care* (UNICEF and Earthscan 1997), Harry Shier, Marisol Hernandez Mendez, Meyslin Centeno, Ingrid Arroliga and Meyling Gonzalez, 'How children and young people influence policy-makers: Lessons from Nicaragua' (2014) 28 *Children & Society* 1, and Lotem Perry-Hazan, 'Children's participation in national policymaking: "You're so adorable, adorable, adorable! I'm speechless; so much fun!" (2016) 67 *Children and Youth Services Review* 105.

188 See the guidance on the meaning of this for states issued in UN Committee on the Rights of the Child, *General comment No. 12 (2009): The right of the child to be heard*, UN Doc CRC/C/GC/12.

their age and maturity",[189] while the later National Framework for Children and Young People placed greater emphasis on children's contributions.[190] In 2015, Ireland became the first state in Europe to adopt a National Strategy on Children and Young People's Participation in Decision-Making.[191] This specifically identifies the hearing of children's voices in relation to social service provision, and in the courts and legal system as priority areas.[192] This is underpinned by a clear recognition of children's agency; they are recognised not as "'beings in becoming', but rather [as] 'citizens of today'".[193]

These broad policy objectives were first put into action in the early 2000s but became much more frequent after 2006.[194] Two examples focused on child protection issues will suffice for present purposes, one of which looks at the legislative entrenchment of new participation duties in the delivery of child welfare services, while the other looks at how young people's participation directly influenced legislation itself. In terms of new participation duties, the Child and Family Agency Act 2013 represents an acknowledgement of the importance of children's views in delivering the kind of child protection and welfare service that children at risk feel would meet their needs. This took child protection responsibilities away from the HSE and gave them to the newly established Child and Family Agency which was obliged to adopt a welfarist approach by having regard to the best interests of the child when discharging its functions,[195] and to regard the child's best interests as paramount when engaging in child protection work.[196] Yet it must also engage with children in a more participatory fashion, as it is further obliged to ascertain and give due consideration to the views of children in delivering its services.[197] These legal obligations mirror the contention by McGregor that the establishment of the Agency is part of a shift in the dominant official discourses in child protection work, which have a new emphasis on children's rights as one of the dominant themes.[198] This shift clearly positions children as agents, capable of influencing the direction of the welfare and protection work in a more systematic way than before.

189 Department of Health and Children, *Our Children, Their Lives: The national children's strategy* (Government Publications 2000) 11.
190 Department of Children and Youth Affairs, *Better Outcomes, Brighter Futures: The National Policy Framework for Children and Young People* (Government Publications 2014) 7.
191 Department of Children and Youth Affairs, *National strategy on children and young people's participation in decision-making 2015–2020* (Government Publications 2015).
192 Ibid 3.
193 Ibid 12.
194 Ibid 65 and Deirdre Horgan, 'Consultations with Children and Young People and Their Impact on Policy in Ireland' (2017) 5(3) *Social Inclusion* 104, 107.
195 Section 9(1) of the Child and Family Agency Act 2013.
196 Section 9(2).
197 Section 9(3) and 9(4).
198 Caroline McGregor, 'Why is History Important at Moments of Transition? The Case of "Transformation of Irish Child Welfare via the New Child and Family Agency' (2014) 17(5) *European Journal of Social Work* 771, 775–776.

The second example of participation, this time demonstrating how children directly participate in the design of child protection laws themselves can be seen in a number of legislative provisions. The exemptions from mandatory reporting found in both the 2012 and 2015 Acts point to young people possessing some agency over whether concerns are reported if they either object to reports being made, or the relationship giving rise to concerns is not characterised by intimidation. Crucially, these exemptions were not granted by legislative drafters in an act of unprompted munificence, but after the recognition by legislators that children themselves could have some meaningful input into the development of the relevant rules. While this exercise of agency is incorporated into the legislation, a more direct example of participation shaping legislation itself was seen in the 2017 reform of age of consent legislation.

In 2006, the Office of the Minister for Children undertook a consultation exercise involving 210 teenagers on a variety of aspects of the reform of sexual consent laws.[199] This novel consultation highlighted concern among young people that non-exploitative peer relationships were currently capable of giving rise to criminal prosecutions, and suggested that a two year age difference between sexual partners would be a fair and reasonable gap indicating the presence or absence of exploitation.[200] This eventually found its way into the provisions of the mandatory reporting statutes, as well as the Criminal Law (Sexual Offences) Act 2017, which specifically exempts young people in relationships like this from criminal liability, even though one or both parties are under the age of consent. The difference in approach between the open engagement with young agents and the secretive deliberations of the Carrigan Committee and the Dáil committee which drafted the provisions of the 1935 Act, when children were regarded as passive objects and at risk from the moral dangers of dance halls, could not be starker. It indicates that children's rights had become integral to the institutional design of child protection law, woven into its very constitutive fabric. In doing so, children are marked out as agents, in much the same way as Oswell does in his ophthalmic clinic analogy – by exerting influence on service design and delivery, and the legal framework itself, children have become agents of change.

Conclusion

This chapter has highlighted how reflexive modernization ultimately came to shape the development of the contemporary child protection framework, and vice versa. While earlier chapters highlighted the early onset of this process, the period covered in this chapter shows how deeply late modernity came to be reflected in legal and social work reforms. The sociological indicia of late

199 Office of the Minister for Children, *Report on the Outcome of Consultations with Teenagers on the Issues to be Considered by the Minister for Children when Examining the Age of Consent for Sexual Activity* (Department of Health and Children 2006).

200 OMCYA (n 81) 11.

modernity – detraditionalization and individualization, risk, and agency – were all present in the reforms pioneered in this era. People occupying previously trusted positions of power and respectability – priests, teachers, coaches and families – were reconstructed as potential dangers, as risks. As the risks associated with, and indeed embodied in, these individuals and loci of power came to have greater prominence in public discourse, they altered and undermined the traditional environments in which they first emerged. What the material covered in this chapter shows is that the assumptions relating to traditional sites of trust have been opened to public discussion and then subjected to new modes of regulation inspired by a desire to control risk. This was evident in the increasing legal emphasis on the role of individuals in positions of trust and authority, especially in the context of the criminalization of exploitative sexual conduct and the legal regulation of risk management strategies such as mandatory reporting and vetting, on the basis that these individuals were themselves risks.

However, the recognition of agency was also a prominent factor lying behind legislative change. This allowed for the interests of children to be partially decoupled from the interests of their families, more than had been the case during the period of simple modernity, and for a public conveyance of a message that children's rights mattered. At the level of institutional design, the interests and rights of children are now regarded as the overriding factors driving the operation of the statutory child protection agency and the guiding principle in the operation of child protection law; a clear expression of a message that children's rights are to be taken seriously, even if all rights are not fully recognised, or even if recognised rights are not fully or consistently implemented. Young people were asked for their views on how one the most difficult aspects of a person's sociological biography, the regulation of intimacy, ought to be dealt with, even where one or both people concerned are under the age of consent. What is more, those views were broadly accepted and enshrined in legislation. In doing so, the state recognised them as possessing agency in the sense of being allowed control over their own bodies and biographies without fear of the imposition of criminal law, so long as certain protective preconditions are met. Between 2006 and 2017, the child protection system yielded to the forces of reflexive modernity.

References

Beck U, *World Risk Society* (Polity Press 1999).

Birchard M, *The Birchard Inquiry: Report* (The Stationery Office 2004).

Brosnan K, *Monageer Inquiry: A Report Presented to Ms Mary Harney TD, Minister for Health and Mr Dermot Ahern TD, Minister for Justice, Equality and Law Reform* (Stationery Office 2007).

Buckley H, 'Duty to Care: Reducing Risk in Childcare Settings' 2006 9(3) *Irish Journal of Family Law* 3.

Buckley L, 'Can the Criminal Law Put an End to the "Cover-Up" of Clerical Sexual Abuse?' (2014) 24(2) *Irish Criminal Law Journal* 98.

Bunting L, Lazenbatt A and Wallace I, 'Information Sharing and Reporting Systems in the UK and Ireland: Professional Barriers to Reporting Child Maltreatment Concerns' (2010) 19(3) *Child Abuse Review* 187.

Children's Rights Alliance, 'Response to the Report by the Office of the Ombudsman for Children, Children First: National Guidelines for the Protection and Welfare of Children' <http://www.childrensrights.ie/index.php?q=knowledgebase/child-protection/response-report-office-ombudsman-children-children-first-national-gui>

Commission to Inquire into Child Abuse, *Report of the Commission to Inquire into Child Abuse* (Stationery Office 2009).

de Londras F and Kelly C, *European Convention on Human Rights Act: Operation, Impact and Analysis* (Round Hall 2010).

Department of Children and Youth Affairs, *Children First: National Guidance for the Protection and Welfare of Children* (Stationery Office 2011).

Department of Children and Youth Affairs, *Better Outcomes, Brighter Futures: The National Policy Framework for Children and Young People* (Government Publications 2014).

Department of Children and Youth Affairs, *National Strategy on Children and Young People*'s *Participation in Decision-Making 2015–2020* (Government Publications 2015).

Department of Education and Science, *Child Protection Guidelines 2001* (Stationery Office 2001).

Department of Education and Science, *Child Protection Guidelines 2006* (Stationery Office 2006).

Department of Health and Children, *Our Children, Their Lives: The National Children's Strategy* (Government Publications 2000).

Ferguson H, 'Abused and Looked After Children as "Moral Dirt": Child Abuse and Institutional Care in Historical Perspective' (2007) 36(1) *Journal of Social Policy* 123.

Ferriter D, 'Suffer Little Children? The Historical Validity of Memoirs of Irish Childhood' in Joseph Dunne and James Kelly (eds), *Childhood and its Discontents* (The Liffey Press 2002).

Fisher E, *Risk Regulation and Administrative Constitutionalism* (Hart Publishing 2007).

Freeman M, 'Why it Remains Important to Take Children's Rights Seriously' (2007) 15 *International Journal of Children's Rights* 5.

Furedi F and Bristow J, *Licensed to Hug: How Child Protection Policies are Poisoning the Relationship between the Generations* (Civitas 2008).

Ganiel G, *Transforming Post-Catholic Ireland: Religious Practice in Late Modernity* (Oxford University Press 2016).

Garrett PM, 'Excavating the Past: Mother and Baby Homes in the Republic of Ireland' (2017) 47(2) *British Journal of Social Work* 358.

Habermas J, 'The Concept of Human Dignity and the Realistic Utopia of Human Rights' (2010) 41(4) *Metaphilosophy* 464.

Hart R, *Children's Participation: The Theory and Practice of Involving Young Citizens in Community Development and Environmental Care* (UNICEF and Earthscan 1997).

Hennessy M, 'Backbenchers briefed on plan' *Irish Times* (Dublin, 1 June 2006) 6.

Hogan G and Gwynn Morgan D, *Administrative Law in Ireland* (4th edn, Round Hall2010).

Hogan G and Whyte G, *JM Kelly: The Irish Constitution* (4th edn, Butterworths 2003).
Holmquist K, 'Flower power' *Irish Times* (Dublin, 3 June 2006) 107.
Horgan D, 'Consultations with Children and Young People and Their Impact on Policy in Ireland' (2017) 5(3) *Social Inclusion* 104.
Joint Committee on Health and Children, *Report on Children First (Heads of) Bill 2012* (Houses of the Oireachtas 2012).
Joint Oireachtas Committee on Child Protection, *Report of Joint Oireachtas Committee on Child Protection* (Houses of the Oireachtas 2006).
Joint Oireachtas Committee on the Constitutional Amendment on Children, *First Interim Report of the Joint Oireachtas Committee on the Constitutional Amendment on Children* (Houses of the Oireachtas 2008).
Kilkelly U, 'Learning Lessons from the Past: Legal Issues Arising from Ireland's Child Abuse Inquiries' (2012) 12(1) *Irish Journal of Applied Social Studies* 8.
Lally C, 'Thousands gather with white flowers at short notice' *Irish Times* (Dublin, June 3 2006) 8.
Lundy L, '"Voice" is Not Enough: Conceptualising Article 12 of the United Nations Convention on the Rights of the Child' (2007) 33(6) *British Educational Research Journal* 927.
McAleese M, *Report of the Inter-Departmental Committee to Establish Facts of State involvement with the Magdalen Laundries* (Stationery Office 2013).
McAlinden A-M, 'Vetting Sexual Offenders: State Over-Extension, The Punishment Deficit and the Failure to Manage Risk' (2010) 19(1) *Social and Legal Studies* 25.
McAlinden A-M, *'Grooming' and the Sexual Abuse of Children: Institutional, Internet and Familial Dimensions* (Oxford University Press 2012).
McAlinden A-M and Naylor B, 'Reframing Public Inquiries as "Procedural Justice" for Victims of Institutional Child Abuse: Towards a Hybrid Model of Justice' (2016) 38 *Sydney Law Review* 277.
McCárthaigh S, Woulfe J and Deegan G, 'White flower day: Thousands across the country' *Irish Examiner*, <http://www.irishexaminer.com/ireland/icrime/white-flower-day-thousands-across-the-country-5104.html>.
McDonagh M, 'Mother gets seven years in jail for abuse of children' *Irish Times* (Dublin, 23 January 2009) 6.
McGarry P, 'President tells abuse survivors of heartfelt sorrow' *Irish Times* (Dublin, 29 June 2009) 1.
McGarry P, 'Christine Buckley helped shift Ireland's cultural axis on child abuse' *Irish Times* (Dublin, 12 March 2014) 14.
McGarry P, 'A woman of extraordinary courage' *Irish Times* (Dublin, 14 March 2014) 10.
McGregor C, 'Why is History Important at Moments of Transition? The Case of Transformation of Irish Child Welfare via the New Child and Family Agency' (2014) 17(5) *European Journal of Social Work* 771.
Moriarty N, '"Telling My Story": An Analysis of How Disclosure to the Irish Commission to Inquire into Child Abuse is Constructed' (PhD Thesis, University of East London 2013).
Mother and Baby Homes Commission of Investigation, *Second Interim Report* (Stationery Office 2017).
Murphy Y, *Report into the Catholic Archdiocese of Dublin* (Stationery Office 2009).

Murphy Y, *Commission of Investigation Report into the Catholic Diocese of Cloyne* (Stationery Office 2011).

O'Brien C, 'Profound moment of validation for forgotten children' *Irish Times* (Dublin, 11 June 2009) 6.

O'Brien C, 'Child deaths in care or in contact with services now at 188' *Irish Times* (Dublin, 5 June 2010) 1.

O'Brien C, 'Tears and Fury as institutional abuse victims march on Dáil' *Irish Times* (Dublin, 10 June 2010) 1.

O'Doherty C, 'Abuse victim's brother plans altar protest during Easter Sunday Mass', *Irish Examiner* (Cork 30 March 2010).

O'Malley P, *Risk, Uncertainty and Government* (Glasshouse 2004) 318–19.

O'Malley T, *Sexual Offences* (2nd edn, Round Hall 2013).

O'Neill L, 'Protesters ready to express anger at Leinster House' *Irish Times* (Dublin, 2 June 2006) 8.

O'Reilly A, 'A mass grave of 800 babies' *Irish Mail on Sunday* (Dublin, 25 May 2014) 1.

Office of the Children's Ombudsman, *Investigation into the Implementation of Children First: National Guidelines for the Protection and Welfare of Children* (Stationery Office 2010).

Office of the Minister for Children, *Report on Consultations with Teenagers on Issues to be Considered by the Minister for Children When Examining the Age of Consent for Sexual Activity* (Stationery Office 2006).

Office of the Minister for Children, *Report on the Outcome of Consultations with Teenagers on the Issues to be Considered by the Minister for Children when Examining the Age of Consent for Sexual Activity* (Department of Health and Children 2006).

Office of the Minister for Children and Youth Affairs, *National Review of Compliance with Children First: National Guidelines for the Protection and Welfare of Children* (Stationery Office 2008).

Office of the Minister for Children and Youth Affairs, *Implementation Plan for the Commission to Inquire into Child Abuse* (Stationery Office 2009).

Office of the Minister for Children and Youth Affairs, 'Press Statement by Ms Frances Fitzgerald TD, Minister for Children and Youth Affairs - Launch of Children First 2011 – National Guidance for the Protection and Welfare of Children, 15 July 2011' <https://www.dcya.gov.ie/viewdoc.asp?Docid=1595&CatID=11&mn=&StartDate=01+January+2011>.

Perry-Hazan L, 'Children's Participation in National Policymaking: "You're So Adorable, Adorable, Adorable! I'm SPEECHLESS; So Much Fun!"' (2016) 67 *Children and Youth Services Review* 105.

Rafferty M and O'Sullivan E, *Suffer the Little Children: The Inside Story of Ireland's Industrial Schools* (New Island Books 1999).

Review Inquiry Team, *Review Inquiry on any matter pertaining to Child Protection Issues touching on or concerning Dr A* (Stationery Office 2008).

Rorty R, *Contingency, Irony, and Solidarity* (Cambridge University Press 1989).

Rorty R, 'Human Rights, Rationality and Sentimentality', in Stephen Shute and Susan Hurley (eds), *On Human Rights: The Oxford Amnesty Lectures 1993* (Oxford University Press 1994).

Roscommon Child Care Inquiry, *Roscommon Child Care Case Report of the Inquiry Team to the Health Service Executive* (Stationery Office 2010).

Shannon G, *First Report of the Special Rapporteur on Child Protection* (Stationery Office 2007).
Shannon G, *Third Report of the Special Rapporteur on Child Protection* (Stationery Office 2009).
Shannon G, *Audit of the Exercise by An Garda Síochána of the provisions of Section 12 of the Child Care Act 1991* (An Garda Síochána 2017).
Shier H, Hernandez Mendez M, Centeno M, Arroliga I and Gonzalez M, 'How Children and Young People Influence Policy-Makers: Lessons from Nicaragua' (2014) 28 *Children & Society* 1.
Smyth J, 'HSE revises figures for deaths of children' *Irish Times* (Dublin, 9 December 2010) 3.
Steele J, *Risk and Legal Theory* (Hart Publishing 2004).
Stevens K, 'An Overview of the Law Governing the Age of Consent for Sexual Activity in Ireland with a View to Reform' (2015) 25(4) *Irish Criminal Law Journal* 90.
Wallace I and Bunting L, *An Examination of Local, National and International Arrangements for the Mandatory Reporting of Child Abuse: The Implications for Northern Ireland* (NSPCC 2009).

Conclusion

Reflexive modernity has altered social conditions – and hence child protection – radically. The structures of traditional orders shaped by conditions of simple modernity presented limited abilities to alter the course of one's life, but in late modernity agents have a wider creative space in which to write their own biographies.[1] This newfound ability to choose, however, takes place in a risk society, where uncertainty has become a part of everyday life. Agency, risk and uncertainty, therefore, define the late modern condition. This is certainly true for children. Once conceptualised as passive objects of concern, or the source of social threats, children now exercise decision-making powers to a greater extent than in the past, influencing the world around them. Oswell's understanding of agency as being like the operation of a clinic, where children can influence structures without having to actively choose to do so, shows us the multiple ways in which this agency can be exercised,[2] and the guarantee of agency is protected by the recognition of legal rights which also help to loosen children from control by others. This does not mean that all children are always regarded as having full capacity to exercise agency and make life choices – this would ignore children's developing capacities.[3] Even though children's rights have been recognised, not all of these rights are fully enforceable.[4] Yet the change in children's status brought about by the onset of reflexive modernity has been radical.

Yet alongside this stands the new perceptions of risks, produced by the changing construction of childhood itself, including the risk that their newfound agency

1 See generally, Ulrich Beck, *Risk Society: Towards A New Modernity* (Sage 1992), Ulrich Beck, Wolfgang Bonss and Christoph Lau, 'The Theory of Reflexive Modernization: Problematic, Hypotheses and Research Programme' (2003) 20(2) *Theory, Culture & Society* 1, Anthony Giddens, *The Consequences of Modernity* (Polity Press 1990), Anthony Giddens, *Modernity and Self-Identity: Self and Society in the Late Modern Age* (Polity Press 1991).

2 David Oswell, *The Agency of Children: From Family to Global Human Rights* (Cambridge University Press 2013) 77–78.

3 See generally, Gerison Lansdown, *The Evolving Capacities of the Child* (UNICEF Innocenti Research Centre 2005) and Michael Freeman, 'Why it Remains Important to Take Children's Rights Seriously' (2007) 15 *International Journal of Children's Rights* 5.

4 See, in the context of children's socio-economic rights, Aoife Nolan, *Children's Socio-economic Rights, Democracy and the Courts* (Hart Publishing 2011).

may be exploited by people in positions of authority, as well as new risks associated with technological development. Child protection work has changed from a moralistic enterprise aimed at eliminating threats to one aiming to manage risks while promoting children's interests.[5] As the role of social workers has expanded, in many ways their discretion has contracted, because legal rules have begun to govern new areas of social life and even professional practice. It is apparent from my research that the claims made by advocates of reflexive modernity have been borne out, at least in the context of the development of child protection law. Public understanding of child abuse has been heavily influenced by the processes of detraditionalization, and the resulting decline in trust in old hierarchies, and also by the subpolitical activity of survivors of child abuse, people who once existed at society's margins. The family has become increasingly individualized, and indeed juridified, as the recognition of children's agency has led to the granting of constitutional and legal rights to children who were previously regarded as objects of parental authority. Risk has become a dominant theme in how the state engages in child protection work, but its work has also become democratised to an extent, given that working with risk is not seen as a concern for centralised institutions alone.

The changes experienced in recent years in law and policy around child protection in Ireland provided the initial impetus for this work. Sensitised to the likelihood that broader sociological factors which have generally not been explored in the legal literature on child protection had influenced the development of those laws, this book has been framed around the question of the extent to which child protection law and policy was influenced by the forces of reflexive modernity. In answering this question, and by using Ireland as an example throughout, I have sought to make two overarching and mutually reinforcing arguments: first, that a complex understanding of how lawmakers thought about children, childhood and risk can be seen when child protection laws are examined with an eye to the nature of modernity itself, and, second, that the concept of reflexive modernity is a useful analytical framework for the examination of child protection law and policy.

As a result, I have looked at child protection statutes in a narrower sense than previous studies, forsaking the examination of related ideas like infanticide and illegitimacy. The emphasis has instead been placed on those statutes mandating state intervention on behalf of children to protect them from abuse and criminal laws governing sexual contact with children. Tracing the evolution of criminal liability and sentencing, it becomes clear that the system relating to criminalisation of sexual contact with young people has become far more elaborate, and reflective of the concerns of late modernity. First, there has been a movement away from seeing criminal law relating to children as a means of exercising moralistic control over sexuality, and indeed, control over young people's own bodies. Second,

5 Caroline McGregor, 'Why is History Important at Moments of Transition? The Case of "Transformation of Irish Child Welfare via the New Child and Family Agency' (2014) 17(5) *European Journal of Social Work* 771.

children have gradually been exculpated from any sense of responsibility for their abuse, with the moral burden of culpability being shifted onto abusers. Third, a wider range of conduct has been made subject to criminal law. At one time, physical contact with a child was necessary in order to establish liability for child abusers; now liability can arise from preparatory acts designed to lead to abuse, or from engagement with online material depicting abuse. As such, the justifications for imposing liability now include the exploitation of a relationship of trust with a child in addition to the physical and psychological harm arising from an act of abuse. Fourth, maximum available sentences for sexual offences against children have become harsher, coupled with the development of a range of post-sentence supervisory measures. Finally, young people themselves have had a meaningful input into the operation of some of these laws through reform of evidential rules, which allow them greater participation in the courtroom process, and even in the design of laws, acting as agents in the construction of rules relating to liability.

In relation to child protection measures rooted in civil law mechanisms, there has been a movement away from measures designed to institutionalise children, coupled with the development of a much more nuanced set of available legal responses. The Child Care Act 1991 sought to foreground children's best interests, a concept that has been given a clear constitutional status since the 2012 referendum. This means that children's own interests, and not the interests of a wider moral or social order, nor the interests of their parents, should determine the outcomes of child protection work. Moreover, this focus on best interests is now regarded as a right held by children, who also possess rights in respect of participation which must form part of the legal decision-making relating to their care and protection. The idea of rights has also informed a constitutional realignment so that children are now to be regarded as equal, and equally entitled to protection based on their individual needs, regardless of their parents' marital status. A further innovation in the development of legal responses to child protection is the way in which control over information has increasingly been seen as part of the child protection enterprise and its use governed by legal rules. Thus, the introduction of mandatory reporting and a new vetting system in the last decade show an increasingly legalistic approach to child protection, radically different from that which existed in the early twentieth century.

Since the early work on the role of reflexivity in child protection,[6] limited attention has been paid to the concept despite the significant changes that have

6 Harry Ferguson, 'Child Abuse Inquiries and the Report of the Kilkenny Incest Investigation: A Critical Inquiry' (1994) 41(4) *Administration* 385, Harry Ferguson, 'Protecting Irish Children in Time: Child abuse as a social problem and the development of the child protection system in the Republic of Ireland' (1996) 44(4) *Administration* 5 and Harry Ferguson, 'Protecting Children in New Times: Child protection and the risk society' (1997) 2(4) *Child and Family Social Work* 221, Fred Powell, 'The Professional Challenges of Reflexive Modernization: Social work in Ireland' (1998) 28 *British Journal of Social Work* 311, Caroline Skehill, 'Reflexive Modernity and Social Work in Ireland: A Response to Powell' (1999) 29 *British Journal of Social Work* 798.

occurred in both the legal framework governing child protection and public perceptions of children and child abuse. These changes made it vital to revisit and reassess reflexivity as a concept. I have shown how aspects of reflexive modernization can be readily observed in the discourse surrounding child protection law and policy. Individualization and detraditionalization have become extremely evident in Irish life over the last 20 years. The social factors which traditionally shaped one's life – family and religion in particular – have either declined in importance or have been altered significantly in the ways in which they influence how people live their lives. There is greater individual choice and freedom, and importantly in the context of child protection, the deference to trusted sites of authority has diminished. The family is no longer regarded by the state as a space into which it cannot step for fear of violating Catholic social teaching on subsidiarity. Family is also no longer regarded as a unitary concept, with individuals within the family now regarded as having interests and rights of their own, separate and distinct from the family as unit.[7] This is linked to the rise of agency, even for children and young people, who can now not only influence individual legal proceedings but even policy formation relating to the most intimate expressions of individual choice.

Risk has been such a prominent feature of the legal and political response to all of these revelations that it is now possible to characterise Ireland as a risk society, as exemplified by its response to child protection issues. Earlier in Ireland's legal history, attempts were made to eliminate risks through institutionalising children, increasing punishments for offenders due to a belief in deterrent effect and through the attempted restriction of supposed sites of risk, such as dance halls, cars and cinemas. Risk in this era was seen as emanating from definitive sources – young people engaged in supposed sexual immorality, or "neglectful" mothers. As revelations of the real, lived realities of abuse victims emerged, however, it became clear that risk was more frequently recognised in modern times and was also managed differently. The home was now regarded as a site of risk, as were schools, sports clubs and religious bodies. Fear of stranger-danger still permeated political debates, but policy-making now problematized previously unproblematic aspects of social life, through the imposition of new reporting rules and pre-employment vetting mechanisms. Risks could not be eliminated but were to be managed. Yet the risk was not centralised through governmental decision-making in a simple manner, but democratised, made subject to individual choice. The operation of the vetting system, for example, cedes control of risk management to appointed officials within organisations to make decisions on the basis of the available information, with the constant fear that the risk may be mishandled or misidentified. Reporting of risks of child abuse to the child protection authorities is now mandatory. Risk is now everybody's business.

Certain limitations must, however, be placed on these claims. The claims made in this book are made on the basis of certain kinds of evidence – parliamentary debates, legislation, case law and responses to official inquiries, media reports and

7 See generally, Ulrich Beck and Elisabeth Beck-Gernsheim, *The Normal Chaos of Love* (Polity Press 1995).

other adult-centred sources. As such, it has had limited access to children's own voices. It also, as recognised in the Introduction, did not attempt to disaggregate different experiences of childhood, conditioned by issues such as gender, to any great degree. Significant space could not be afforded to this issue without diminishing the attention paid to risk and reflexive modernity. This is not to deny or sideline the important role that gender plays in child protection, or to understate the changes in thinking about gender which have occurred in the period under examination. Under conditions of simple modernity, the social role of women and girl children was rarely within their own determination, as sex instead bound these women to a fixed social identity. It also resulted in them being subjected to both male sexual privilege, and the desire to present them as risks to the social order, even from a young age. Especially during the earlier twentieth century, and no doubt later as well, a disciplinary attitude to female sexuality can be seen, while child abuse also took on a very specifically gendered dimension. Yet gender, like childhood, underwent a significant reconstruction as a social category in the transition to late modernity. The conditions of simple modernity, which made institutions such as Magdalene laundries possible, have been largely superseded by the social conditions of late modernity. Under these more reflexive social conditions, institutions in which female victims of abuse were detained were closed and later subjected to investigation; adult women and girls have both greater levels of autonomy and are less frequently regarded as responsible for the sexual violence that they still face. Sexual violence still predominantly victimises women and girls. Yet a system is developing which attempts to manage the risks that they face through new forms of legal regulation of the social spheres in which they encounter risk, changes explored in depth in Chapters 7 and 8. That this includes the family home is an extremely significant shift in our understanding of the interaction between gender and risk.

The use of reflexivity and risk theory also presents new opportunities for child protection research. The question of different historical childhoods, for example, can be explored especially in conjunction with concepts such as gender, class and race. Despite the increasing importance of risk in political and legal discourse, little attempt has been made to understand how courts think about and act on risk in the child protection context. Recent valuable work has been undertaken examining first instance child protection court decisions made under the Child Care Act 1991,[8] but these do not focus on risk. Risk to children arises in a variety

8 See for example, Conor O'Mahony, Caroline Shore, Kenneth Burns, and Aisling Parkes, 'Child Care Proceedings in the District Court: What Do We Really Know?' (2012) 15(2) *Irish Journal of Family Law* 1, Conor O'Mahony, Kenneth Burns, Aisling Parkes and Caroline Shore, 'Child Care Proceedings in Non-Specialist Courts: The Experience in Ireland' (2016) 30 *International Journal of Law Policy and the Family* 13, Conor O'Mahony, Kenneth Burns, Aisling Parkes and Caroline Shore, 'Representation and participation in child care proceedings: what about the voice of the parents?' (2016) 38(3) *Journal of Social Welfare and Family* 302 and Conor O'Mahony, Aisling Parkes, Caroline Shore and Kenneth Burns, 'Child Care Proceedings and Family-Friendly Justice: The Problem with Court Facilities' (2016) 19(4) *Irish Journal of Family Law* 85.

of other legal contexts – such as in private child law proceedings, and in international child abduction proceedings. The importance of working with risk in the specific context of a reflexive, late-modern society is acknowledged in the following quotation from *Bedford County Council v M; A v Child and Family Agency*:

> We need a more mature conversation about risk. Child protection is a matter of risk management, not risk elimination. The populist idea that risk can be removed, or that child protection tragedies must never happen again, is fundamentally misconceived. Child protection is always a question of balance and proportionality and must not degenerate into a spurious and self-serving process of exposure minimisation.[9]

Despite the emphasis in this book on the theoretical concepts of modernity and risk, it is childhood, however, that has remained at the centre of my research. I have argued that our understanding of childhood has developed under conditions of, and has been influenced by, the related ideas of reflexivity and risk. Yet this should not be understood as an overly optimistic progression towards a "better" childhood. It is vital that the present state of thinking about childhood cannot be presented as more enlightened than the ways of previous eras, or as meaning that children will have "better" lives now that the problems posed by simple modernity belong to the past. There is a danger in such complacency. Ozment argued that "the hubris of an age reaches a certain peak when it accuses another age of being incapable of loving its children properly".[10] If reflexivity is to be of any value, we must be aware that such hubris can only make us blind to the risks in our own age.

References

Beck U, *Risk Society: Towards A New Modernity* (Sage 1992).

Beck U and Beck-Gernsheim E, *The Normal Chaos of Love* (Polity Press 1995).

Beck U, Bonss W and Lau C, 'The Theory of Reflexive Modernization: Problematic, Hypotheses and Research Programme' (2003) 20(2) *Theory, Culture & Society* 1.

Ferguson H, 'Child Abuse Inquiries and the Report of the Kilkenny Incest Investigation: A Critical Inquiry' (1994) 41(4) *Administration* 385.

Ferguson H, 'Protecting Irish Children in Time: Child Abuse as a Social Problem and the Development of the Child Protection System in the Republic of Ireland' (1996) 44(4) *Administration* 5.

Ferguson H, 'Protecting Children in New Times: Child Protection and the Risk Society' (1997) 2(4) *Child and Family Social Work* 221.

Freeman M, 'Why it Remains Important to Take Children's Rights Seriously' (2007) 15 *International Journal of Children's Rights* 5.

9 [2017] IEHC 583, [123].

10 Steven Ozment, *When Fathers Ruled: Family life in Reformation Europe* (Harvard University Press 1983) 162.

Giddens A, *The Consequences of Modernity* (Polity Press 1990).
Giddens A, *Modernity and Self-Identity: Self and Society in the Late Modern Age* (Polity Press 1991).
Lansdown G, *The Evolving Capacities of the Child* (UNICEF Innocenti Research Centre 2005).
McGregor C, 'Why is History Important at Moments of Transition? The Case of "Transformation of Irish Child Welfare via the New Child and Family Agency' (2014) 17(5) *European Journal of Social Work* 771.
Nolan A, *Children's Socio-economic Rights, Democracy and the Courts* (Hart Publishing 2011).
O'Mahony C, Shore C, Burns K and Parkes A, 'Child Care Proceedings in the District Court: What Do We Really Know?' (2012) 15(2) *Irish Journal of Family Law* 1.
O'Mahony C, Burns K, Parkes A and Shore C, 'Child Care Proceedings in Non-Specialist Courts: The Experience in Ireland' (2016) 30 *International Journal of Law Policy And The Family* 13.
O'Mahony C, Burns K, Parkes A and Shore C, 'Representation and Participation in Child Care Proceedings: What about the Voice of the Parents?' (2016) 38(3) *Journal of Social Welfare and Family* 302.
O'Mahony C, Parkes A, Shore C and Burns K, 'Child Care Proceedings and Family-Friendly Justice: The Problem with Court Facilities' (2016) 19(4) *Irish Journal of Family Law* 85.
Oswell D, *The Agency of Children: From Family to Global Human Rights* (Cambridge University Press 2013).
Ozment S, *When Fathers Ruled: Family Life in Reformation Europe* (Harvard University Press 1983) 162.
Powell F, 'The Professional Challenges of Reflexive Modernization: Social work in Ireland' (1998) 28 *British Journal of Social Work* 311.
Skehill C, 'Reflexive Modernity and Social Work in Ireland: A Response to Powell' (1999) 29 *British Journal of Social Work* 798.

Index

www.ingramcontent.com/pod-product-compliance
Ingram Content Group UK Ltd.
Pitfield, Milton Keynes, MK11 3LW, UK
UKHW022026061126
477531UK00002B/67
9780367276317